Bicentennial USA

Pathways to Celebration

ROBERT G. HARTJE
with a foreword by Louis L. Tucker

Nashville: The American Association for State and Local History, 1973

To John and Carol, Tom, Jim, Phil, Paul, Beth Anne, and MARTHA—*who gave up father and husband to his travel, research, and writing*

The author and publisher gratefully acknowledge
the support of
THE NATIONAL ENDOWMENT FOR THE HUMANITIES
and
THE BICENTENNIAL COUNCIL OF
THE THIRTEEN ORIGINAL STATES

Foreword

In the early 1960's friends and fans of Lawrence "Yogi" Berra, longtime New York Yankee baseball star, held a special program to pay tribute to his spectacular career. Berra, whose talents with bat and ball far exceeded his skill in handling the spoken word, responded to the accolades with the memorable statement "Thank you for making this day necessary."

Berra's singularly appropriate response has a fitting application to this nation's bicentennial birthday on July 4, 1976. Across the land, legions of speakers will be praising, with hyperbolic intensity, the Founding Fathers of the Revolution and the new nation. They will make many eloquent speeches (and some not so eloquent), and the essence of their impassioned oratory will assuredly be "Thank you for making this day necessary."

The thought deserves to be pondered. The Founding Fathers did indeed make the bicentennial commemoration of their achievements "necessary." Just as Berra, by his brilliant athletic performance, forced his fans to pay him homage, so did those who inspired the first of the great revolutions and created a new nation compel future generations of Americans to honor them. Almost two hundred years have passed since the revolt from Britain began and the American republic took form, yet these consecutive achievements continue to rank as great moments of world history. In the context of eighteenth-century life, they were extraordinarily significant happenings, since they introduced a new phase in the political evolution of mankind.

The Revolution itself remains a central phenomenon in the national life of the American people, assuming richer meanings and growing larger in the consciousness of each passing generation. An event in which all Americans can take pride, the Revolution transcends the individual's particular political persuasion. Like the modern British monarchy, it is the great unifier, the common bond, the essential link with the past. Some of the more perceptive Founding Fathers, notably Jefferson and John Adams, were aware that the Revolution would affect not only future American life but the history of the world as well.

Historians frequently have seen fit to compile lists of events which have helped shape the distinctive character of the United States. The Revolution usually heads such lists. From this experience came the conviction that America and authoritarian government were mutually exclusive concepts, and the notion that ours is a country with a special destiny, a land of second chance for the oppressed and destitute, an "asylum for mankind." The Revolution reaffirmed the earlier Puritan vision of the New World as "a Citty upon a Hill," a fresh model for emulation. Much of the American's Messianic zeal to reform is derived from the Revolution. The writings of Jefferson, John Adams, and other Argonauts of the Revolution are replete with statements that their struggle against Britain was but the first stage in a universal development, the opening battle of a long war against tyranny. Writing nearly fifty years after the Revolution began, the immortal Jefferson expressed a hope which has achieved reality innumerable times in the past century and a half: "May it be to the world, what I believe it will be, (to some parts sooner, to others later, but finally to all,) the signal of arousing men to burst the chains under which monkish ignorance and superstition had persuaded them to bind themselves, and to assume the blessings and security of self-govern-ment."

It is an odd paradox that the bicentennial of a historic hap-pening which has inspired, and continues to inspire, the hopes and aspirations of all "oppressed" people should occur at a time when cynicism and disillusionment have become the prevailing mood of much of the world. Modern man lives in eschatological despair. The world seems infested with evil spirits. The prophets of gloom and doom hold center stage. The idea of progress, which the Revolution helped to foster, is no longer in vogue. In this context, a massive national birthday party hardly seems appropriate.

Yet, as Hartje notes, the occasion *will* be observed, whatever the current mood. The Revolution's symbolic significance will transcend the mutable moods of man.

For those of us who bear responsibility for planning and exe-cuting Bicentennial programs on the state and local levels, these are indeed times that try our patience, if not our souls. With the collapse of the proposed Philadelphia Bicentennial Exposition in 1972, the focus of celebration has shifted from one urban center to every state and local community in the na-tion. The Bicentennial now belongs to all of the people, from Anchorage, Alaska, to Augusta, Maine; from Minneapolis, Minnesota, to Miami, Florida. Not even the original thirteen states can lay a proprietary claim upon it.

In its traditional role of serving state and local historical agencies, the American Association for State and Local History (AASLH) has been granted a rare opportunity to provide a vital service to the nation. State and local historical societies (both public and private), local historians, history museums—these are the agencies and the people who are best qualified to plan and execute meaningful commemorative programs. They must offer a large part of the leadership if the Bicentennial is to realize its potential as a force for good in the life of the na-tion.

With opportunity comes responsibility. The AASLH is acutely aware that if the Bicentennial is allowed to degenerate into a mindless doodle-dandy celebration characterized by blatant commercialism and tawdry programs, it may well achieve the dimension of disaster predicted by detractors. To prevent such an occurrence, the AASLH has developed this book, which is designed, first and foremost, for planners at the state and local levels, and principally for historical society personnel and local historians.

Santayana's well-known admonition that "those who cannot remember the past are condemned to repeat it," has a special credibility for all Bicentennial planners. The fundamental purposes of this book, then, are to alert planners to the dangers they face and to guide them to the proper "pathways of celebration." Hartje's method is most appropriate for those who value the discipline of history. He has operated on the principle that Man can learn from the past. He has examined past celebrations, selecting and anatomizing a number of prototypal commemorations. He has sought to discover why certain programs were successful and why others failed. He has made critical distinctions between substantive and banal programs. Above all, he has underscored the importance of uniting cerebration with celebration.

The AASLH has been joined in this venture by the National Endowment for the Humanities (NEH), which provided a generous research grant. There is a logical congruity in the union of the AASLH and the NEH, one a non-profit educational service organization, the other a unit of the federal government. Both are preoccupied with the achievements of Man. Both are committed to strengthening the role of the humanities in our national life.

The humanities have been defined as "the study of that which is most human," and their fundamental role is to form, preserve, and transform "the social, moral, and aesthetic values of every man in every age." The study of history is the very core of the humanities, and it is the principal *raison d'être* for the AASLH, as stated by its Executive Director, Dr. William T. Alderson: "Fundamental to the Association's work is a strongly held conviction that a knowledge of the past enriches man's existence and is essential to his perspective on the political, economic, and social problems he must face as a responsible citizen." The prime objective of the NEH closely parallels the angle of vision of the AASLH: "to provide the American people with a better basis for making judgments of value in private and public life by improving access to the thoughts and activities of human beings in the past."

This book faithfully adheres to the principles and objectives of both agencies. Its immediate aim is to help Bicentennial planners find the appropriate forms of commemoration; its ultimate aim is to influence planners to develop programs which will open up the human capacities of the American people to the highest degree.

In sponsoring this publication the AASLH fervently hopes that this contribution will help restore to our national consciousness the conviction held by our Founding Fathers: that America is an idea greater than its name.

> Louis Leonard Tucker
> State Historian of New York
> President, American Association
> for State and Local History

Albany, New York
February 1973

Contents

Preface

1976! A year to remember in our nation's history—a time of celebration, when Americans recall two hundred years of independence and nationhood. The Bicentennial year will be a time of achievement, a time to remember the past, to enjoy the present, and to build for the future.

Hopeful that it could help stimulate sophisticated leadership and participation in Bicentennial events, the American Association for State and Local History early concerned itself with the planning for 1976—and beyond. This book, generously supported and encouraged by the National Endowment for the Humanities and Wittenberg University in co-operation with the AASLH, was written with the hope that it would remind the general public of the meaning of the American Revolution and help our nation celebrate the Bicentennial with dignity and understanding. While the book should be of particular value to members of Bicentennial Commissions and contains special chapters for their consideration, its scope is such that all Americans interested in the Bicentennial—and all should be—may find it worthy of their attention.

Except for one chapter containing suggestions of activities, the book avoids the "how-to" approach in favor of case studies showing what other centennials have accomplished. After opening chapters on the meanings of the American Revolution, celebrations in general, and the coming Bicentennial in particular, I have sought to present through case studies the widest possible cross-section of celebration at the national, state or provincial, and local levels. Of course, the creative planner may adapt activities to any level.

Although some preferences may be obvious, I have, in general, avoided any firm recommendations. My study of other centennials, however, has led me to the conclusion that for the Bicentennial to be complete, it must be for all the people; it must be accepted as an important "once-in-a-lifetime" affair; and its planners must recognize man's search for identity, his needs for festivity, and his innate urge to create. The Bicentennial should also bring greater understanding and appreciation of the American Revolution as an important aspect of the heritage of this nation. The selection of centennials for case study from the many that have taken place in the United States and Canada, therefore, relates to these emphases. Though other celebrations may have been just as interesting, informative, and successful, the ones selected for this book were important ones for large numbers of people. They offer contrast on national, state, and local levels of celebration, as planners struggled to meet the demands of their particular situations.

The Civil War Centennial and the Centennial of Canadian Confederation were recent national celebrations that attracted much attention. They offer remarkable contrast in leadership and achievement, and they show different directions that planners took to achieve their results. Since the coming Bicentennial is a national celebration, planners on all levels—local, state, and national—should be aware of the many interrelationships involved in setting up their own programs.

The state centennials selected were distinguished by purpose, variety, good planning, and capable leadership. Those in New Jersey and Illinois were unusual year-long affairs which involved large numbers of people and grappled with problems that Bicentennial planners will soon know. Their committees also left records that permit studies of each of these in some depth. The six vignettes of state and provincial centennials give further contrast in style and manner of celebration. Though they may not have been as successful as many other state celebrations, they offer contrasting patterns of organization, fund-raising, public relations, and programs. Each had a different emphasis; each eventually followed a different direction toward its ultimate goals.

Chapter IX emphasizes the local level in centennial celebration. Though the nation's attention will be concentrated on large national programs and objectives, most of the action will take place at the local level. For these local planners, Chapter X offers examples of projects, programs, and events of other centennials—items that round out the profile of a centennial. The items listed show only what others have done in celebration, but I hope that they will inspire others to do even more significant things in the Bicentennial. The listing of an item does not necessarily suggest my approval, though I have eliminated events and programs that appeared to overlap or repeat other themes or lacked the dignity appropriate to such an important national occasion. While our majestic goals of celebration may be better reached through some programs more than others, I hope that these case studies will lead my readers to be more discriminating in their own selection of programs and events for the 1976 celebration.

Chapter XI, a brief conclusion, suggests the larger challenges and deeper meanings implied in a Bicentennial of the American Revolution and urges planners to recognize these concerns in their programs.

This book owes much to many people who helped to bring the ideas together. The thoughts of those persons across the United States and Canada who so generously submitted to interviews speak through the pages that follow. The ideas of those who answered a questionnaire or wrote letters are also incorporated, though not often personalized. To William T. Alderson, Director of the American Association for State and Local History, who shared in this effort from its beginning, I am grateful for professional counsel, innovative ideas, enthusiasm, and patience. I also worked closely with an advisory committee which met five times to evaluate the book in the research and writing stages. The committee consisted of Louis L. Tucker, Assistant Commissioner for State History, New York Department of Education, chairman; Professor John Armstrong, Department of History, Boston University; Professor Samuel Proctor, Department of History, University of Florida and Editor of the *Florida Historical Quarterly;* Richard C. Shultz, Executive Director of the Rochester Museum and Science Center; James Morton Smith, Director of the State Historical Society of Wisconsin, and Robert A. Weinstein, Vice-President, Ward-Ritchie Press, Los Angeles, California. These men contributed much to the organization and format of this publication, and their editorial assistance has been invaluable. The strong points of this book are the results of their suggestions; the weaknesses are mine alone. Editorial assistance came from Paula Hiles and Juanita Isherwood of the American Association for State and Local History, but the editing of Mary Lee Tipton of AASLH deserves special commendation for invaluable suggestions and numerous changes. Without the assistance of Jeanette Woodward, whose patience increased with the typing of every draft, the project would have been more difficult. I wish to thank the National Endowment for the Humanities for the generous grant which made this project possible, Wittenberg University for sabbatical and leave time which allowed me to engage in research and writing, and the Bicentennial Council of the Thirteen Original States for a publication grant. Thanks also to a family that allowed husband and father to be absent for over a year in research and writing.

    Like Francis Bacon's "Theater of Man's Life," a centennial

appears to be a time "reserved only for God and angels to be lookers on." Indeed, few Americans will be lookers on. Most will be paiticipants in the multitude of programs that will commemorate our national heritage. This book appears in the hope that it may direct celebrating Americans of all persuasions to serious concerns and worthwhile endeavors in the Bicentennial Era.

Springfield, Ohio   RGH
4 December 1972

Celebrating a Bicentennial
In the United States of America
In the Seventies
Is much like attacking
A two-headed leviathan
Breathing fire from two sets of nostrils
Facing in opposite directions—
Left and Right.

Enlightenment and achievement
Meet challenges and hopes
Head-on!
But even in the exalted moments
Of praise and thanksgiving
The joys of celebration
Must be tempered
By the realities of the possible—
Which are always changing.

1972

I

The Bicentennial:
Why Celebrate?

P REPARING for a large birthday party is seldom easy. When the party is for the two-hundredth birthday of a nation as vast and complex as the United States, the problems increase as the interest mounts. What can such a nation do to commemorate that which it is? What can its people do to give recognition to people and events that contributed to its growth and achievements? How can they relate its heritage to the uncertainties of its third century?

The birthday party of which we speak is the American Revolution Bicentennial. Its title creates an important distinction from a mere celebration of our national independence. The Revolution was the first great American cultural legacy, and it still commands public admiration and curiosity. But what does this Revolution mean in the nation's history? What do Americans celebrate on the anniversary of such an event? Even though they speak their opposition to revolution, Americans appear to be seeking a new revolution patterned after theirs two centuries ago. Rhetoric about such a revolution will fill commentaries and speeches in the days ahead. Orators will urge Americans to embrace the new spirit of '76.

Historians themselves have never agreed on the meaning of

this revolution, nor are they likely to. As each generation of scholars finds new answers, new questions arise. The Revolution has been seen as an overthrow of an oppressive government, a colonial war for independence, a failure of British policy, a problem of inept British leadership, a conflict of "home rule" against "who should rule at home." Seemingly achieved in an ivory tower, the Revolution has been called "the orderly transference of allegiance" from one set of rulers to another. Some have even contended that there was no revolution at all.

Soon after the Revolutionary War, John Adams sensed the complexity of meaning of the Revolution when he described it as being as varied in principle as the colonies involved and the individuals who participated in it. Historians have agreed with Adams: Robert R. Palmer calls the meaning of the conflict "ambivalent" after nearly two centuries;[1] William H. Nelson uses the term "downright elusive";[2] and Lawrence H. Leder suggests that the "cataclysmic nature" of the Revolution has brought about a variety of interpretations.[3] Was the Revolution, as Adams reflected late in life, "effected before the war commenced"[4] in the minds of people long before the first shot was fired at Lexington? Or was it merely the first act in a continuing process, as Adams's contemporary Benjamin Rush intimates?[5]

Whatever this Revolution was, it has been an important in-

---

1. Robert R. Palmer, "The American Revolution: The People as Constituent Power," in Irwin Unger, David Goodman, and Paul Brady, eds., *The Record of American History* (Waltham, Massachusetts: Xerox College Publishing Co., 1971), 159.

2. William H. Nelson, "The Revolutionary Character of the American Revolution," *American Historical Review*, 70 (July 1965), 998.

3. Lawrence H. Leder, ed., *The Meaning of the American Revolution* (Chichago: Quadrangle Books, 1969), 3.

4. Quoted in Hannah Arendt, *On Revolution* (New York: Viking Press, 1963), 115.

5. Address of Dr. Benjamin Rush, reprinted in Alden T. Vaughan, ed., *Chronicles of the American Revolution* (New York: Grosset and Dunlap, 1965), 334.

gredient in determining the national outlook. Henry Steele Commager says that the country was "founded squarely on the right of revolution, on the right to alter or abolish government," to change an existing order.[6] This is an exciting doctrine of change, but it is a dangerous one, which must be tempered with reason. In final analysis, the American Revolutionaries went beyond mere change to create instruments which gave life and meaning to revolutionary principles without causing the bloodbath that has accompanied so many other revolutions. Revolution in the American tradition, therefore, became a reaffirmation of values rather than mere protest, the triumph of reason and human dignity. It created a new government—"a very complex political machine . . . federalist, pluralistic, constitutionally restrained republicanism . . . the supreme culmination of the American Revolution," preserving individual liberty with "republican rule."[7] Adams described the new unity in noble language: "Thirteen clocks were made to strike together —a perfection of mechanism which no artist has ever before effected."[8] Tom Paine called attention to the timeless and cosmopolitan nature of the new doctrine: "Tis not the affair of a city, or county, or province, or a kingdom," he wrote, "but of a continent . . . not the concern of a day, a year, or an age; posterity are virtually involved."[9]

In light of all these interpretations, then, what does the Revolution signify today? What does it say to a generation preparing for a Bicentennial commemoration? Certainly the Revo-

---

6. Henry S. Commager, "Our Declaration Is Still a Rallying Cry," in Leder, ed., *The Meaning of the American Revolution,* 123.

7. James Morton Smith, "The Transformation of Republican Thought," *Indiana Historical Society Lectures 1969–1970* (Indianapolis: Indiana Historical Society, 1970), 58.

8. Quoted in Merrill Jensen, *The Founding of a Nation* (New York: Oxford University Press, 1968), xii.

9. Quoted in Avery Craven, Walter Johnson, and F. Roger Dunn (eds.), *A Documentary History of the American People* (New York: Ginn and Co., 1951), 154.

lution produced "tolerance of change," and a new reconciliation of liberty and order. It stressed the limitations of power and forecast the guarantee of civil rights. It showed how certain abstract doctrines, such as the rights and sovereignty of peoples, could be pragmatized by representative government; it triggered egalitarianism, social and cultural transformation, a new concept of colonialism, and the advance of learning; and it welded a people together as a nation by stimulating a feeling that the new nation had, from its beginning, "been destined to play a special role in history." [10] The Revolution, wrote Arnold Toynbee, "bore the fruits of reform, release, and rejuvenation," asserting human rights "for all human beings and right of self-determinism for all people." [11] An early mountain man, James P. Beckwourth, stated it simply: the Revolution "raised the dignity of man, and taught him to be free." [12]

Three documents—the Declaration of Independence, the Constitution, and the Bill of Rights—signify the nature and goals of the American Revolution and provide a continuity to the American experience, but it is the Declaration that epitomizes "the divergence between fear and faith that characterizes American life," [13] and makes the most profound statement of the human rights that underlie all national deliberations. Though the present political, economic, and psychological structure of the world often canonizes inequality among men, the Declaration of Independence still stands as a model of hope for better things. The achievements of the American people through two hundred years of nationhood include important successes in fulfilling its expectations. Still, in the midst of cele-

10. Bernard Bailyn, *The Ideological Origins of the American Revolution* (Cambridge, Mass.: Harvard University Press, 1967), 133.

11. Arnold J. Toynbee, "The Continuing Effect of the American Revolution" [Address on the occasion of the celebration of the Prelude to Independence] (Williamsburg, Va.: Institute of Early American History and Culture, 1961), 7.

12. Delmont R. Oswald, ed., *The Life and Adventures of James P. Beckwourth as told to Thomas D. Bonner* (Lincoln: University of Nebraska Press, 1972), 13.

13. Leder, *The Meaning of the American Revolution*, 109.

bration, we must remember that in spite of the bold signature of John Hancock, the classical statements of Thomas Jefferson, and the enthusiasm that John Adams had for the document, there was slavery!

Predictably, annual celebration in the past has concentrated on the anniversary of the Declaration of Independence, the Fourth of July. Since the early nineteenth century, speeches, fireworks, and other festivities have marked Independence Day. Even in the midst of civil war, Federal troops paused in the field to commemorate this day with barbecue, music, speeches, and a host of visiting ladies. For years the Tammany Society of New York required its membership "to assemble at the wigwam" every Fourth to listen to lengthy speeches and a reading of the Declaration. The perspiring members endured only through their knowledge of "the delights of the oasis" in the basement below.[14]

John Adams deserves some credit for this type of celebration. He spoke of a "Great Annual Festival," to be celebrated "as the day of deliverance, by solemn acts of devotion to God Almighty . . . with pomp and parades, with shows, games, sports, guns, bells, bonfires and illuminations from one end of this continent to the other, from this time forward, forever more." [15] An act from a Boston town meeting of 1783 encouraged similar celebration: "The Fourth of July shall be constantly celebrated by the delivery of a Publick oration . . . in which the orator shall consider the feelings, manners, and principles which led to this Great Capital event as well as the important and happy effects . . . which already have and will forever continue to flow from the auspicious epoch." In such spirit Americans have continued to celebrate for nearly two centuries. "Everybody has his own way of letting the American eagle loose," colorfully recounted

---

14. William L. Riordon (recorder), *Plunkitt of Tammany Hall* (New York: E. P. Dutton, 1963), 70.

15. Quoted in Page Smith, *John Adams* (Garden City, N.Y.: Doubleday, 1962), I, 271.

the Steubenville (Ohio) *Weekly Gazette* in the Centennial year. "Some boys are satisfied with a ten cent flag, while others will not be satisfied unless they get full of raging . . ."

The deaths of Adams and Jefferson on July 4, 1826, the fiftieth anniversary of the signing of the Declaration of Independence, portended Divine Providence and added profound meaning to Fourth of July observances. Historian Page Smith says that America came of age on that day. The lives of Adams and Jefferson "encompassed the revolutionary experience. . . . The burden that they laid down, successive generations must pick up anew." [16] Their contemporary, William Wirt, confirmed this new direction: "Hitherto, fellow citizens, the Fourth of July had been celebrated among us, only as the anniversary of our independence, and its votaries had been merely human beings. . . . But at its last reoccurrence—the great jubilee of the nation—the anniversary, it may well be termed, of the liberty of man—Heaven, itself, mingled visibly in the celebration, and hallowed the day anew by a double apotheosis." From this day forward, says historian Daniel Boorstin, the Fourth of July did not simply "commemorate the nation's birth," it "affirmed national purpose." [17]

Here was the culmination of nationhood: America, born in the Revolution, maturing in the passing of two of its greatest architects—a nationhood that exhibited "a confessional and creedal quality" but also "a surprising verve and exuberance." [18] This was a new system in the ways of men, this America— "rigid, moralistic, and self-righteous sometimes," said William Nelson, "yet with an ultimate respect for the rules of reason and a saving capacity for self-criticism." [19]

---

16. *Ibid.*, II, 1138.
17. Daniel Boorstin, *The Americans: The National Experience* (New York: Random House, 1965), 390.
18. William Nelson, "The Revolutionary Character of the American Revolution," 1014.
19. *Ibid.*

The Centennial of 1876 added another contour to the patterns of celebrating nationhood. At the end of its first century, the United States was well on its way toward achieving status on the international scene, yet so young that its heritage seemed only a shadow when compared to that of the older European nations. Celebration, therefore, had to be of *achievement,* one hundred years of growth unparalleled in human history—progress in a material age. Optimistic Americans looked at their civilization and smiled with approval, then celebrated their Centennial as a sort of long, drawn-out Fourth of July, with a magnificent Exposition in Philadelphia the highlight of a year of glamorous and sometimes meaningful pageantry. Americans were proud of the achievements they had made: their science and art, the appliances of human ingenuity, and the gadgetry they beheld at their Fair. In 1876 the frontier was fading in the rise of a new industrial empire. The people in that year could look back at an agrarian heritage and mythologize it into a permanent place in the American mind; but they also looked ahead to a new technological society, exemplified at its best and at its worst by the Great Exposition.

Closer observation by those Americans might have sobered other judgments about their first century of progress, especially if they had looked at the plights of Black Americans, Indians, recent immigrants, subsistence farmers, and underpaid day laborers, or at the confusing political and economic situations that had followed war and depression. They might have noticed the growing urban complexes, the unrelenting cycles of "boom and bust," the continuing dehumanization of Blacks, Indians' resentment of white encroachment on western land, and the rapidly closing public domain—which would soon end Jefferson's fond dream of a longtime "empire for liberty." To point up a particular continuing discrepancy in the national experience of the first century, Susan B. Anthony and an escort of four other ladies assembled in Independence Square on the Fourth and read their own liberalized "Declaration of Independence."

Certainly some Americans concerned themselves with the problems of their times; but most were euphoric and the Declaration of Independence of 1776 continued to symbolize to them even greater opportunities for progress in building, changing, moving, growing, and creating. Their festive mood testified to their hopes for even greater successes in the nation's second century. "Thomas Jefferson still lives!" If these were truly John Adams' words, he was speaking for generations beyond his own.

Another hundred years have passed, and again Americans approach a centennial with high hopes—some for solemn and fruitful commemoration, some for commercial opportunities, some just for fun. A centennial is a once-in-a-lifetime affair, a chance to step outside the routines of daily living and look at the past—to evaluate, appreciate, and preserve that which gives the nation and its people identity. "A nation needs . . . to have a consciousness of itself; to cherish heroes, to recall its past, and to gather to itself the loyalty that goes with heroes and memory." [20] These possibilities may materialize in a centennial properly celebrated. A centennial can be a dynamic process, involving people, resources, and environment. If faced realistically, it can become a milestone in the life of a nation.

The Bicentennial, like the Centennial, offers such opportunities, even as it symbolizes another significant transition in American history—the end of the pre-industrial, pre-technological, pre-behavioral period, and an introduction to a new man in a new age. Signs point to ever-changing methods and approaches for handling old problems—changing patterns of management, radical new concepts of education, humanistic concerns beyond the imagination, and international co-operation that may eventually blur national boundaries. Therefore, the big question is how to celebrate a historic revolution and its results in a new age of revolutionary change. How should

20. Walter Notestein, *The English People on the Eve of Colonization* (New York: Harper and Row, 1954) , 6.

Americans "celebrate" or "commemorate" the occasion of two hundred years of nationhood to give it fullest expression? The word commemorate seems hardly to express the sentiment craved, but it does imply a much-desired restraint. Celebration is probably the better term, but it too quickly draws to mind a type of excessive display that would be well avoided. Perhaps to celebrate in its theological sense—to remember, to rededicate, to reaffirm—offers the greatest meaning in these troubled times.

National birthdays, like human birthdays, offer opportunities that citizens of this country should not take lightly. Birthdays symbolize more than our birth and the passing of our days. They symbolize achievement and growth, remind us of the past that shapes our present, and give hope for a productive future. The big question is not *whether* America will celebrate its national birthday; it is *how* our nation will deal with this important moment in history. Will this be a solemn occasion for rededication, the commemoration of accomplishments, a reassessment of where we are and where we are going; or will it be marked "by frying chickens, firing away damaged powder, or fuddling our noses over tavern wine"?

One of the most difficult assignments of any planner, then, is to determine the nature of his program. Human beings are festive creatures, and the festive spirit is rooted deep in history. Much of the history of the Egyptians, Persians, Greeks, and Romans deals with ceremony, pageantry, and festivity. The medieval peasant interrupted his dull routine with celebrations of almost everything—the birth of a son in the manor house, a religious holiday, a good harvest.[21] These festivities went beyond expression of the mere joy of living: "such ceremonies also promoted tribal unity and strengthened the loyalty of the individual to tribal traditions.[22] This is the spirit that prompts

---

21. Eileen Power, *Medieval People* (Garden City, N.Y.: Doubleday, 1924), 29.
22. H. B. Parkes, *Gods and Men: The Origins of Western Culture* (New York: Random House, 1959), 29.

many of us to celebrate. "For life to be fruitful," writes humanist essayist Albert J. Nock, "life must be felt as a joy; that is by
the bond of joy." This is the joy of the festival, as man becomes involved with his fellow man expressing zest for life.
This is the joy that deflates balloons of prejudice and pride
with homely wisdom and humor.

Centennial planners must understand that, in celebration,
ritual takes on meaning according to the tastes and desires of
individual participants and the availability of materials. Some
persons feel that celebration must be on the loftiest plane. The
imagination, originality, sophistication, and enthusiasm that
they apply will determine the true measure of their program.
Others prefer frivolity; parades, pageants, re-enactments, beard-
growing, and beauty contests may dominate the celebration at
the expense of more serious endeavors. Whatever the case, men
have always taken time from routine for gala affairs, and they
will do so in 1976. One of the challenges of every planner is
how to harness this festive spirit to best effect.

Much of the success of managing the moods of celebration
in a centennial depends upon the themes selected by planners,
and here the Bicentennial faces its most serious challenge. In
our present days of painful self-examination, almost any theme
tends to polarize rather than to bring people together. One suggestion, however, is to turn to the list of America's ten contributions   to   civilization   compiled   by   historian   Arthur
Schlesinger, Sr. These were the right of revolution, the principle of federalism, the consent of the governed, the status of
women, the melting-pot idea, freedom of worship, the public
school, voluntary giving, technology, and the concept of evolutionary progress.[23] Through many of these topics face serious
re-evaluation in the light of current practices, they are principles that sprang from the actions of the Revolutionary genera-

---

23. Arthur Schlesinger, Sr., "Our Ten Contributions to Civilization," in
Albert Karson and Perry E. Gianakos, eds., *American Civilization Since World
War II* (Belmont, Cal.: Wadsworth Publishing Co., 1968), 75–82.

tion, and they may lend themselves to any celebration, either as isolated program topics or as multiple themes for more complex elaboration. In nearly every case symbols already exist, and a program director can either use them or develop new ones.

Some planners may prefer to celebrate more general themes, such as the Revolutionary generation's love of liberty, its willingness to face the realities of revolution, the sacrifice and devotion of individuals to a particular cause, the fellowship in ideals and arms both within America and between America and France, its concerns 'that this land remain a land of the free, its creation of a tradition resting firmly on a base of moral principle, and its willingness to accept equality as an article of faith. Others will stress themes of liberty and equality, the open society, equality of opportunity, the sanctity of private property, the protection of the rights of the individual against the state—civil rights— or the wide array of choice available to Americans. Some may concentrate on such themes as freer expression in literature and art, broadening the base of dissent in American politics both at home and abroad, and maintaining freedom in the midst of technological change. Some may find nothing more to consider than hopes deferred.

The Bicentennial is a time for a reconsideration of our heritage. A nation is showing its maturity when it can look objectively at its history. Our national history from its beginning was a struggle for a new way of life. "The equality of all men, their inherent and inalienable rights, and the sovereign right of peoples to institute their own governments" were now realities, a new and sometimes fitful experience for this nation's "new man," as he was branded by the French visitor Hector St. John Crèvecoeur. At what better time than during our Bicentennial may Americans increase awareness of this cultural and social heritage—this unique experiment? What better time is there to gain greater understanding of the Revolution and its meaning? We study the past and return to the complicated world of the present more aware of our former outlooks on history. The Bicentennial Era is a time of intensive study of the past: scholars should explore new paths of understanding in light of new evidence, sophisticated techniques, and expanded viewpoints; libraries should make available for general reading the standard works, as well as newer anthologies and popular books, not only on the Revolution, but on local heritage; the news media, particularly television, should also employ their talents both to interpret the past and to develop local pride and participation. Colleges and high schools should focus on research projects, collateral reading, exciting electronic programs, as well as tours to sites of historic interest and importance, to supplement interest gained within and outside the classroom.

To give themes a personal dimension, planners might symbolize complicated themes and ideas by singling out several key persons in the drama of the American Revolution. Thomas Jefferson, George Washington, John Adams, and Benjamin Franklin come immediately to mind. Who but Thomas Jefferson "formulated the ideas of democracy with such a fullness, persuasiveness and logic"? Jefferson is "our best historic symbol of the universal, in time of struggle for human freedom against tyranny in any of its forms." [24] While he symbolizes individual independence, Washington symbolizes "national independence," leadership of the highest order in a nation that demanded the services of its greatest citizens. John Adams gave dignity and meaning to conservative principles in a generation of revolutionaries. Though faith in the future was easier for Jefferson than it was for him, Adams never lost heart, even in the darkest days of uncertainty. The versatility and universality of Benjamin Franklin make him and Jefferson "true children of the enlightenment."

To understand ourselves better and to enable most Ameri-

---

24. Saul Padover, "Jefferson Still Survives—," in Glyndon G. Van Deusen and Herbert J. Bass, eds., *Readings in American History,* 2 vols. (New York: Macmillan, 1963) , 108.

cans to identify with the Revolution on a personal level, we would do well to look beyond the leaders of the Revolution to the common folk of that generation—men and women who faced an uncertain future in a nation lacking territorial and administrative unity, and with no demonstrable unity of will or purpose—as they struggled to maintain their simple ways of life in a changing world. Not only did these Americans survive, they set a firm foundation for a nation that, for all its failures, has cherished human values and freedom to a degree hitherto unknown. Their accomplishments still work a ferment in the American society and in the American mind and give hope for the future.

On any level of celebration, prospects for programs are complicated by the current mood in America and the world. The celebration of a generation ago may no longer be possible, as celebrating as Americans did in 1876 certainly is impossible. In many ways the nineteenth century was a more comfortable time: progress had a universal ring; patriotism was the American's highest calling. There is less assurance in America today, so what we celebrate is at least in part transitory and even illusory. Planners should take note of pitfalls that may mar the celebration. Citizens of some Western states, Indians, Blacks, and other ethnic groups—whose roots seem far removed from our eighteenth-century memories and whose heroes are not included in traditional lists of Revolutionary heroes—may show little enthusiasm for developing programs, even feel that they have no role in celebration. They may feel that the Revolution has no bearing on their own history; they may not want to involve themselves in commemoration of a period so remote and alien to their present mode of life. State and local historians, however, with their enormous storehouse of knowledge, talent, creativity, and diversity, can help to solve this problem. Working closely with these groups, local historical societies may provide the link that will bring them into the spirit of commemoration.

State and local historians may be the voices of influence that will effect the broadest possible participation of citizens, private organizations, special groups, businesses, educational institutions, historical societies, libraries, and museums. It is in the context of the community that most people seek fulfillment. It is at home that they find the best prospects for an understanding of their own historical tradition. Local historians deal with the individual where he is—in tenement, farmhouse, mansion, apartment, or suburban ranchhouse. By study and preservation of local heritages within the larger contexts of national and international change, local historians may be able to broaden participation in Bicentennial activities so as to include the most disparate of groups.

In fact, the Bicentennial may present an unusual opportunity for state and local history, "once practiced with carefulness, zeal, and even pride . . . but later despised by the supporters of general history," to regain its rightful voice in the affairs of men. Josiah Royce spelled out this important direction when he wrote "we need . . . in this country a new and wiser provincialism . . . which makes people want to utilize, to adorn, to ennoble, to educate their own province." [25] One of the first obligations of the local historian should be to encourage programs that educate citizens to the meaning and the details of their own local heritage as well as of the American Revolution. This is the time for local historians to offer materials, guidance, and leadership: to work with libraries to create Bicentennial bookshelves and displays, for both adults and children; to inform themselves and others about available films, the best biographies, and the resources available from agencies specializing in Bicentennial affairs; to know and publicize the most helpful journals; and to be familiar with the Bicentennial projects of the Library of Congress, the National Archives, the National Trust for His-

---

25. Quoted in Pierre Goubert, "Local History," *Daedalus*, 100 (Winter 1971), 113.

toric Preservation, other historical associations, and additional groups whose primary concerns relate to a scholarly interpretation of America's revolutionary heritage. Working with productive themes and materials, the local historian will command new attention as source, leader, and participant.

II

The Bicentennial Era Begins

ON July 3, 1971, President Richard Nixon proclaimed to a nationwide television audience and a few select guests the beginning of the "Bicentennial Era," a period of preparation for and celebration of America's two-hundredth anniversary. In a simple ceremony at the National Archives, the President, Chief Justice Warren Burger, and House Speaker Carl Albert, representing the three major divisions of the federal government, spoke of their hopes for commemorating the occasion. While these national leaders spoke, television cameras, dramatically blending past and present, shifted from their faces to the original Declaration of Independence in its impressive case to the mural of the signers of the Declaration covering the large wall at the rear of the room. Almost as if to break the spell, the Army choir sang "America the Beautiful" as a benediction. The cameras moved on as the choir spanned the years of history in song. The music faded; the dignitaries left the stage. The Bicentennial Era had begun.

Plans to commemorate the Bicentennial of American independence officially began in 1966, when Representative Charles Mathias of Maryland and Bradford Morse of Massachusetts introduced legislation that led to the creation of the American

Revolution Bicentennial Commission. "We believed," Mathias said, "not only that the revolution was the most important event in our history but, even more, that the ideas and ideals of the revolution are as real and relevant today as they were two hundred years ago." To these congressmen, a Bicentennial is a "rare opportunity" for the nation to renew a commitment made two centuries ago by the Americans who first had the national dream. On July 4, 1966, President Lyndon Johnson signed Public Law 89–491, establishing the American Revolution Bicentennial Commission (ARBC), "to plan, encourage, develop, and coordinate the commemoration of the American Revolution Bicentennial." In November the President appointed seventeen members of the new Commission, instructing them to bring back specific recommendations for celebration no later than July 4, 1968. Hampered by lack of funds, and lack of presidential and congressional support, the Commission accomplished little before the end of the Johnson administration.

After some delay and a change of personnel, President Nixon reconvened the Commission under a new chairman, Dr. J. E. Wallace Sterling, Chancellor of Stanford University. Subcommittees on media; science; arts and humanities; commerce and labor; events and expositions; volunteer, military, and service organizations charted some positive directions. To supplement ARBC planning further, the President also appointed the National Goals Research staff, a small group of consultants to work with "the problems of forecasting the alternative choices for the physical, social, and individual life environments in American cities." [1] The staff of the National Goals Research Staff was made up of experts in the collection, correlation, and processing of data relating to social needs and in the projection of social trends, who report to the ARBC.

Three guidelines for the Bicentennial emerged from the early activity of ARBC. It would be *national* in scope; it would

---

1. North Carolina Bicentennial Commission, *American Revolution II* (Raleigh, 1971), 41–42.

continue to 1987 with the focal year 1976, the focal date July 4 of that year; and it would be a time "to *review* and *reaffirm* the public principles upon which the nation was founded." The immediate goal called for forging a new national commitment, "*a new spirit for '76,*" a spirit to utilize "the ideals for which the revolution was fought . . . /and/ unite the nation in purpose and dedication to the advancement of human welfare as it moves into its third century." The Commission also decided upon three basic themes for the Bicentennial Era. *Heritage '76* recalls the past; *Festival USA* (formerly *Open House USA*) directs attention to the present and to other nations of the world; and *Horizons '76* anticipates the challenges of an uncertain future. *Summons, opportunity,* and *challenge* were the key words in ARBC's search for a national scheme of commemoration.

To publicize its activities, and to serve as a sounding board for other centennial planners, ARBC began the publication of a monthly newsletter entitled *Bicentennial Era,* which was followed later by a weekly supplement called *Bicentennial News.* Under ARBC's encouragement nearly every state has established a Bicentennial commission; these in turn urge communities to form committees to prepare for their own celebrations. Two federal grants support this program.

Early Bicentennial planning generally failed to produce a firm pattern for fruitful celebration. When Dr. Sterling resigned from the chairmanship under the pressures of a heavy work load, President Nixon named David J. Mahoney, president and board chairman of Norton Simon, Inc., as the replacement. Criticism from Congress and from the press continued to point up shortcomings until the Commission was forced to make important changes. On July 3, 1971, the President envisioned goals more universal than the original ones by speaking of peace; progress; full employment; the "restoration of our heritage of clean air and water"; law; better education, health, and housing for all Americans; necessary governmental reform;

and "unlimited opportunity for every American citizen whatever his background." If these are indeed the true goals throughout the celebration, and proper steps are made to implement them for all Americans, social action programs will dominate much of the action of the Era, and tangible concerns may be rail systems, pollution, and new processes for living, among many others. In this connection ARBC should be a source and a guide for planners looking for projects, programs, and materials—as well as a sort of weather vane to sense new directions and hopes on other levels of planning and to keep planning within announced bounds.

ARBC has continued to move very slowly, and, though their own publications speak of involvement, its critics still speak of what the Commission has not done. In answer to some criticism, ARBC increased its membership, adding Blacks, women, a Mexican-American, and young people. Regional offices have been established in Atlanta, Boston, and Chicago, with plans for several others. Other actions have been significant in a narrow perspective, but the large picture is still blurred. The Commission endorsed Niagara Falls, New York, as the nation's first Bicentennial city, encouraging better Canadian-American relations in this connection. They endorsed Mt. Rushmore as the first Bicentennial regional site—an appeal to Western states that suggests historical considerations beyond the American Revolution period and the scenes of its actions. They have assisted in the establishment of state and territorial Bicentennial Commissions and have shared materials with these new commissions—including two grants of $45,000 to each of the fifty states. Probably the most ambitious project has been the most controversial. In early 1972, the Commission proposed a complicated park program, with a Bicentennial park for every state. These parks would be focal points in a state's celebration of the Bicentennial and would remain thereafter as permanent reminders of the anniversary. They would answer ecological needs, provide facilities for traveling national and international touring artists and exhibitions, offer recreational complexes unrivaled in the United States, be available for family camping, and provide a Bicentennial pavilion for historical exhibits, displays of American arts and crafts, and special films. Each park would have a rapid transit system, a craft bazaar to inject local color and ethnic uniqueness, a state crafts workshop for local artists to develop and display creativity, and a large outdoor amphitheater to provide programs by symphony orchestras, folk and rock groups, bands, dancers, jazz combos, repertory theater, and other performing groups.

Three other proposals of national significance include the South Street Seaport, a multi-million dollar restoration of New York City's wharf, support for *Foxfire,* the innovative educational program of a group of Georgia young people designed to preserve past American history and culture, and an exhibit entitled "Bicentennial Exhibit of the Chicago Museum of Science and Industry," which will trace contributions and evolution of America's science and technology throughout its two hundred years.[2]

More realistic to historians and to others interested in the past was the proposal to create a National Historic Records program, to "involve the creation of appropriate mechanisms for making matching grants to assist states, committees, groups, institutions, and individuals in locating, preserving, making available, and developing better utilization of the nation's public and private historic records."[3] In addition to formal grants, this program would provide money to states, communities, and individuals for locating, preserving, making available many public and private historical records heretofore lost to researchers. Receiving the endorsement of the presidents of the Amer-

2. American Revolution Bicentennial Commission Special Bulletin to Congress, September 11, 1972.

3. Robert K. Webb (American Historical Association), Statement before the Standing Subcommittee on Federal Charters, Holdings, and Celebrations, Senate Committee on Federal Charters, August 1, 1972.

ican Association for State and Local History, the Organization of American Historians, the American Historical Association, the American Society for Legal History, and the Society of American Archivists, this program holds great hope for the future of historical research.

ARBC has also expanded its horizons in arts and in travel programs. In early 1972, forty-seven prominent Americans from the fields of travel and hospitality, the creative and visual arts, and the performing arts held a series of advisory meetings in New York City to discuss the performing arts, the creative and visual arts, and an invitation to the world to attend the American celebration.

With ARBC struggling to determine choices and directions for the national Bicentennial future, other commissions and organizations have stepped into what appeared to be a vacuum and followed their own inclinations. The Afro-American Bicentennial Corporation, a non-profit Black group formed in 1970, is dedicated to the encouragement of minorities in Bicentennial activities. Its announced basic goal is to promote the "continuing revolution," defined as "a process of decolonization, a movement toward self-realization and self-government by 'people determined not to be kept in a subject status.' " [4] Using some funds from the federal government, the corporation identified first areas of interest as housing programs, selected publications of Black history, and preparation of historic sites honoring Black contributions to our national heritage.

The Peoples American Revolution Bicentennial Commission in the nation's capital is a more radical organization, representing a more liberal point of view. They have emphasized the "revolution of '76" to help create "an atmosphere of confidence among people and their ability to shape the future, to explore and enter unfamiliar areas of experience." [5]

4. *Preservation News*, 12 (August 1972) , 6.
5. Washington *Post*, October 15, 1971; Jeremy Rifkin, "The Red, White and Blue LEFT," *The Progressive* (November 1971) .

Federalism Seventy-Six is a non-profit, tax-exempt, educational corporation whose announced goal in Bicentennial commemoration is "to increase public understanding of our American federal system of self-government so that every citizen will be able to participate intelligently in the advance of this system." [6] Members are working for "a greater realization of the ideals set forth in the Declaration of Independence and . . . the high objectives expressed in the Preamble of the Constitution of the United States." This group is working toward involving American people in nationwide civic educational programs, hoping to associate better understanding of the governmental process with Bicentennial meaning.

Many state and local groups have accepted the challenge and are working on programs. The thirteen original states have taken the lead, planning separately and through a special cooperative commission—the Bicentennial Council of the Thirteen Original States. Programs currently under way in Connecticut will relate to the results of a $45,000 grant from the General Assembly to study the feasibility of establishing a state historical museum and park complex as a permanent Bicentennial memorial and to purchase land for several historical restorations. State planners have also negotiated contracts with publishers for the production of thirty to forty monographs and booklets on Connecticut during the Revolutionary War, and have plans for a color motion picture on the same subject.

From its initial meetings in 1969, New Jersey planners placed heavy emphasis upon history, following patterns set earlier in the Tercentenary, with special projects including library workshops, elementary school "colonial fairs," an extensive publications program, a history symposium, traveling exhibitions, an outdoor drama on the battlefields of Trenton and Princeton, new historical markers and a State Visitor Center, and Bicentennial discussion on every level of planning. As with its Tercente-

---

6. Brochures from Federalism Seventy-Six, Inc., 1700 Pennsylvania Avenue, Washington, D.C.

nary state officials are again requesting "broad and active public participation at the local level." [7] Paterson's goals illustrate this interest—the renovation of the Mill Race System; several historical restorations; the development of a museum of science and technology; and construction of walkways, recreational facilities, and vistors' facilities.

Early planning in Virginia concentrated upon publications, with special attention to seven booklets on the Virginia signers of the Declaration of Independence, nine booklets on Virginia in the Revolutionary War, eight booklets on military men in that war, and twelve source booklets on the American Revolution. New York's dynamic program, already under way, includes important new publications, a "Fabric of the State" annual series of exhibitions of early crafts, several color films, and a fine newsletter. Maryland has a Revolutionary Era Trail booklet underway, among other publications, and research has begun to develop the state's Iron Furnace sites. Pennsylvania has floundered a bit, trying to decide how to involve Philadelphia, but now is active in promoting new programs, as are North Carolina, Rhode Island, Massachusetts, Delaware, Georgia, Maryland, and South Carolina.

Beyond the thirteen original states, Florida and Texas have moved rapidly in outlining programs. Florida's state commission emphasized historical backgrounds and concentrated upon publications to emphasize this direction. That state's planning has also been the concern of interama, a Miami project whose promoters visualize as providing "a place which millions of people each year will come to understand what is and what could be for the people of the Americas, . . . a permanent community of cultural, entertainment, educational and trade activities, . . . a showplace of learning and participation for all

---

7. Bernard Bush, "New Jersey's Historical Programs for the American Revolution Bicentennial" (New Jersey Historical Commission paper).

of the western hemisphere." [8] Sometimes Interama's plans seem at cross purposes with the state planning commission, but its plans for cultural exhibits, trade shows, amusements, business and trade activities, sports, and special entertainment and recreation are extensive.

Texas, like Canada in its Centennial, is fortunate to have a citizens' committee working with its regularly constituted legislative commission. Each group quickly provided directions for Texans in early planning sessions. Objectives, which point to realizable hopes that the Bicentennial will be a time for growth and change, include an intensive publicity campaign; a speakers' bureau; extensive competitions for school-age children in essay-writing, art, music, and drama; research and publication; and programs and projects stressing Texas backgrounds, state historical figures, exhibitions, and artistic productions. Houston's Americana Center, a unit affiliated with Rice University, indicates the larger directions of Bicentennial efforts. This center is described as providing "ultimate modern facilities for research, learning, teaching, and dissemination," and housing the most sophisticated computerized techniques as a service center "to help solve problems created by the information explosion." [9] In this center will be housed super computers, telecommunications, video display, mass laser storage, microfilm computer storage, and digital verbal installation designed to store, interpret, and communicate knowledge about every state in the Union to every level of government, major traditional library collections, and agencies of knowledge in the private sector. Fascinating and frightening—modernity at its ultimate to open a new century! San Antonio is working on a year-long open house for 1976 with emphasis on bringing together Mexicans and Americans in an annual fiesta dedicated to the Bi-

8. "Action Program for Interama," (Miami, Florida: Inter-American Center Authority, 1971).

9. "1776–1976" (American Revolution Bicentennial Commission of Texas, 1972).

centennial. Dallas has initiated a complex "Goals for Dallas" program which includes neighboring planning sessions, task forces to study programs and projects, and an extensive number of diversified programs for the Bicentennial year. Other Texas officials have looked to local history as subject matter, but the larger emphasis seems to be on the cities' developing at least one permanent Bicentennial project.

In looking toward a state Centennial and the Bicentennial in the same year, Colorado's legislature set a pattern of action that might well serve as a model for other states struggling with Bicentennial planning. A nine-member state commisson works without pay, receiving only actual and necessary travel expenses. All groups and institutions in the state are urged to re-examine origins, values, and the meaning of the American heritage while also setting forth accomplishments, dramatizing historical development, and forging new commitments through remembrance and discovery of the state's heritage. A $25,000 initial appropriation signified a seriousness of purpose in a legislative act that also called for demonstrated concern for "human welfare, happiness, and freedom." [10] Though the state voted down the Winter Olympics as a feature of 1976, the state still looks to extensive Bicentennial participation. Early plans in Washington, D.C., included constructing a new town, Fort Lincoln, as a model community; transit improvements, including a metro station at Arlington Cemetery; a National Visitors' Center; Bicentennial gardens; a national air and space museum; an art and industries building to house the exhibits of the original United States Centennial; and many other programs to meet the needs of a changing world.

In Wisconsin the Heritage Committee of the Wisconsin American Revolution has recommended that Old World Wisconsin be considered as a national Bicentennial project in lieu

---

10. Colorado House Bill No. 1092.

of the proposal of ARBC for a State Park.[11] Californians are planning the largest equestrian event in the state's history, retracing the old trails of El Camino Viejo. Wyoming has proposed a National Women's Hall of Fame at Cheyenne as a special project. "Pioneer Arizona," an outdoor living museum of reconstructed history, is a project of that southwestern state. South Dakota has designated Deadwood as its first Bicentennial historic city. Utah, one of ten states selected by ARBC to be surveyed for special Bicentennial pilot studies, has mapped out the Escalante-Dominguez expedition for special study and commemoration. Spokane, Washington, is planning an extensive beautification program combined with an information center to interpret the city's history and culture. Ohio is celebrating the Bicentennial with an assortment of projects, including a special folklore program whereby selected primary and secondary teachers will devote one unit to bringing their students into direct contact with the folklore of their own communities through interviews, collections of verse and song, and research. In setting directions for celebration, Alaska's commission expected to give its emphasis in planning "to the ideas associated with the American Revolution which have been important to the development of the United States and Alaska in world affairs and in mankind's quest for freedom." [12] Other states are also active, and their stated programs a potpourri of what the Bicentennial year will be. Other states procrastinate—and time runs out.

Though commercialism appears to be getting up a good head of steam, some special programs of substance are already appearing under the sponsorship of American businesses. Though melodramatic and overdrawn at times, Union Oil's "Spirit of '76" advertisements recount interesting historical vignettes.

11. "Old World Wisconsin Endorsed as State Project for Nation's Bicentennial, *Wisconsin Then and Now,* 19 (September 1972) , 6.

12. American Revolution Bicentennial Committee, *Bicentennial Newsletter,* 6 (August 1972), 5.

American Heritage has taken advantage of the Bicentennial by announcing two narratives—*The Revolution* and *The American People*—stressing maps, documents, and American music. This company also advertises a 1784 map of the United States, appropriately framed; a large American eagle; and a George Washington bowl—copied from a rare piece of eighteenth-century Liverpool ware. Before its demise, *Life* sponsored a Declaration of Independence photography contest with a $25,000 grand prize.

On other government levels, the National Parks plan to extend their own centennial observances of 1973 into the Bicentennial, with an emphasis upon developing a park philosophy for the nation. The Smithsonian Bicentennial plan includes major projects in the nation's capital including an outdoor park exhibition of the Revolutionary War, a spacearium in the National Space and Air Museum, a recreation of the 1876 Centennial in the Arts and Industries Building, and a special inventory of American painting. The Library of Congress and the National Archives have initiated important publications, exhibitions, and lecture series. One of the latter, the Library's Symposium on the American Revolution, has already established itself as an event of importance.

Organizations and individuals are also counteracting commercialism with positive program-planning. The Shackamoxon Society of Philadelphia began with a program of "Living History," which included a museum of the American soldier. One feature calls for twenty-five students to live in a fort in the same style that Revolutionary soldiers lived two centuries earlier. The 4-H Clubs of South Dakota are planning a state beautification program as a Bicentennial project. The New York State Council on the Arts is one of the sponsors of a series of annual shows exploring the different crafts of the state in the Museum of American Folk Art in New York City, a series that will include exhibitions on paper, wood, ceramics, and metal. Stamford, Connecticut, has purchased land to restore a

Revolutionary fort. Two exciting television shows have appeared, and others are expected. Alistair Cooke's series *America* is the narrator's charming birthday present to his adopted country and will serve as a topic of discussion and debate as well as illustrative material for history classes for many years to come. Chet Huntley's narration of *The American Experience* is not as colorful, but offers another perspective of the American past.

Bicentennial celebration, even though it utilizes our best talents, can be marked by pitfalls. There is the possibility of overexposure—too many events and too much involvement over too long a time. We are beginning the Bicentennial Era early, and we may tire of continuing references to "revolutionary" history. Genius and dedication will be needed to sustain interest and promote worthwhile programs if Bicentennial observances continue to 1987. Emphasis on trivia in themes and materials is a danger, as is concentrating too heavily on single issues, emphasizing narrow chronological and geographic concerns. The early surge of interest in the thirteen original states hints strongly that the Bicentennial may be developing a regional tone. To bring in the other states, larger themes must be explored—their own pasts and their own contribution to national growth and development over more than two centuries. Co-operation among the states, sharing of resources, programs, and ideas and the use of events throughout the entire two hundred years of American history will be required to bring the largest number of people into celebration. The focus must always be on the entire two centuries of national history.

Planners should be alert to the possibilities of use of the Bicentennial theme to advance causes. New Left advocates are excited about the implications that commemoration of revolution may have for their programs. They will reflect with enthusiasm on Jefferson's statement that "the tree of liberty must be refreshed from time to time with the blood of patriots and tyrants. It is its natural manure." Partisans of the extreme

Right are also excited about commemorating the American Revolution. This will be their time for flag-waving, "America First" speeches, and "Love it or leave it" sentiments. Too many citizens will emphasize family trees, social status, and economic achievements as criteria for judging a person's worth. Too often people will bask in the reflection of national deeds and overlook the crying needs of a changing world, forgetting that the ideals, hopes, and aspirations of the Founding Fathers are for *all* people.

The focus of the Bicentennial must ultimately be humanistic. Groups that are often neglected in our society—ethnic, youth, and senior citizens—should have their day. The eleven problems of today's world, as identified by *Common Cause*—war, pollution, government, discrimination, criminal justice, poverty, health care, education, housing, family planning, and urban transportation—must also be concerns for Bicentennial times. To be true to the themes of the Revolutionary generation, we must now stand against all that dehumanizes in an age when our national potential stands at its greatest. "Pity for misfortune is one of the tests of a civilization." [13] Human values must share the spotlight of celebration. The Bicentennial is indeed "a time to take stock of our heritage and accomplishments and to eradicate blight and pollution wherever they exist." [14] The Bicentennial is our test. It is not a time to escape from the present but a time to employ our crafts to stimulate bipartisan actions to alleviate pain and extend the possibilities of human dignity to all within our national range.

---

13. Walter Notestein, *The English People on the Eve of Colonization,* 14n.
14. Editorial, *Preservation News,* 11 (July 1971), 4.

III

A Concert of People: The Canadian Centennial of Confederation

We met together
On city square,
By roaring stream or far-off plain,
Beneath an ancient ivory tower—
We met to celebrate a nation's Dream
Or mold one from our past.

We met to celebrate the trails we crossed,
The lives lived out beneath our sun—
Those who won and those who lost.
We met to share our Dream,
To seek the lives that missed the dawn of day,
Or those who once had known our Dream—
Then watched it slip away.

They met in joy, sometimes,
Dancing in the shadows of days
That gave the Dream its worth.
They met as victors one time,
If only o'er themselves,
When in the words that spoke their deeds
The greatest words were Peace—

Peace to all the Earth—
And Joy to those who celebrate!

IF their performance in centennials is a determining factor, the Canadian people must possess some indefinable mystique for celebration. This apparently instinctive knowledge may relate to the fact that Canadians live so close to nature—the land, the sea, winter's blasts of wind and snow, the charm of seasonal living may make Nature's children more willing to pause, even in the face of tribulation, and celebrate life. Or the talent may result from Canadians' keen sense of history—a deep appreciation of their past. Whatever the case, when Canadians celebrate, history and festivity join in a sometimes fitful embrace, but seriousness of purpose often triumphs even in moments of lighthearted revelry.

Few centennials have captured the imagination, stirred the emotions, or aroused the enthusiasm of celebrants as did the 1967 Centennial of Canadian Confederation.[1] The Canadians had something to celebrate. As a nation, Canada was emerging from a sprawling rural, agrarian frontier to a booming business-industrial culture. Her first century had been marked by change and progress, sometimes agonizing, sporadic, and frustrating, but always fraught with the desire to expand and improve. Growth had been Canada's hallmark—in cities, buildings, engineering projects, roads, airports, bridges, dams, powerhouses, railways, population, and more recently in education, social action, the fine arts, and international rapport. But it was her people—their ingenuity, skills, and dedication—that had brought the nation through its first century, and the Centenary reflected their pride of personal involvement in growth and maturation.

Canada's celebration exploded upon the frozen northland

---

1. Canadians use both "centennial" and "centenary" to describe a hundredth birthday, though they generally prefer the latter.

just after the first stroke of midnight of the Centennial year. Bells rang out from nearly every community—"Wild Bells," they called them—bonfires shot sparks into sub-zero skies, cannon boomed, fireworks exploded, bands and orchestras played stirring music. Crowds warmed to the sights and sounds of celebration. Freezing hands waved banners and flags from open windows, and husky voices rang out in paeans of self-congratulation. Parades, pageantry, and pow-wows—and the inevitable long-winded speeches recounted accomplishment and heralded the future.

The other major celebration recognizing the Confederation anniversary—a mildly impressive three-day commemoration of sixty years—took place in July 1927. Little in the programs of Boy Scout encampments, a hook-up of a series of radio stations, runners carrying messages of good will across the nation, commemorative stamp issues, celebration dinners, and anniversary balls promised lasting memorials or permanent change. Yet a central theme—the emergence of Canada as a sovereign state—underlay these 1927 programs. The Centenary of 1967 built upon that theme.

The Centenary foundations were also laid in the British Columbia Centenary of 1958, for it was in Vancouver that a small group of thoughtful people first seriously discussed the possibilities of a national celebration. From the beginning they talked of a planned program with participation on every governmental level—local, provincial, and national. In the midst of the British Columbia celebration, Brooke Claxton, then President of the Canada Council, fanned the embers for a larger Centenary with a speech in which he urged centennial projects that would embrace social and cultural concerns— "slum clearance, better community recreation facilities, and a series of major festivals of all the arts." [2]

Continuing the discussion, two organizations, the Canadian

2. Anne Hanna, *The Canadian Centenary Council* (Ottawa, Ontario: 1968), 11. Hereinafter cited as *Canadian Centenary Council*.

Association for Adult Education and the Canadian Citizenship Council, endorsed the idea of a Confederation Centennial celebration that would "contribute constructively to the growth of the Canadian nation," with citizens' groups playing "a significant role in achieving this ideal." [3] Confirming the seriousness of their interest, they appointed eighty delegates from volunteer organizations all across Canada to the Canadian Centenary Council (usually referred to as CCC) to set the framework for a commemoration. This council of the private sector, which eventually expanded to more than 900 delegates representing more than 250 organizations and 600 corporations, became the single most important factor in putting Centenary planning into motion.

For suggestions and advice on how to organize for a celebration, CCC sought counsel from the leaders of the nation's businesses, organizations, government agencies, and clubs. Suggestions poured in. Inspired by this display of interest, leaders of CCC then called on the federal government to implement these first efforts and to initiate plans on the national level.

The government moved slowly at first, a problem not uncommon in national celebrations. As early as November 5, 1959, non-government groups pushed Prime Minister John Diefenbaker into meeting with provincial premiers to discuss the Centennial at the national level. Although this meeting never materialized, pressures continued, especially from the Canadian Centenary Council, and the government responded in late 1961 with passage of the National Centennial Act. This act formed the Centennial Commission, which is best described as the heartbeat of the Centenary.

The Centennial Commission became a reality in January 1963, with the appointment of John F. Fisher as Commissioner and poet Robert Choquette as Deputy Commissioner. Spurred by CCC, the Commission moved, building its organization and

---

3. *Ibid.*, 8, 12.

programs upon the beachhead already established by the private
sector enthusiasts. Sometimes the Commission and the CCC
worked together in harmony; sometimes they were at logger-
heads, but both seemed always to stress the same basic objective
—celebration was important, and it had to be for all Canadians.

Organizing for a national celebration of the dimensions pro-
jected in Canada was a complex phenomenon that called for
leadership on several levels. In Canada there were three major
divisions—federal, provincial, and local—with subdivisions
usually visible within each structure.

Despite the initial strength of the Canadian Centenary Council, the most impressive authority in terms of material assistance
was, without a doubt, the federal government. Its large invest-
ments in grants and stipends, its special project financing, its
counseling services, and its programs and projects stimulated
interest and participation everywhere. Government leadership
came primarily from three areas—the national leaders, the Centennial Commission, and the various departments of state.

Authority for national planning rested with the Department
of State, but the Centennial Commission was ultimately responsible for goals, directions, and expenditures of national
funds. Though each of the twenty-two different departments
participating was ultimately responsible to the Centennial Commission, each went its way, planning programs that promoted
its special interests.

Provincial leadership worked to carry out federal policy
while adapting to local preferences. Each province had its own
executive director and commission, appointed and financed
within. Later in the planning the Centennial Commission financed a special advisor to each province who served as
coordinator between province and national authorities. Sometimes there was tension between province and the federal agencies, as in the case of British Columbia; but more often the
provinces accepted federal support with enthusiasm.

Leadership in local communities operated at the level of the people, and the better the leadership represented the moods and interests of the community, the more probable was the success of its program. Recognizing local integrity was a strength of Canadian planning, a "concert of people," Georges Gauthier called it, and Canadians on all levels took part. Central planners did invite national attention toward Ottawa, Canada's capital city, for certain programs but not at the expense of local initiative. Provincial ceremonies were often just as impressive as those in the national capital, and people took the same interest and pride in local celebration as they did in programs promoted by national agencies. Members of the Centennial Commission established rapport with many communities by personal visits, both before the Centenary, to help in organizing, and afterward, to celebrate with the local community. Of course, large federal money grants were important in promoting good relations.

The Canadian Centenary Council continued its role as planner and motivator, even as other agencies assumed responsibilities. Though some of its initial leadership was transferred to the Centennial Commission, the Council continued to serve throughout the Centenary year as both a national clearinghouse for project ideas and as an information center. Its "regional blitzes"—members traveling over the nation helping local communities organize and develop programs—were important in spreading the celebration beyond the major arteries of communications. Operating on funds solicited from businesses and other interested sources, CCC held tenaciously to an independence that allowed wide latitude in Centennial planning. Secretary of State Judy LaMarsh paid tribute to the CCC's effectiveness as a Centenary force when she praised it for being "in the forefront" of most of the action.[4]

Strong personal leadership appeared on every level of authority. Nowhere is this better demonstrated than on the Cen-

---

4. *Canadian Centenary Council*, 34.

tennial Commission. John Fisher, Georges Gauthier, Robbins Elliott, Peter Aykroyd, and Charles Prevey provided model leadership and no doubt are responsible for much of the Centennial's success.

Fisher, a man of charming personality, boundless energy, and possessed of a deep and abiding affection for his country, became the personal embodiment of the Centenary—"Mr. Canada"—from the Atlantic to the Pacific. Formerly the executive director of the Canadian Tourist Association and a public relations expert, Fisher combined professional expertise and personal charisma in his leadership.

Gauthier, who replaced Choquette as the Deputy Commissioner, was the stabilizing force. A government servant for many years, he drew heavily upon past experience and contacts to unify the divisive elements in his country. He was effective in promoting *rapprochement* between the French and English Canadians and worked deligently to promote a bipartisan political atmosphere. By approaching Chambers of Commerce, service clubs, associations, and other organizations, he ironed out differences and resolved tensions that often threatened to disrupt Centenary proceedings. His dispassionate leadership was a model of efficiency and effectiveness.

Robbins Elliott, a founder and one of the most active members of the early CCC, left that organization in 1963 to become the Commission's Director of Planning. He was the "idea man" in Centenary programming and seemed always to be in the forefront of the action. Elliott never tired of stressing the fact that the Centenary was "a once-in-a-lifetime" experience which he hoped would provide his countrymen with a series of lasting "sensations and experiences."

Peter Aykroyd, the Commission's Director of Publicity, was a calm humanist whose publicity campaigns stressed national unity, national pride, and harmony among diverse peoples. Aykroyd believed in Centennial magic, a sort of transcendental force which prompted thoughts of both progress and humanistic values. His publicity therefore placed heavy emphasis on cultural and social concerns as profound measures of man's achievement and growth. Aykroyd also believed that bureaucracy can stall and even atrophy planning unless enlivened from time to time by the unusual. Always, to Aykroyd, the centennial was the unusual—a time to revise and even revitalize the bureaucracy.

Charles Prevey, described by his colleagues as the "watchdog" of Centenary funds, was the Comptroller. Well informed in accounting procedures and budget-balancing, Prevey also had an uncanny understanding of his fellow workers. In every circle, planners remember him as one who questioned every expenditure, but who also accounted faithfully for the details of planning—even while shuffling accounts to give planners the greatest possible latitude in spending. In the end his meticulous labors prevented any suggestion of fraud or indiscretion in the handling of Centenary funds. Such a person is a valuable member of a centennial team where there is great opportunity for "pork-barreling" in the handling of public funds.

Hundreds of others played vital roles in the Centenary—federal, provincial, local, ethnic, and group leaders; workers in libraries and museums, schools, clubs, and businesses; men and women who gave time, money, energy, and enthusiasm to Centenary causes. Some received salaries for their services—members of the Centennial Commission, federal representatives assigned to special jobs, and provincial directors and their work staffs—and some received per diem and travel expenses. Many more, especially at the local level, worked at personal expense— a situation not unusual in centennial involvement.

Dignified leadership at the top in Canada helped set the direction of the national program. Both John Diefenbaker and Lester B. Pearson, successive Prime Ministers, promoted the Centenary in speeches, personal appearances, and in soliciting legislative support. As Prime Minister during the Centennial year, Pearson breathed a spirit of bipartisanism, national unity, and international accord into the festive occasion. Peter Aykroyd's public relations department spread the word and stimulated interest in the "once-in-a-lifetime" affair, blanketing Canada with Centennial information for months before the kickoff program. Using national radio and television as the major media for extending information to far distant communities, the public relations department flooded the public mind with Centenary news, features, and personalities, depending heavily upon art, colorful language, and appealing themes to tell their story. "Chimo," a popular cartoon character created to symbolize the Centennial, cavorted on television until his features were familiar in nearly every Canadian household. Newspapers published almost anything associated with Centennial proceedings. Editorials personalized local interests and generally offered strong support for innovative planning on all levels. Full-page advertisements, picture features, program announcements, and descriptive articles made newspapers a constant reminder of the coming festivity. Sunday specials provided extensive records of the proceedings.

Aykroyd's department provided information and materials to the newly created public relations offices in the local communities, arranging speaker appearances wherever and whenever requested, setting up symposia and seminars, distributing flags and banners, and encouraging publicity. It distributed widely the many movies and short features produced for the Centennial by the National Film Board, including the popular *Helicopter Canada* and *Centennial Fever*—both of which attempted to attract visitors to the Centenary.

The Canadian Centenary Council also helped to publicize the celebration. Early in the planning it began publication of the *Bulletin,* a public relations-oriented journal that carried up-to-date planning information to its members. CCC produced and distributed two guideline brochures: *Project News,* a publication which outlined the most current Centennial facts and figures; and a "project analysis service," a confidential reporting system on program developments and plans. Together, CCC and the Centennial Commission published the final edition of *Project News* in 1966, a 150-page summary of all Centenary planning that offered valuable suggestions to communities caught in the throes of their own initial planning.

Another medium of publicizing the national celebration was *Expo '67*, Montreal's World's Fair. Through a separate administrative function from the Centenary, *Expo* often extended Centennial themes and objectives in its publicity and programs. In soliciting support and interest in its own activities, *Expo* carried part of the burden of Centenary public relations.

In reality, nearly every citizen of Canada became a member of the public relations team. People from all walks of life were becoming familiar with the nation's plans for commemorating the hundredth anniversary of confederation and its themes: telling the story of the nation's past, undertaking projects "of a lasting nature" in many fields, providing programs for greater knowledge and understanding of the country, and extending the celebration across the nation. The large number of people who appeared at commemoration events made it obvious that the word did get out.

Canada's programs themselves were publicity material. The range of subject matter, the appealing themes, the substantial effort that went into production, and the elaborateness of costumes and designs provided programs that few could resist. The number, variety, and quality of these programs offered something for everybody.

Just as it had been an agent of publicity, so also was *Expo '67* a model for Centennial programs. *Expo* was indeed a grand affair, probably "the tremendous success" its publicity claimed. Its theme, "Man and His World," and the exhibits and programs surrounding it brought praise from authorities and the less informed. A "marvelous adventure," *Expo '67* exploited color, movement, sound, national pride, and modern technology to create an imaginary world filled with a glamour and excitement that few world's fairs of this century have captured. Its range of man's involvement with his world was so wide that its real theme was Man—from the potential of his achievements to the story of his being caught in a trap "devised by his inhumanity." Program-planners everywhere kept in mind the activities on Montreal's Island as they outlined their own feature attractions.

Federal programs also offered models for local planners to work with. They were organized into four major categories: governmental department programs, the Centennial Projects Program, the Confederation Memorial Program, and the Major National Projects. In the first category each of twenty-two departments operated independently, procuring and funding its own resources for programs. The latter three were under the jurisdiction of the Centennial Commission.

Department programs were many and diverse. The Department of Agriculture dedicated a new rose garden on its experimental farm; the Department of Finance produced a new one-dollar bill, initiated special Centennial designs for federal cheques, postal money orders, and warrants, and issued a special set of bonds and Centenary coin sets. The Post Office Department sponsored several commemorative stamp issues. Air Canada produced nine films, four bilingual, most in color, all concerned with spreading news of the Centenary. Other departments sponsored publications, booths at *Expo '67,* community exhibitions, restorations, lecture series, and contests.

The Centennial Projects Program was an extensive building program whose projects included parks, recreational structures, community centers, recreational areas, municipal buildings, libraries, museums, and art galleries. Also included were playgrounds, band shells, beaches, picnic areas, hockey and curling rinks, swimming pools, golf courses, nature trails, carillons, fountains, town clocks, and theaters. Federal grants of more than $16 million provided partial funds for about 2,300 projects that eventually cost more than $88 million. The federal government paid up to one-third of the cost of any single project, on the basis of one dollar per capita as determined by the 1963 population census. The province and the local community absorbed all remaining costs. Local groups or individuals initiated most of the projects, but approval from the provincial committees preceded submission to the federal government. As these projects were completed they became lasting legacies, and their construction stimulated interest and enthusiasm of a high degree.

As a part of the Confederation Memorial Program, the federal government offered a maximum $2.5 million to each province toward the cost of construction of a major Memorial project, usually in the province's capital city. All provinces participated in this program, with constructions including Newfoundland's Centennial Arts and Cultural Centre, Prince Edward Island's Fathers of Confederation Memorial Building, Sir Charles Tupper Medical Building in Nova Scotia, New Brunswick's Centennial Administrative Building, Le Grant Theatre de Quebec, Ontario's Centennial Centre of Science and Technology, the Winnipeg Concert Hall in the Manitoba Cultural Centre, Regina's Performing Arts Centre and Saskatoon's Centennial Auditorium in Saskatchewan, the Alberta Museum and Archives Building, the British Columbia Museum and Archives Building, the Yukon Territory Museum of Local History and Civic Administration Building, and the Northwest Territories Regional Library.

The Centennial Projects Program and the Confederation Memorial Program were important manifestations of the Centenary spirit. These projects cost millions of dollars, which the people will have to pay in the years to come, but they provided facilities for research, study, entertainment, and cultural enlightenment that defy a mere dollar evaluation. They are now legacies that will probably long influence patterns and attitudes toward architecture, city planning, educational objectives, use of libraries and archives, and fine arts. But as important features of the Centennial, they also recognized the individual integrity of each province and each community, providing much-needed funds to implement local needs and desires. Few nations have experienced such a cultural outpouring in a comparable period of time, while still catering to local interests.

The key to the success of the Major National Projects came in the recognition of and appeal to the diversity of Canadian talents and interests, not only as scholars, scientists, economists, statesmen, and world leaders but also as creative artists, performers, and teachers of the arts. The intent was to develop a series of programs whose scope and variety would make it possible for every Canadian "to participate or benefit." The projects included in the twenty-three categories appealed to man's festive spirit and to his historic sense, providing new experiences in music, drama, art, and literature, as well as a wide variety of spectator and participation sporting events. The federal government allotted $20 million for these projects.

Pageants, exhibitions, re-enactments, student and adult exchanges, medallions for the school children, among other activities, provided something for every Canadian. These programs highlighted folk arts, ethnic culture, community improvement and beautification, personal health, and international cooperation. They extended culture and entertainment—drama and musicals, operas and operettas, classical and popular music, military "tattoos," sporting events, historical pageants—to those in the far reaches of the nation deprived of such activities by poor transportation and communication systems. They provided financial assistance for publications, visual arts, educational programs, and films. Some programs denoted the ultimate in man's creative abilities; some were just plain fun.

Each of these projects had its special appeal. The Centennial Train, fifteen decorated railway cars crisscrossing the nation telling Canada's story in colorful exhibitions, documents, pictures, and other items, and the eight Caravans, each with eight 72-foot tractor trailers carrying their exhibits beyond the normal routes of communications to audiences who seldom knew such fare, were viewed by half of all Canadians. In them the viewer saw his nation—its mountains, rivers, and shimmering lakes, its cities and its people. He felt his history in exhibits which opened up his nation's past. Standing before the life-like models, he saw Canada born. He explored the horizons of yesterday, watching immigrants moving westward into the mystery of a new world, the railway cars and wagons returning filled with grain, timber, beef, and minerals. He watched Canada change in the teeming days of the Industrial Revolution; he felt the drama of revolution in the city streets, the rising factories, and the new roads. He grimaced at the scenes of horror in the Canadian trenches at Verdun. Then, suddenly, he returned to the present—to the shadow of bomber raids and a mushroom cloud, engulfed in a panorama of towering skyscrapers, giant jet planes, and smoke belching from factories.

Young and old remember these traveling exhibitions. They were expensive—the train alone cost $10 million—but in their corridors Canadians discovered, understood, and appreciated their heritage—and they mingled with fellow citizens as they waited their turn for viewing. Neither the train nor the caravans still exist. The caravans were sold to various concerns in the nation for many uses, including several to the Ace Foundation of Calgary, Alberta, which now uses them to transport exhibitions.

A 100-day voyageur canoe pageant also built upon history, recreating the lusty life of the early explorers who conquered the treacherous streams of unsettled Canada in their frail canoes. In fiberglass canoes named for some of the more illustrious voyageurs, modern-day adventurers retraced 3500 miles along the voyageurs' routes.

A program with a special appeal for young people was "This Land Is Your Land," a youth exchange arrangement. Boys and girls, ages fifteen to seventeen, visited in distant provinces at government expense or by private sponsorship. *Centennial*

Travelers, produced by the National Film Board of Canada, recorded some of these adventures—"the warm camaraderie of young people traveling together and then meeting a new world in a far-off province." This program, which benefited 30,000 students, was considered successful enough for continuation beyond the days of the Centenary.

Major National Projects planners grappled with the complex ethnic structure of the nation—"the Canadian mosaic." Planners in any Canadian celebration had to take note of this mosaic, yet to single out every different group in Canada for special recogntion in the Centenary would have violated larger themes of national unity. The Commission thus encouraged ethnic groups to set their own limits on participation, but to share the richness of their culture with their nation. Federal funding assisted in the planning and presentation of programs that promoted and publicized cultural heritages as part of a greater Canada. Some ethnic groups responded cautiously to this approach, their leaders courteous but unenthusiastic about such involvement. Some preferred to preserve folkways and mores in the isolation of their home communities. Some performed only to propagandize a particular grievance or to magnify a culture bias—and some, it appears, had very little to offer. Planners never ceased exploring possibilities, however, and folk arts was always a popular form of festivity, both for performer and audience. Many of their efforts reached fruition as part of the project labeled "Folk Festivals." Revealing remarkable talent, many groups performed their native songs and dances, played their musical instruments, and re-created their native heritages in dress and ceremony.

Planners trying to encourage ethnic involvement found the Canadian Indians to require special consideration. Geographical barriers and distance often isolated Indians from each other and from the rest of the nation. Some Indians had acquired an invisibility not unlike that often experienced by Black Americans in the United States. Centennial leaders found that they not only had to fund the projects that portrayed Indian culture and folklore, but they had to encourage the Indians to participate. This meant bringing the Indian into the larger Canadian community while identifying and preserving traditions and folklore that sometimes separated them from that community.

Across Canada the Indians participated in many Centenary programs. They continued their popular powwows, they met in conferences to discuss their roles in Centennial affairs, and they submitted their paintings, carvings, displays, and other art work for display in many of Canada's cultural centers. Projects for Indians included new publications, films, and booklets explaining the heritage and culture of the various tribes. New scholarships, public and private, offered Indian youth chances at higher education and travel. Communities constructed special museums for Indian artifacts, set up campsites for the Indian reservations, built playgrounds, community halls, libraries, curling and skating rinks, and sports and recreation centers. Four thousand dollars of federal funding promoted a national Indian Princess Pageant. Additional funding set up an important cultural workshop in British Columbia. Indian newspapers received funds for special cultural editions, and there were Indian canoe pageants and folk festivals that added the spice of festivity. Special grants went to residential schools, an Indian hall of fame, an Indian agricultural society, Indian parades, Indian girl and boy scout activities, and in special exhibitions across the country, including a Hiawatha pageant in Ontario and special Indian Days in Kamloops, B.C.

In many cases Canadian planners successfully released Indians to find their own themes and build programs around them. At *Expo,* Indians used "straight talk" to explain their situation to visitors. At the Indian exhibit, twelve pretty Indian hostesses spoke of the harsh treatment their people had received at the hands of the whites. A special exhibit emphasized this mistreatment. A large totem pole carved by British Columbia

Kwakiutl Indian artist Henry Hunt portrayed six brilliant Indian cultures before an enlarged photograph of tattered, dirty, unhappy, Indian children surrounded by smaller photographs of white Canadian children playing in suburbia's finest comfort.

Exhibits in *Expo's* pavilion and in Centennial exhibits elsewhere portrayed the Indians' constant rivalry with the white man, the interracial wars of the nineteenth century, the low level of Indian participation in the national affairs, and the "white betrayal." "Give us the right to manage our own affairs," screamed a large *Expo* pavilion sign.

Programs were not always satisfactory nor were they all well received. Including the Indians in the Centenary meant a recognition of two cultures that had lived side by side without assimilation. To their credit, Canadian planners did acknowledge such social problems and attempted to find solutions. Though they never promoted a spectacular rebirth of Indian dignity and pride, nor brought a final *rapproachement* between white and Indian, planners did make an effort to involve all cultural groups. Sometimes harmonious interplay increased understanding; sometimes tensions dominated, with the result mere juxtaposition of the two cultures.

Other Major National Projects included *The Dream,* a reenactment of the original founding of the Confederation in Quebec City, the Maritimes, and Newfoundland; the Ladies of the Provinces Confederation Parade in Charlottetown and St. Johns, a costume presentation of a historical event of the era; an Armed Forces Tattoo in forty cities—a spectacular military pageant of music in which men and horses performed intricate drills and formations. Also included were a four-part athletic program for school children, university students, international events, and special Centennial sporting events; the Centennial International Development Program which called upon Canadians to share their celebration by providing gifts of food, medical supplies, clothing, books, tractors, money, fellowships, and scholarships to underdeveloped countries; and a large and complex program of community improvement and beautification. There were Centennial medallions for 6,000,000 Canadian youngsters; a major film program spearheaded by the National Film Board; miscellaneous projects that included an interchange of community leaders among the major cultural groups of the nation; a series of special programs for isolated communities; a national exhibition of color photography; and special recognition awards for Canadians who reached their hundredth birthday in 1967 and for parents of babies born in the Centennial year.

Themes of the past appeared in other programs—pageants, folk art programs, and numerous subsidized publications. Novels, histories, and encyclopedias recalled former men and deeds. Libraries added new collections, revised exhibitions, and encouraged new scholarship ventures. The Commission engaged two teams of distinguished writers to write "festival plays"—pageants that combined history and festivity. Another grant underwrote a university series of historical seminars to study select areas of Canadian history with emphasis upon controversial topics. The universities also sponsored notable lecturers and artists in special programs on the campuses.

As diverse as its programs were, Major National Projects would not be complete without the color, sound, and beauty of the arts, which fascinated observers to whom such presentations were often new experiences. John Fisher hailed "an extravaganza of performing arts of every description . . . music, dancing, opera, song." [5] Add drama, folk-singing, pageants, festivals, painting, new architectural designs, and the wide dimensions of art celebration become more apparent. Georges Gauthier expressed satisfaction at the new intercultural unity the arts produced, as well as their emphasis on the profitable use

---

5. Speech in Centennial Files, Canadian National Archives, Ottawa, Canada. [Hereinafter referred to as Centennial Files.]

of leisure time.[6] Artists "must create an environment that looks ahead, that promises growth and expansion," said Nicholas Goldschmidt, chief of the Performing Arts Division of the Centennial Commission.[7]

Actually the arts were of primary importance in almost every aspect of Centennial activity, influencing both the Centennial Projects and Memorial Projects in styles of building patterns and as rationale for project selection. Federal departments and provincial agencies relied on the arts to improve their programs. Nowhere were the arts more in evidence than in *Expo '67*, in the many exhibits that probed the nature of "Man and His World," and in the beauty and style of its many other programs and events. Its architecture alone was a feast of artistic creativity. "Man the Creator" presented collections of some of the world's great paintings, photographs, and sculpture —medieval art, popular art, and all periods between. One writer called *Expo* a literal "garden of art." [8] Seven of the twenty-three divisions of the Major National Projects depended heavily upon the arts for fullest expression. Three others— Festival Canada, the Canadian Festival of the Folk Arts, and the Visual Arts Program—were exclusively in the "fine and lively arts" category, each revealing a different dimension of artistic expression.

Festival Canada, the Commission's program of the performing arts, brought some of the world's great musical and theatrical companies and artists to theaters and auditoriums where people had never known this form of entertainment. It also included local talent performing both at home and in other provinces. Festival Canada on tour and at home was the drama

---

6. Interview with Georges Gauthier, September 2, 1971, Ottawa, Ontario, Canada.

7. Address to the Port Arthur Club, January 1966, Centennial Files, Canadian National Archives.

8. Robert Collins, "Man in His World, A Magic Era," Calgary *Herald*, February 19, 1966.

company Ann of Green Gables presenting a musical version of the novel by the same name. It was Don Messer and his Islanders performing popular old-time country music, Holiday Theater with its exciting and widely known Children's Theater, and Le Theatre du Nouveau Monde performing Moliere's *Le Bourgeois Gentilhomme* all across Canada. It was the exciting Feux Follets—the fabled Fireflies—a youthful national folk-dancing company headquartered in Montreal but always performing on the road; the National Ballet of Canada interpreting *The Nutcracker* or *Les Sylphides;* and the National Theatre of Great Britain, with Sir Laurence Olivier performing Georges Faydeau's *A Flea in Her Ear.* Festival Canada also included performances by the National Youth Orchestra of Canada, the New York Philharmonic under Leonard Bernstein, the Neptune Theater in a Sean O'Casey play, or the Stratford Festival Company playing Shakespeare's *Twelfth Night* or Gogol's *The Government Inspector.* It was popular radio and television personality Alan Mills singing "Canada's Story in Song," or Le Theatre de l'Escale providing Canadians with entertainment on a floating riverboat theater. It was the *Best of Barkerville,* an oldtime variety show of the famous Canadian goldrush days, its songs and dances providing the authentic vaudeville variety show touch; or *One Hundred Years of Musical Comedy,* a group wearing colorful costumes and featuring songs of musical comedy the world over. It was also the folk rock and "rhythm and blues" music for young people. But Festival Canada was more than just performance. Its special grants program provided money for posters, travel, pamphlets, and brochures, as well as for recording programs, a monthly magazine of the arts, a consultation service, research, liaison, and for preparation of special directories.

In the Canadian Festival of the Folk Arts the Commission scheduled one hundred folk festivals to be presented all across Canada, eventually involving more than 35,000 Canadians. This festival highlighted cultural exchanges, representative ethnic group programs, and visiting groups from other parts of the world displaying their talents on Canada's Centennial stage. The 1967 program actually followed a successful pilot series of provincial folk festivals the year before. Eventually, however, folk festivals took place in every province, displaying prominently the local talent and culture that each province claimed as its own.

The Visual Arts Program had three basic thrusts: a grant program "designed to assist all galleries, art museums and art circuits in developing special exhibitions of art, or other projects";[9] "Perspective '67," which offered young artists 18 to 35 opportunities to compete for prizes in painting, sculpture, prints, and drawings; and a program of grants for traveling exhibitions of art works across Canada, making the art available to the people living far from the cultural centers. Special grants were also provided for arts programs in the various provinces, such as "People of the Salmon and Cedar," an exhibition of west coast Indian art in the Vancouver Art Gallery; "Canadian Art 1967," an exhibition of native artists' work in the Norman MacKenzie Art Gallery in Alberta; "Mother and Child," the exhibition of works of Marc Chagall in the Winnipeg Art Gallery; and "Ten Decades 1867 to 1967—Ten Painters," an unusual exhibition of artists at thè peak of their creativity exhibited in the New Brunswick Museum. At least 35 other major exhibitions appeared across the country during the Centennial year.

In all of these programs the fine and lively arts appealed to the festival spirit in people—offering excellent entertainment, giving people a chance to discuss their experiences and exchange viewpoints, and helping Canadians discover themselves. That is really what the arts are all about, said Gauthier, "super channels of communication—the carriers of content that would

---

9. *Centennial Facts*, vol. 4, *Performing and Visual Arts*, (Ottawa: Centennial Commission, 1967) , 23.

overload mere language and numerical systems." [10] The singing, the dancing, and the new understanding of culture through art, music, and literature made the Centennial not only an interesting time but an exciting one. "The Centennial year has brought Canada's cultural pattern—the exercise and enjoyment of the fine and lively arts—to a point of genuine national importance," said Goldschmidt.[11] "What cultural future will be cannot be foreseen but the prospect is promising and full of good omens."

The Major National Projects created a stir in Canada that extended from the Atlantic to the Pacific, involved a fantastic number of people, and underlined the Centennial with a satisfying festival spirit. Some would say that money was wasted, and certainly some was. Still, one culture transmits its values to another through many media, and these projects explored many different methods of transfer. Some people may have been insensitive to culture so transmitted, but others experienced moments of beauty and truth they had never known before. The folk sing, the beautiful music from the Winnipeg Orchestra, and the appearances of Sir Laurence Olivier or Leonard Bernstein on the Centennial stage provided audiences with moments of grand and fleeting exhilaration. In far-off towns where ballet was only a dream or an old movie, citizens watched the National Ballet display its superb discipline and training. In the outpouring of music and drama to celebrate an anniversary, Canadians across a broad nation found satisfaction and new understanding in national and cultural diversity.

Leadership of CCC and the Centennial Commission extended the Centenary to Canadian people everywhere, from the cities to the hinterlands where sometimes there was not even electricity to power the borrowed projectors to show Centennial films. Hundreds of communities, large and small, engaged, and the Canadian Archives and local newspaper files bulge with Centenary records, reports, and official programs. The several

10. Gauthier interview.
11. Goldschmidt address.

volumes of the *Programme of Events,* produced jointly during the year of celebration by the Commission and the Canadian Broadcasting Company, recorded community and provincial programs of that year; their pages were filled with a variety, complexity, and multiplicity of events.

The Hundredth Summer and *Centennial Fever,* two Centenary films, recorded typical small community centennial activities. *The Hundredth Summer* was the story of three Prince Edward Island villages putting together their programs in the face of many obstacles, including the usual shortage of funds. Despite the limitations, citizens found excitement in celebration, in the music, bunting, and strange wares. Parents joined their children in the community tug-of-war, in which teams struggled vigorously to defend community pride but took victory or defeat in the spirit of the season. Later, contest victors made their way to the judges' platform amidst the cheers of their supporters, to be rewarded for Centennial deeds. Then costumed waiters served food to hungry citizens who later danced to the music of their yesterdays and todays. Festivity ruled as the three communities remembered their pasts—sometimes hardly aware they were part of the larger Confederation celebration. As the stars came out to light the early evening, the newly crowned queen of the pageant looked out over her subjects—soon again to be only one of them—but her momentary radiance cast a spell symbolic of something greater than that moment.

Centennial Fever recorded the celebration in St. Paul, Alberta, where more than sixty projects took shape. Few towns commemorated the Centenary as vigorously or with such diversity. This film captured the festive spirit of the times in vivid vignettes: a scene in a hairdressing salon where Centenary art works had replaced old calendars, a local doctor and his wife encouraging Indians to complete Centennial art works, street scenes showing the celebration excitement interrupting daily routines. St. Paul had music, flag-waving, bright colors, period costumes, beards, and a parade. Even raising money was a Centennial event—the old mission bell tolled at a dollar a ring, the curling rink charged for penalties, and a goat was sold over and over again at auction, the proceeds going to the town's fund for the construction of a school for handicapped children.

Other communities had their own programs, and by the end of 1967 practically every Canadian had celebrated his nation's birthday. He may have been a member of a planning group, an actor in a dramatic production, or only a spectator at an international sporting event. If the end-of-the-year newspaper editorials provide a true sample of public opinion, he probably had few regrets that the Centenary was over. Frivolity had probably highlighted the average Canadian's Centenary, but his nation had made more substantial gains, not only in buildings, publications, cultural and historical innovations, but in a new spirit of what it meant to be a Canadian.

Why had this celebration gone so well, and why do Canadians look back upon it as a turning point in their national history? Passing judgment on the success or failure of a centennial is a precarious assignment at best, but several points of the Canadian Centenary emerge as strengths that other planners might seek to emulate: It was well organized with good leadership on many levels; it involved government spending in productive and innovative projects, always recognizing local integrity in project selection; it included arts and history prominently in its entire format, thus releasing creativity and identifying important traditions of the past. Beyond this, flexibility that allowed for the distinctive contributions of race, creed, language, and personal interests dominated project-planning and execution.

Other reasons also contributed to the success of the Canadian Centenary. Of great importance was the role young people played in many programs besides the exchange visits. Youth showed interest in the folk festivals; they saw and became involved in plays, musicals, and pageants; they enjoyed the train, the caravans, and the excitement of the athletic field. They participated in large numbers in the special Centennial athletic awards program for students between the ages of six and eighteen which was designed to motivate Canadian youth to higher levels of physical fitness. They appeared prominently in mountain climbs, highland games, canoeing, camping, and winter sports. Special programs for retarded children were also very popular.

The Centenary produced a psychological ebullience that crossed ethnic, age, and social lines. Centennial leaders stimulated Canadians into a new belief in themselves and their nation as contrasted to their former somewhat paranoiac feeling about themselves and the world in which they lived. Well-planned programs, good publicity, and sound objectives appealed to deeper strengths within these citizens and helped build a new interest in the nation. Another strength appeared in the residual carryover at every stage and on every level. Fairs, parades, and pageants were never enough. Books, buildings, scholarships, art works, and community objectives carried Centennial themes well beyond the year of celebration—these and other projects had been a major part of the initial discussions that set off the Centennial. Canadians found a fine blend in their Centennial—the festival, creating a mood of awareness; the commemoration, a search for understanding in an exciting new spirit of "becoming"; the celebration, extolling the past while making new commitments to the future; and the dedication, long-range programs to be remembered when dancing shoes were in the closet again.

Besides all this, the Centennial was fun. Canadians climbed mountains; poled their rafts over the streams discovered by early explorers; paddled their canoes between portages; rode bicycles, wheelchairs, covered wagons, and old jalopies across the country. One man shot the rapids with a live boa constrictor draped around his neck; and a group of twenty-eight teen-agers recorded a new world record of one hundred straight hours on the trampoline.

There were, indeed, moments of frustration—the prima donnas in Festival Canada making new demands before every performance, the atrocious art works that appeared at exhibitions everywhere, the "Centennial Fever" that picked up only in warm weather, the high prices for performances that were supposedly being subsidized by the state, the threats against the Centennial Train by the French Canadians who felt they were not properly represented, the protests that biases and not objectivity determined the train exhibits.[12] The fabulous "sound and light" show in Quebec hardly made the impression expected of it because its script was too weak, and the producers' attempt to simulate the burning of the Parliament building was "a bit much," said one of the participants. There were the usual mixups in correspondence, the distribution of Centennial "goodies" to the favored, late arrivals and unexpected absences in Centenary programs, ill feelings caused by jealousies of high position, and the irritation of many at the monthly expense of $2500 to $3000 for running a Centennial office. Finally the abrupt dismissal of Centennial employees left a bad taste with many who had given devoted service to planning and administration—a circumstance that could have been avoided by some long-range planning in employment needs.

If Canadians had a major criticism of their Centennial, it centered around the vast expenditure of money. Originally officials had anticipated a million dollars for each of the hundred years of growth. Funds petered out toward the end, however, and the final figures reached only $90,000,000. Some felt that years of heavy taxation would pay the cost of a "year of folly," but the government defended its actions by calling it a planned expenditure. In addition to government expenditure, provincial and local governments also authorized extensive spending, as

---

12. The western papers record an interesting controversy over substituting the picture of Chief Sitting Bull for Crow Foot in the panorama of Indian life.

did private groups, associations, organizations, and individuals. *Expo '67* must also be considered in the total program—$230 million could well be a warning to planners on any level of the precariousness of the exposition as a centennial venture— though some can certainly argue that *Expo* increased the income of city, province, and nation; stimulated the spirit of centennialism; and revealed the excitement of creation in its exhibits.

Despite its limitations, the long-range effects of the Centennial upon Canadians must have been good, for many provinces continue to plan centennials of their own. In final analysis the Centennial of Canadian Confederation was probably a people's centennial—a "grassroots" affair, involving nearly every citizen. To many Canadians it was a bangup, a noisy birthday party with lots of splash and color, but for many others it was an occasion for pausing and reflecting, a time for personal stocktaking. This gave the Centenary introspective overtones, stimulating an atmosphere that made building as important as feasting and dancing.

The traveler crossing Canada today sees the impact of the Centenary upon Canadian life. The word "Centennial" shines forth in the names of parks, public buildings, and hundreds of community projects. The Centennial flame burns brightly before the public buildings in Ottawa. Visitors enjoy the beautiful Nikka Yuko Centennial Gardens in Lethbridge, Alberta, built as a Centennial project to honor the citizens of southern Alberta who are of Japanese ancestry. Beautiful memorial projects command attention in every province. The federal government still subsidizes youth travel programs, as well as a new "commune" program which allows young people to get away from the urban life which stifles so many.

In other places smaller features command attention. John Fortier, one of the Centennial planners, felt that even a new fountain added something to the architectural character of a town. Peter Aykroyd emphasized the spirit of doing. He recalled that on the occasion of his return to his hometown community of about 500 people, the first thing he noticed was the new addition on the old courthouse-townhouse-municipal building. The community had resisted such a project for years, but in the enthusiasm of Centennial action they had built the addition—and over the door was the symbol of the Centennial. Aykroyd called this one of the greatest thrills of his year of involvement.

No single feature of the Centenary sets it apart from other celebrations. No single name is a reminder of its many events. The depths of its impact upon the nation have not yet been probed, but John Fisher suggested that "by our own accomplishment . . . our generation will be judged." Judy LaMarsh summed up the Centenary's larger dimension in a speech at Quebec City in August 1967:

From all this, hopefully, we will finally learn that those differences which seem so often to plague us, differences of race and language, of history and geography—need not be the divisive forces we too frequently assume they are. Surely we will see that unity need not be synonymous with uniformity, that people can be Canadians and still retain something of their heritage of culture and region.

IV

The Civil War Centennial

Bloody conflict,
Cutting 'cross our history
Like a vivid scar,
Weaving dark lines
Into the mystery
Of the complex mosaic
That is our national heritage—
How do we see thee now?
Poet,
Scholar,
Mystic,
Americans commemorating—
Seek to understand,
Fail to agree,
Even on original premises.

A DARK swath across our national history, the Civil War brought victory—the triumph of national unity over sectional division, freedom from slavery—but karma—the tragedy of unhealed wounds, families divided, and economic, social, and psychological dismemberment. War is an event to remember, to recall with compassion and admiration those who showed courage and dignity in the face of calamity. But it is hardly an event to celebrate. Too often participants in our Civil War Centennial of 1961–65 failed to recognize this dichotomy, and we remember this commemoration with some misgiving.

Hardly the exciting and creative time the Canadians knew in their Centennial of Confederation, the Civil War Centennial nevertheless offers some valuable lessons to planners engaged in preparing another national commemoration—the Bicentennial of our Independence. Some of the lessons we learn from the Civil War Centennial are harsh ones: it taught us what to avoid, what perspectives to change, how leadership failed and sectional loyalties reappeared. The failure of the Civil War Centennial to capture our imaginations or bring us together as a nation reflects the absence of a theme of celebration for *all* Americans, and its divisive issues rekindled old flames that still smoldered as embers. Unity, rather than separation, might have been promoted by "a more effective teaching of history in our schools . . . enhanced attention by the mass media to colorful segments of our national record; [and] . . . the achievement of a number of our ablest writers in making the war period live again, vivid and poignant," [1] but the opportunity was lost.

In the decade following World War II, there was, indeed, great interest among Americans in their Civil War. They compared crises of their own time with the confrontations and tensions of war, peace, and reconstruction of the past. The death of President Franklin Roosevelt in the midst of preparations for peace returned their thoughts to Abraham Lincoln, dying in his moment of victory, his task also unfinished. As civil rights concerns blossomed in the fifties, Blacks, especially, traced other roots deep into the nineteenth-century sectional conflict. This same generation was also noting the passing of the last Civil

---

1. *The Civil War Centennial, A Report to Congress* (Washington, D.C.: U.S. Civil War Commission, 1968) , 3.

War veterans and searching for meaning in the war which gave these old men a special place in history.

The Civil War Centennial officially began in 1957 when Congress enacted Public Law 85–105, which created the United States Civil War Commission. In response to an "unmistakable demand on the part of the American people," Congress charged this Commission "to provide for appropriate and nationwide observances." To co-ordinate the many ceremonies of commemoration expected, they also gave consideration to the actions of state, civic, patriotic, hereditary, and historical organizations. The appropriation of $100,000 which implemented this legislation was the first of several grants that offered encouragement to planners. Congress also appointed the Commission—twenty-five members, including the President and Vice President of the United States, four Senators, the Speaker and four members of the House of Representatives, and twelve additional members.

The Commission held its first meeting on December 20, 1957, in the offices of the Department of Interior. There, by unanimous consent, they chose as their first chairman Major General Ulysses S. Grant III, octogenarian grandson of the illustrious Civil War general. Grant was a dedicated American, proud of his personal and national heritage but understanding the feelings of Americans whose fathers had fought under another flag. Informed about the Civil War, Grant took seriously his responsibilities as chairman. The Commission chose Karl S. Betts, founder and past president of the important District of Columbia Civil War Roundtable, as executive director. Betts brought to the Commission the experience of long and active service in advertising, public relations, and investment banking fields.

Under the leadership of Grant and Betts, the Commission began at once to define objectives and formulate goals and programs. Theirs was the large responsibility—handling matters of policy, publicity, finance, and program-making, as well as offering ideas, programs, and encouragement to state and community groups across the country—a task complicated by remnants of sectional bitterness and by the crucial civil rights concerns that erupted during these tumultuous years. Arbiter and referee as well as source of knowledge and of materials, the new Commission faced an awesome responsibility. The Department of Defense, the Post Office Department, the Library of Congress, the National Archives, the Smithsonian Institute, and the U.S. Information Agency worked closely with the Commission, making special contributions with programs, publications, and encouragement. A large, cumbersome national advisory committee made up of leading Civil War authorities, political figures, and businessmen periodically offered counsel.

The Commission worked primarily through its general meetings, usually monthly, and its annual National Assemblies, which rotated their meeting places among important cities of the Civil War period. The first, in the nation's capital in 1958, launched Centennial planning. The 1959, 1960, and 1961 meetings, held in Richmond, St. Louis, and Charleston respectively, devoted panel discussions and conferences to "major projects, the progress made the difficulties encountered." [2] In these deliberations, Assembly actions became the springboard for most national planning in the months immediately preceding the official Centennial kickoff date—January 8, 1961.

Shaping a national commemoration was a delicate and demanding task for the Commission, and its members struggled diligently to offer more than pap to the nation. Some of their most productive efforts during the planning stages included the production of a 16mm, 35-minute film on the Centennial, which clubs and schools showed steadily in the months preceding the kickoff, the forming of speakers' bureaus, the successful solicitation of five commemorative stamp issues, and the establishment of close working ties with Congress. Commission members were in contact with automobile clubs, NATO, the

2. *Ibid.,* 8.

railroads, and travel bureaus concerning plans to stimulate tourism. They encouraged oil companies and other business firms concerned with travel to produce appropriate documentary films for national distribution. They worked with the Department of Health, Education, and Welfare to insure an educational emphasis. They encouraged writers and directors to produce pageants that would employ orchestras, choruses, ballet, and dramatic groups. They inspired local organization and action that led to 6,500 state and local Centennial events. Few of the Commission's actions were as important as the establishment, in early 1959, of a Committee on Historical Activities, led by the personable and able Civil War historian Bell I. Wiley of Emory University. This committee stimulated the scholarly thrust so often neglected in centennials, and much of the research and writing of the Centennial years stemmed from its encouragement.

While publicity posed some problems, all media soon became involved in presenting Centennial happenings to the American people. Newspaper articles and features aroused interest in the Civil War, and several papers began regular series of reproductions of Civil War items. Many used the Sunday supplement to capture the drama of the past. Radio and television offered news reports, spot programs, drama, and interviews. State and local commissions and newspapers published weekly or monthly newsletters, with North Carolina providing a noteworthy example. *100 Years After,* the publication of the Commission, was also an exemplary newsletter, and its back issues now form part of the record of the proceedings of the Centennial years. *Civil War Times, American Heritage,* and many popular magazines depicted the Civil War in stories, personality sketches, and colorful illustrations.

The close association many organizations had with the Civil War also stimulated public relations efforts. The American Red Cross called attention to Clara Barton and her war work and featured the Centennial in its speakers' kit. The YMCA began its own Centennial observance with a series of community, regional, and national events honoring the many thousands of Americans who served in the Armed Forces during the Civil War and afterward. Probably no groups publicized the Centennial more than did the Civil War Roundtables that sprang up over the country, in large cities and in small. Active Roundtables even appeared in Virginia and Maryland prisons and a California veterans' hospital. Though activities varied in quality with the resources and leadership available, roundtable members were almost invariably enthusiastic. They conducted tours, restored buildings and beautiful sites, contributed articles and photographs to the news media, distributed books to school children, recalled local and family heroes, held cookouts and picnics, and discussed the Civil War in forums open to anyone interested in that war—or in meeting interesting people.

On January 8, 1961, as scheduled, the official commemoration of the Civil War began. Churches across the nation responded to a Presidential Proclamation by opening the official ceremonies with the ringing of bells, special prayers, and sermons with themes that tied in with Centennial emphases. Later in the day, special dedicatory services took place at the tombs of Generals U. S. Grant and Robert E. Lee and at the military academies. Elsewhere, special programs set the tone for commemoration. In one of them, Executive Director Betts recounted the great domestic and international benefits and privileges the nation enjoyed as a result of the Civil War. In his opinion, the Centennial was the event that Americans had long awaited.[3] President Dwight D. Eisenhower's official proclamation of the day called the war "America's most tragic experience . . . [but] an enduring lesson and profound inspiration."[4]

The statements of these two men denoted the early sentiments of commemoration. Popular author Bruce Catton spoke

---

3. Commission papers, Civil War Centennial files, National Archives, Washington, D.C. [hereinafter referred to as Commission Papers].

4. *Civil War Centennial Report*, 11.

in a similar spirit a few weeks later in an address to the Chicago Historical Society. "The Civil War is the central theme of our existence," he said. "We are bound to look back . . . to see what war did to us and what we got from it." But, he continued, the Centennial was more than just a time to remember. It was a time to move ahead, to appreciate national greatness, and to contend with new national and international responsibilities. It was a time for sober reflection and new understanding. These thoughts ring just as true today, as Bicentennial planners begin their search for meaning.

To some, the first year of commemoration was "the most eventful in the life of the National Commission." [5] Programs materialized in nearly every state, changes in the organizational charts of both national and state commissions brought more stability and better planning, and interest increased in the wake of continued activity.

Still, something was obviously wrong. Throughout the country the Centennial was not making the impact expected. Celebration would not jibe with the tragedies of war. The problem of "civil war" seemed too divisive to be resolved in commemorative services. Protests appeared—from individuals, organizations, and the media—criticizing Commission actions. The Connecticut Daughters of the American Revolution called for an immediate end to all proceedings. An editorial in the outspoken Manchester (New Hampshire) *Union Leader* called the Centennial a "ghastly celebration." An editorial in the Arizona *Daily Star* was equally critical: "The excuse that our children should know more about this terrible war questions the quality of the teaching that goes on in our schools and colleges." Too little emphasis was being placed, this editorial contended, "on the fact that it was the uncompromising of extremists of both sides who brought on this lamentable tragedy." After the Commission issued a call for the churches to

---

5. *Ibid.*, 11.

cooperate in beginning the Centennial on a serious note, a Catholic priest from Philadelphia protested: "This priest is sick and tired of attempts . . . to pervert the message of the Christian church . . . to use the Christian church for a signal for anything other than that of glorifying All Mighty God." A note to the Commission in late 1960 was even more emphatic: "I would destroy all monuments, memorials, emblems, mementos, tokens, symbols of any and all descriptions, both in the North and in the South." Bruce Catton identified "a distressing pattern" of the "Strawberry Festival," disguising real issues with "syrupy sentiment," in the proceedings. He felt that the Centennial was becoming "a lighthearted celebration that leaves us feeling that the whole affair was nothing more than a regrettable but vastly entertaining misunderstanding between people who were never really angry about anything in particular." [6] Many of the participants experienced the feeling that despite enthusiasm, dedication, and hard work, the leaders of the Commission were not moving the country toward the proper spirit of commemoration.

Though Grant and Betts took these criticisms seriously, they always countered with the defense that the war should be commemorated because it had drawn the country together. It was the lives of men and their deeds of valor that demanded the occasion, said Grant.[7] They failed also to answer the continued charges of commercialism bruited against the Centennial. In reference to the growing sale of souvenirs, relics, and other materials, he commented: "While the sale of such articles does carry an unfortunate commercial flavor, it must be remembered that it also carries the remembrance of the Civil War story to a very wide public and especially to the young citizens of tomorrow upon whose wise patriotism our country must depend in

---

6. Bruce Catton, "Lest We Forget . . ." *American Heritage*, 12 (August 1961) , 26.

7. Commission Papers.

the future."[8] Grant insisted that the Commission had not co-operated in any commercial enterprise, though he did admit that the members had encouraged commercial groups to tie in their advertising with Civil War themes when possible. Such defenses failed to abate the storm, and even as late as 1963 television commentator David Brinkley was leveling new charges of increasing commercialism in Centennial planning.

Unfortunately for the Centennial, many of its problems reflected the inadequacies in the leadership at the top, especially Grant and Betts. Personal problems became a major factor in the general's leadership. His wife's lingering illness took a heavy toll of his time and energy and often removed him from his command post in Washington. Also, though Grant was very active for his eighty-odd years, he often appeared inflexible. His speeches and correspondence often demonstrate a tenacious unwillingness to depart from a set position on controversial views as well as an unwarranted sensitivity to criticism. These characteristics appear at their extreme in an incident that created an immediate stir of some significance which lingered on for months to haunt the general and the Commission.

Sometime in 1959, Grant presented to the members of a special military order in which he held membership copies of an article entitled "Abraham Lincoln and the Rothschilds," which accused the Jewish people of Europe of having supported both sides in the Civil War for financial gain. Although this was not a new article, this distribution antagonized Jewish people everywhere and resulted in a sharp rebuttal by the Anti-Defamation League. Grant's answer to continuing criticism hardly helped to resolve the tension. "Evidently I made a tactical error," he confessed. Though he apologized for an indiscretion, he still called the criticism "unjust and vicious," contending to the end that there was "much truth" in the article.[9] When Senator Kenneth Keating questioned him on the

8. *Ibid.*
9. *Ibid.*

impropriety of his action, Grant promptly cited his "right of free speech," suggesting that some people had even praised him for distributing the article. The general seemed to miss the point that because of his position on the Commission, his actions suggested official as well as personal views.

Karl Betts' leadership also came into question. In the opinion of many participants, his actions strongly suggested a Madison Avenue approach to Centennial planning, as well as a somewhat naive interpretation of what the real meaning of the commemoration was. "It is our hope," he once said, "that every community, no matter how large or small, will have some sort of commemoration during the Centennial to show its appreciation for the principles and heroism displayed by our forefathers regardless of the side on which they fought." [10] Though both Grant and Betts spoke enthusiastically of commemoration, their stress on cohesiveness ignored the reality of social tensions in 1961, which were exacerbated by developing civil rights concerns. It was difficult to include Blacks in any commemoration that stressed unity at the time they were meeting such strong resistance in their bids for equality, and tensions increased with the continued references to a nation brought into harmony by the Civil War.

From its inception the Commission had soft-pedaled Black involvement in Centennial proceedings. As early as February 26, 1958, the executive committee agreed not to ask Blacks to serve on the advisory council unless they were selected with some care "so as to avoid political nuances or risks or the risk of bringing embarrassment to the Commission." [11] There was also a haunting fear that the commemoration might become a formidable weapon to be used against the Blacks. Whatever the case, the Commission, in its early days, did miss many opportunities to extend participation to the race which had been so important in the war that was being commemorated. When a

---

10. *Ibid.*
11. *Ibid.*

group of Blacks in Arkansas requested an exposition in their state on Black contributions to state history, Betts showed little understanding of the validity of their request: "I regret very much," he wrote, "that our Commission has no materials which we can send to assist you in the formulation and carrying on of your program. At this moment we are preparing for publication and distribution a small brochure on the Emancipation Proclamation itself." [12] He then spoke of a ceremony being planned, *in Washington*, that would relate to Blacks in American history.

On another occasion, Betts suggested, even more naively, to the manager of Stone Mountain Memorial in Georgia, that he had just recommended "due recognition ... to the magnificent loyalty displayed by the Negro to their masters in the South during the war." [13] This insensitivity to the deeper problems appeared in Betts' reply to a Columbus, Ohio, woman's request for suggestions on how to give Blacks their proper place in history. Betts advised a search for letters, diaries, documents, and publications that portrayed the Black in some capacity—a good suggestion in itself, but hardly enough to satisfy a restless minority. When Pauline Myers, the Director of Public Relations for the National Association for Colored Women's Clubs, suggested that there was "a general tendency to simply neglect to approach the period with the Negro in mind," General Grant advised her to contact the chairman of various state commissions and work out her program suggestions with them.[14]

To his credit, as the civil rights movement intensified, Grant did seek counsel on how to involve the Blacks. A personal letter to President Charles Wesley of Central State College in Wilberforce, Ohio, invited Wesley to Washington to confer with the Commission on this sticky problem. Wesley accepted the offer. In a letter to Betts in January 1961, Wesley detailed his first actions. His emphasis was on research and publication—

12. *Ibid.*
13. *Ibid.*
14. *Ibid.*

the identification of the Black in history—but he also suggested a special celebration for Blacks at the time of the centennial of the Emancipation Proclamation. His suggestions also spawned other actions, including an Emancipation Centennial Lecture Series sponsored by the New School of Social Research; an exhibition, "Slavery and the American Negro, America's Tragedy," by Providence Public Library; and inclusion of a volume, *The Negro,* in an "Impact Series" proposed by the Commission.

These and continued efforts might have helped sustain Commission leadership had it not been for an unfortunate incident at the Fourth National Assembly in Charleston, South Carolina, in April 1961. With "a deplorable lack of vigilance," the Commission committed the meeting to a racially segregated hotel. With a Black woman, Mrs. Madelene A. Williams, on its state commission, New Jersey immediately protested the arrangement which discriminated against its delegate. The official report of the Commission suggests that at this point leaders "failed to take the instant corrective action . . . required." [15] Public sentiment roused quickly, and the incident became a national issue. In the midst of growing unrest, a tactful approach to presidential advisors by several Commission members prompted President John F. Kennedy to intervene—"tactfully but firmly"—by moving the meeting to the unsegregated United States Naval Base outside of Charleston. The damage had been done, however, and the incident punctured the idea that the Centennial would extend the unity theme into mid-twentieth-century America. Several changes on the Commission took place within a few months, including the resignations of both Grant and Betts. Betts' departure related directly to pressures "from the Charleston blunder, as well as other considerations." Grant's resignation was attributed to compelling "family anxieties," brought on by the continued illness of his wife.[16] During the leaderless interim, Representative Fred Schwengel

---

15. *Civil War Centennial Report,* 12.
16. *Ibid.*

of Iowa played a major role in holding the Commission to-gether.

The departures of Grant and Betts from Commission leader-ship closed the first phase of the Civil War Centennial. Within a month Professor Allan Nevins of Columbia University be-came Commission chairman, and Professor James I. Robertson, Jr., of the University of Iowa became the executive director. These men called for an entirely new concept of commemora-tion. In the Grant-Betts phase the emphasis had been on public relations, too heavily involved with "military personages and events," and tainted with charges of commercialism. Under the new leadership, the "social, cultural, and economic history of the war" came under consideration.[17]

Allan Nevins' stature as a historian was of such consequence as to offer unusual opportunity for a new program. One of the nation's most distinguished and productive scholars, Nevins changed the emphasis from a military thrust and a cohesive past to a more scholarly one. In his intial address to the Commission, he explained the new directions: "We shall use our energies and influence to help make the national commemoration of the Civil War both instructive and constructive. To this end we shall discourage observances that are cheap and tawdry, or that are divisive in temperament, or that in other respects fall short of expressed magnanimity of the spirit shown by Lincoln and Lee. . . . We shall encourage observances which will assist the American people to understand the mingled tragedy and exalta-tion of the war, and to draw from its lessons both practical and moral commensurate with its importance." [18]

The new executive director was also a solid addition to the Commission. Robertson, former editor of the scholarly journal *Civil War History*, brought youthful vigor and efficiency into a troubled situation. For nearly three years, he traveled widely across the country, contacting Centennial leaders, encouraging

17. *Ibid.,* 5.
18. Quoted, *ibid.,* 13.

them to produce new programs, finish old ones, and continue efforts to make the commemoration important for all Americans.

Two national programs in Washington, D.C., under the direction of Nevins and Robertson, command attention as dignified and effective commemorations. The first, on September 22, 1962, commemorated the Emancipation Proclamation. The second, on January 13, 1964, honored President Lincoln's Gettysburg Address. A large crowd, including many young people, attended the Emancipation Proclamation program at the Lincoln Memorial, while a larger audience viewed the program on the three major television networks. Later, videotapes carried the program to many others. Nevins presided over the day's ceremonies, introducing the impressive list of participants. Mahalia Jackson, accompanied by the United States Marine Corps Band, sang the National Anthem. Archibald MacLeish read his special poem, "At the Lincoln Memorial: A Poem for the Centennial of the Emancipation Proclamation," and the Marine Band followed with the first performance of "Forever Free: A Lincoln Chronicle," composed especially for the occasion by Ulysses Kay, present on the stage with the other dignitaries. After remarks by New York Governor Nelson A. Rockefeller and Judge of the U.S. Court of Appeals Thurgood Marshall, Ambassador to the United Nations Adlai E. Stevenson delivered the memorial address. Stevenson related the philosophy of the second phase of commemoration to the Emancipation Proclamation with these words: ". . . once more we feel as men did in Lincoln's day, that the future of mankind itself depends upon the outcome of the struggle in which we are engaged." Videotape remarks by President Kennedy followed, and the program ended with the singing of the "Battle Hymn of the Republic."

Nevins also presided at the Gettysburg Address affair, a symposium of distinguished American writers and thinkers. Poet Robert Lowell read several of his compositions, including one on the Address. John Dos Passos, Arthur L. Goodhart, Reinhold Niebuhr, and Paul H. Douglas spoke on different aspects of the Address. Bad weather limited the size of the crowd, but the University of Illinois Press later published these remarks, together with a paper by Professor Nevins elaborating on the program.

In other important national programs, Congress arranged ceremonies in 1961 and 1965 marking the First and Second Inaugurations of Abraham Lincoln. These programs followed formats similar to those sponsored by the Commission, with dignitaries including Bruce Catton and poet Carl Sandburg, Senators, Congressmen, and other national officers. At the 1965 commemoration, Adlai Stevenson delivered an eloquent description of the background of the Second Inaugural Address.

The largest number of programs emerged at the state and local level, however. These programs reflected the interest and wishes of the man in the street rather than those of a national Commission. As early as 1958, the Governor's Conference, meeting in Miami, had unanimously endorsed the resolution of Virginia's Governor J. Lindsay Almond, Jr., urging appointment of state Civil War Commissions to stimulate interest in the Centennial. Encouraged by the National Commission, these state commissions formed rapidly and began to develop their programs. Eventually there were commissions in forty-four states. Under their supervision, hundreds of local committees were formed to become the backbone of community planning.

As state and local committees formed, more and more programs and projects emerged. On this level the change in Commission leadership and the subsequent changes of emphasis appeared less serious than on the national level. States and communities generally went their own ways, and though Nevins and Robertson influenced them to new actions, they continued their particular expressions of commemoration. Commemoration on the local level often followed regional or state directions more than national. States celebrated their own history and heroes. Many Southerners remained loyal to "the cause," and Northerners honored the "victors." It was logical for Illinois to have Lincoln programs and for Mississippi to honor Jefferson Davis.

A variety of programs emerged on the state and local levels.[19] Kentucky held special ceremonies a hundred miles apart, at the birthplaces of Jefferson Davis and Abraham Lincoln. In the first year of her planning, Georgia erected more than 600 roadside markers which' detailed Sherman's march from Chattanooga to Atlanta and on to Savannah, while in June 1964, she commemorated the Battle of Kennesaw Mountain with battlefield tours, a visit to Atlanta's famous Cyclorama, a medics' exhibition, a long parade, and a noisy hootenanny. Mississippi issued a proclamation of commitment to the Centennial, established a Centennial headquarters, and inspired the enthusiasm of her citizens well before the official beginning of the commemoration. Much of her focus was on the Old Capitol, the most historic building in the state. Many of the ante bellum homes were opened and attracted many visitors.

Alabama appropriated $60,000 for an elaborate week of activity, recalling the inauguration of Jefferson Davis with a parade, official ceremonies, a pageant entitled *The Man of the Hour,* and essay contests, ladies' day, fashion shows, fireworks displays, speaking engagements, and a motorcade. South Carolina re-enacted the *Star of the West* incident and the Secession Convention before the national commemoration began. Later the state co-operated with the national Commission to re-enact the firing on Fort Sumter. Tours, luncheons, dress parades, banquets, speaking affairs, balls, all in the traditions and patterns of the antebellum South, were festivities that marked South Carolina's involvement in the Centennial. One of the highlights in Texas was the dedication of the Supreme Court Building in the fall of 1960 to the more than 100,000 Texans

---

19. Most of the state programs are described in the files of the state in Civil War Centennial Papers, National Archives.

who served in the Confederacy. The state also began construction of a $2.5 million archives building in which the records of the Civil War period would be stored and sponsored a microfilming of Civil War service records.

North Carolina's commission expressed its own personal philosophy of commemoration as well as that of many of the other Southern states in "remembering the valor and sacrifices of its sons who fought and died for principles which they believed eternal and the sons of other states who also made the supreme sacrifice for their convictions." [20] The commission approved both the popular programs and the more scholarly ones. The opening ceremonies spoke to one mood by including a sunrise service, a breakfast, a pageant of flags written by a local North Carolinian, and choruses singing songs the soldiers sang during the days of the Civil War. For the more scholarly, there were programs of research and study throughout the state, exhibitions of pictures, records, and equipment of the Civil War days in libraries and museums, and a Civil War Centennial Conference sponsored by the North Carolina Department of Archives and History, which featured speakers and seminars on Civil War topics.

Arkansas commemorated a new national park at Pea Ridge Battlefield, with a colorful pageant featuring representatives of the five Indian tribes who fought in the battle. In October 1964, Memphis, Tennessee, unveiled the long-planned 1800-pound bronze statue of Confederate President Jefferson Davis. Special programs at Chattanooga in the summer of 1963 commemorated important battles in the Western campaigns.

Virginia, where so many battles of the Civil War took place, celebrated actively. Commemorative services were held at many of the battle sites, and the state honored its heroes in community after community. In a special July 4th program at Berkeley Plantation, historian Clifford Dowdey highlighted the re-enact-

20. Civil War Centennial Papers of North Carolina, National Archives.

ment of the writing of "Taps" by reviewing the circumstances under which this famous tune was written. Perhaps the most important among Virginia's 1,147 centennial events was the construction of a fully equipped Civil War "Centennial Center," an elaborate project which combined a series of exhibitions and an information center with an elaborate motion picture program that constituted a chronological history of the war in that state. The Virginia commission also concentrated heavily upon a stupendous re-enactment of First Manassas, the restoration of several historic sites, and the publication of the wartime papers of General Robert E. Lee.

Outside the South others responded with similar enthusiasm and good intentions. In 1960, New Jersey scholars were searching for unpublished documents, cataloguing and microfilming Civil War material at Rutgers University Library, urging greater local participation, and planning a monument to their state hero, General Philip Kearney. The lighter side of commemoration in New Jersey came in May, 1960, when a balloon similar to the one used in the Civil War reconnoitered high above New Jersey's landscape, announcing new events and new programs. The state's most impressive program, however, was the re-enactment of Abraham Lincoln's visit to the legislature at Trenton en route to his inauguration in 1861. Actor Anthony Quinn, starring as Abraham Lincoln, stirred the large audience with his sensitive interpretation of the President-elect's speech, and an eighty-voice choir sang several Civil War songs. The *Trentonian* of March 6, 1961, commented on a superb effort of the state's planners: "The spirit of a historic moment was felt even by the most casual spectators and the silence that came about in anticipation of Lincoln's address was electrifying."

Connecticut distributed copies of Lincoln's speeches to all its schools and libraries. Within the state several new roundtables appeared, and the state commission raised money to put a unit in the field at the First Manassas re-enactment. New Hampshire's committee conducted essay contests and encouraged publication of unit histories. The state commission also sponsored a trailer carrying Civil War exhibits to communities throughout the state. At Colby College, the New England Civil War Centennial Commission sponsored a conference for school teachers of the state. Maine served as host for a New England Regional Conference in April, 1960, a meeting to develop and co-ordinate programs of Centennial activities for neighboring states. The Maine commission also engaged radio and television stations to produce programs that would highlight Centennial themes. Massachusetts, encouraged by an enthusiastic executive secretary, published and circulated a brochure describing the state's role in the war, and encouraging research and publications on Civil War subjects. The state commission utilized local talent effectively in a program commemorating the Emancipation Proclamation in September 1962. Reading, Massachusetts, demonstrated that town's involvement in the Civil War by setting up a "knothole view of the Civil War," an exhibition of the life of the common soldier.

The Centennial of the Battle of Gettysburg commanded national interest with an impressive program at the battle site in July, 1963. More than 50,000 people watched the ceremonies and a symbolic reenactment of Pickett's charge. Four months later a commemoration of Lincoln's Gettysburg Address took place at the same site, with speakers including Secretary of State Dean Rusk; historian David Donald; and panel members Alistair Cook, David Donald, Archibald MacLeish, Fred Schwengel, and others. Former President Dwight D. Eisenhower lent his prestige to the occasion with a short address, and Marian Anderson brought the crowd to its feet with her singing. A specially taped message from President Kennedy concluded this commemoration on a solemn note of contemporary concern: "Let us rededicate ourselves to the perpetuation of those ideals of which Lincoln spoke so luminously . . . As Americans, we can do no less." This moving tribute to our assassinated president was Kennedy's last public statement before his own assassination in Dallas.

In the Midwest, Indiana invited Civil War Commission members from the adjoining states to a regional conference, where they talked of preserving papers, letters, and photographs and discussed the possibilities of long-range publications. Ohio looked for descendants of her Medal of Honor winners and selected particular shrines upon which to focus Centennial interest. With Louis L. Tucker as program chairman, Cincinnati held a two-day symposium on "The Ohio Valley in the Civil War," with Bruce Catton as keynoter. Illinois reported special commemorations for many of its Civil War leaders, a special re-enactment at Cairo, and a two-day Civil War symposium at Southern Illinois University. Springfield sponsored a workshop in the fall of 1962 for historical society and museum curators. A conference in Des Moines, Iowa, in May 1962, included distinguished speakers, a workshop on teaching Civil War history, and seminars for elementary and secondary teachers.

The states beyond the original bounds of the United States in 1861 were not as enthusiastic about Civil War Centennial plans as were those more immediately associated with the conflict. The failure of the National Commission to grapple with the problem of how to extend the Centennial into the West limited the possibilities for making it a national event. There was activity in the West, however, as some of the states associated their own past with the Civil War period. Though South Dakota stressed her remoteness from Civil War scenes, her commission nevertheless set up several publications, including a succession of monthly brochures for use in schools and clubs. Minnesota memorialized the Sioux Indian uprising of 1862. The Arizona commission published a booklet on the state's role in the war and set up a re-enactment of the Cross-Mowry Duel at Tubac. Colorado sent "troops" to engage in Arizona and New Mexico re-enactments, and Utah concentrated interest on her Mormon battalion that participated in the Civil War. Utah's program, which included songs, luncheons, and speeches, was not unlike some of the programs in the Southern states. Oregon planned a lively Centennial program for the year, with a Civil War float appearing in many parades. Oregon also held commemoration services for Colonel Edward Baker, Lincoln's personal friend killed at the Battle of Ball's Bluff.

Across the country people commemorated the Civil War, some ignoring its tragic dimension, others subdued by the intensity of its meaning. Such a commemoration would hardly appear to be a time for joy, but frivolity appeared often in the Centennial despite serious efforts of planners to dignify this tragic historical event. The Starkville (Mississippi) Chamber of Commerce sponsored a Snuffy Smith Week in May 1962 which began with an archery tournament and a horse show and continued with a lengthy parade, a "coon on a log" contest, a rodeo, an old-fashioned harp-playing, several dramatic productions, an all-night square dance, a style show, a "Loweezy" bridge tournament, a fishing rodeo, a bowling contest, and four Centennial balls. Interspersed among these activities was a continuing fashion show. Fashion shows often appeared as commemoration features in the former Confederate states. In Beaufort County, North Carolina, Civil War dresses, lingerie, and riding outfits were featured; while in the Vicksburg and Warren County (Mississippi) Historical Society Confederate fashion show more than fifty Southern belles modeled costumes worn in ante bellum Vicksburg. An elaborate pageant in Leeksville, North Carolina, celebrated the completion of a railroad link in 1864. In the midst of a heavy downpour in the summer of 1963, the *Belle of Louisville,* loaded with 1,050 enthusiastic passengers, commemorated John Hunt Morgan's crossing of the Ohio River. The annual program of the Theophilus C. Hauser family in Yadkinville, North Carolina, was expanded by assembling family descendants and those of their slaves at the old homeplace for a festive reunion. Women in La Grange, Georgia, created a "hoop-skirt brigade" which traced its origin back to a Civil War home guard unit of women. The uniform was a flowing skirt, "the more colorful the more appropriate." Membership in this brigade, by the way, included two Yankees.

Dinners with menus from the Civil War days were a popular Centennial feature. Ham from hogs "raised within gunshot" of the battlefield; candied yams; field peas with snaps, plantation style; watermelon pickle; chow-chow; homemade biscuits; corn muffins; old South peach cobbler; and coffee were served at a North Carolina dinner. At the commemoration of the Battle of Wilson's Creek, Missouri, the following menu attracted attention: "a fresh cup of pokeberries and green apples, a salad made from young horse corn leaves, sassafras root and bacon fat; an entree of stolen tough turkey and chitterlings, ground acorns and swamp cress; hardtack and cornpone, buggy rut water and roof drippings. For dessert there was mess sergeant's special soggy pie or souffled wild onions." In contrast, a special breakfast at Cape Fear, North Carolina, included hors d'oeuvres, tiny tea biscuits, hot crabmeat balls, pigs-in-the-blanket, and tiny sausages, chicken livers and bacon, olives wrapped in bacon, fresh Carolina shrimp, assorted canape trays consisting of caviar canapes, imported sardines, smoked oysters, anchovy canapes, fancy olives, deviled eggs, assorted cocktail nuts, and champagne.

Ohio preserved more than 400 bullet-riddled regimental flags carried by many of its wartime regiments as a Centennial project. Arkansas put out a special gray and red automobile license plate in 1961. The same year, Harrisonburg, Virginia, opened to the general public a large electric map of Stonewall Jackson's famous valley campaign. Tennessee located and marked the birthplaces of its fifty-one Confederate general officers, commemorating each with a monument. Even a race track materialized as a result of Centennial activity. The Garden State Race Track Association in New Jersey announced that the Centennial would be the theme for a short period of time, and school children were invited to the park without charge to view displays and maneuvers reminiscent of Civil War times. There was also a Centennial running of the Jersey Derby, an event that first began during the Civil War. A centennial commission member in Connecticut set up a private project of his own—recording on tape the sounds of a Minie bullet at 200 yards and other sounds he felt that the soldiers heard during the course of battle over a century ago. A Virginia boy who bore the same first name of a grandfather born during the battle of First Manassas—Battle Manassas Bull Run Brown—was singled out for attention. A young lady wrote President Kennedy in June 1963: "I would like to know what is being done about the situation in Gettysburg. I think this battlefield should be kept up as a national park. As Mr. Lincoln said, this is hallowed ground and I believe it should be treated as such. If nothing else you might take up a collection around the nation, I would contribute at least fifty cents, then buy it." [21]

Important programs on every level of participation, however, marked a more significant involvement with Civil War history. Few Centennial projects attracted as much attention or drew as large crowds as did the many impressive exhibitions that reminded the American people of their Civil War heritage. A few of the more impressive ones illustrate the variations in size, topic, and quality. The Library of Congress opened an extensive display of original drawings, prints, photographs, maps, letters, historical documents, and books on the Civil War and furnished a special catalog to identify each. The National Archives exhibited more than 300 documents, maps, photographs, sketches, and works of art to create a panoramic sweep of the war. A Navy Department museum ship displayed Civil War dioramas, equipment, and other items which illustrated the Navy's role in that war, and the department produced a forty-minute film entitled "The Navy and the Civil War." A traveling Centennial exhibit sponsored by the Army made its initial

---

21. Commission Papers. The letter makes clear the girl's distress at the commercialism that marred the area.

appearance in July, 1961, at Shepherd College in West Virginia. The Armed Forces Institute of Pathology, tracing its own beginnings back to 1862, displayed exhibits of Civil War medicine, wounds, and diseases. Newport News, Virginia, featured a diorama of the first ironclads battle in a *Monitor-Merrimac* wing of the Mariners Museum. Prison life was the topic for an exhibition at the Virginia Centennial Commission Center during much of 1963. The Ansco Division of General Aniline and Film Corporation presented a sequence of a hundred Mathew Brady photographs in a traveling display entitled "Photography and the Civil War."

The Detroit Historical Society featured "Michigan in the Civil War," an exhibition that ran for four years and showed the war's progress year by year. The Civil War Roundtable of Southern California, claiming the first Centennial exhibition in the country, presented an exhibit of weapons, accoutrements, model soldiers, documents, and newspapers. Maine opened the Civil War Museum in Portland with relics ranging from bullets to one of Lincoln's razors. The Ohio Historical Society presented a display of recruiting posters and political broadsides. The Dallas Philological Society presented one of the major exhibits in the Southwest, entitled "The Confederacy: Its Impact on the Cultural Life of Dallas."

The Jewish Historical Civil War Centennial Commission sponsored an impressive exhibition entitled "The American Jew in the Civil War" at the B'nai B'rith Building in Washington, D.C., in 1962. In historical dioramas, photographs, letters, and artifacts, the exhibit attempted to present the civic and military participation of American Jews in the war, their literary and art work, as well as Jewish attitudes toward slavery, the war, the chaplaincy issue, and relationships with Abraham Lincoln. Corning, New York, displayed a special glass collection at the Corning Museum including, among others, a unique *Monitor* and *Merrimac* vase, tumblers with Civil War emblems emblazoned on the sides, dishes bearing General Grant's likeness, three glasses from President Lincoln's state service, and photographs of many other collections of Civil War vintage. Gimbel's Philadelphia store had a major exhibition on the Civil War.

Many traveling displays also carried Civil War themes. Wisconsin and Illinois had historymobiles, whose contents of Civil War memorabilia, dioramas, historical documents, and equipment told continuing stories of the past. The New Jersey National Guard set up a militiamobile, a traveling museum presenting the role played by that state's militia units during the Civil War. Harnette County, North Carolina, used utensils, tools, household linens, trade tools, and other items to present a picture of army life in the Civil War.

Civil War tours were popular. At many sites special guides explained historical events and directed traffic. At other sites, strategically placed recordings recounted events. The National Association of Travel Organizations, which comprised a cross-section of the United States travel industry, aided operations by publicizing the various locations of battlefields and other hitoric sites.

Placing and dedicating landmark plaques was a popular commemoration feature. More impressive, and probably more important for posterity, were some of the restoration projects. The restoration of Fort Ward in Alexandria, Virginia, provided the city with a park with picnic areas, military buildings, and a headquarters for historical information, as well as historic attraction. Washington and Lee University, aided by a grant from the Ford Motor Company, restored its famous Lee Chapel. The Old Randolph House, a Civil War landmark at Farmville, Virginia, had an important face-lifting, with the room where Grant wrote his famous surrender proposal to Lee set up as a museum and showplace. Arkansas concentrated its attention on its Civil War capitol at Washington in Hempstead County, restoring the capitol and other period buildings of that community. Across the country other restorations produced important museums, libraries, and historic attractions which will continue to preserve the heritage of the Civil War well beyond the Centennial period.

Radio and television played their roles in presenting various aspects of Civil War history. Executive Director Robertson singled out CBS's *A Pair of Boots* as one of the most moving and effective dramas of television endeavor. CBS did *Eisenhower on Lincoln—A Military Tribute,* a conversation between the General and Bruce Catton. In a dramatic ninety-minute special, Richard Boone starred in a nationally televised re-creation of the Battle of the Crater. Hollywood produced several Centennial movies. Although *Shenandoah,* with James Stewart, came late, it was one of their best productions. The National Commission presented an award to *The Horse Soldiers,* which starred William Holden and John Wayne. No great movie epic was produced in connection with the Centennial, however, and years after their original release, *Birth of a Nation* and *Gone with the Wind* continue to show to large audiences of Civil War enthusiasts.

State and local commissions and stations shared Centennial television and film interests. The Louisiana Commission sponsored several local programs. The Tennessee Centennial Commission in Nashville produced a filmstrip called *Tennessee and the Civil War.* Lancaster County, Pennsylvania, sponsored *Footnotes of the Civil War,* twenty-five weekly telecasts featuring Pennsylvania or Maryland communities in the Civil War period. Many Virginia stations televised *Stonewall Jackson's Way,* a film produced by the Virginia Civil War Commission which highlighted the activities of that colorful Virginia general. Norfolk, Virginia, viewed the interesting television show *The Last Full Measure,* the work of a retired Marine officer whose hobby was film-making. George Washington University and others offered courses in the Civil War on their television stations. Ohio State University had a three-hour documentary on the war on April 9, 1965, entitled *Ohio Has Saved the Union,* with nearly one thousand pictures and photographic slides helping to re-create the mood and the tragedy of the Civil War period. A fifty-five-minute documentary, *Echo of the Dark Years,* which featured the speakers at the national Centennial Assembly at St. Louis, was the result of efforts of a radio station in Indiana. The film of the re-enactment at Antietam was shown on neighboring television stations. Together, the National Park Service and the National Centennial Commission prepared a film on the Civil War Centennial which was distributed to roundtables and other organizations throughout the country. Maryland sponsored a color and sound film on its legislative activity during the Civil War, which was available to groups without charge.

In final analysis, publications commanded as much attention during the Civil War Centennial as any other single project, and brought the war from the archives into the American experience. The National Commission concentrated on four major projects: the collecting, editing, and publishing of papers of two of the wartime leaders, Ulysses S. Grant and Jefferson Davis, by Southern Illinois University and Rice University, respectively; "an annotated bibliography of the most useful and utilized books about the Civil War," and the *Impact Series,* fifteen detailed studies to trace and analyze "the impact of the Civil War on . . . nonmilitary aspects of American life."

The Library of Congress released a series of useful "resource books," including titles of maps, reading lists, photographs, and motion pictures. The National Archives and Records Service in Scholarship listed to its credit *A Guide to Civil War Maps, A Guide to Federal Archives,* and *A Guide to the Archives of the Confederate States,* and it microfilmed many of its Civil War holdings with an eye toward making them more available to students. From the Smithsonian Museum of History and Technology came a booklet, *Uniform Regulations for the Army of the United States, 1861;* a folio of selected Civil War maps from the Coast and Geodetic Survey was a valuable addition to

Civil War material. The United States Government Printing Office published James T. Robertson's popular *The Civil War,* a sixty-four-page volume which sketched the major campaigns and activities of the war. This little book, which has now sold over 800,000 copies, has been commercially released.

University presses released much new material, including biographies, campaign studies, and interpretive works. Some were also active in reproducing valuable Civil War books and records that had been long out of print. The Civil War Centennial Commission commended the university presses of Indiana, Louisiana State, North Carolina, and Texas for excellent publishing records during the Centennial years. Private presses increased the flood with many volumes on the period.

State commissions also became involved with publication programs. Ohio's series on the Civil War was one of the better ones. Mississippi's commemorative work, *Mississippi and the Confederacy,* was two volumes of more than eight hundred pages of contemporary documents and writings. The Detroit Historical Society underwrote the publication of the Civil War letters of one of its state generals, Alpheus Williams.

No aspect of the Civil War Centennial attracted so much attention or set off such a furor of controversy as did the many battle re-enactments. From the beginning, public opinion was divided sharply as to the wisdom—even the propriety—of such events. Despite divided opinion, major re-enactments took place at First Manassas, Philippi, Wilson's Creek, Antietam, and Kennesaw Mountain; and minor engagements were acted out at Carthage, Winchestesr, Bentonville, Franklin, Nashville, and numerous other places, especially in the South. Enthusiasm for such pageantry reached a high point at the re-enactment of the Battle of First Manassas in July 1961, but this engagement was such a fiasco that it cast a pall on the other re-enactments in the remaining years of the Centennial.

Defenders of such affairs claimed "that re-enactments provided realism, color, and pageantry, that they enabled a great many people to take direct part in the Centennial and that they brought authentic sights and sounds of the Civil War to even greater numbers of persons." [22] Many letters to the Commission indicated enthusiasm for such affairs, as opportunities to re-create scenes heretofore only described in the pages of books, and a chance to get local units into a larger action. Opponents contended that the sentiments associated with re-enactments were "'more theoretical than real," that they were expensive, promoted commercialism and a carnival atmosphere, and "were an affront to good taste and an abuse to history." [23] Re-enactments brought joy to many who rode and "fought" again, in some mystic spirit of the occasion. But they also brought pain to many others, for war has losers as well as victors, and the re-enactments focused heavily on the futility of events that had left too many wounds—or they became carnivals of men on horse-back pantomiming serious moments in history.

The re-enactments were never officially sponsored by the Commission during either phase of the Centennial leadership, though the Grant-Betts phase offered greater encouragement. The general policy throughout the Centennial was to leave re-sponsibility and control in the hands of state or local commissions or committees, or even private individuals. Both Grant and Betts defended the action of the Virginians who prepared the re-enactment of First Manassas, arguing that each state had a right to plan its own programs. Betts even contended that large amounts of revenue would come into the state as a result of a good performance. He wrote the Manassas Chamber of Commerce that the Commission was "wholeheartedly behind . . . plans to re-enact the first battle of Manassas," [24] and stated that the Commission was prepared to lend "all the aid within our power and authority." When Senator A. Willis Robertson suggested that such an action might reopen old wounds by com-

22. *Civil War Centennial Report*, 45.
23. *Ibid.*, 44.
24. Commission Papers.

memorating bitter fighting, Betts acknowledged that while the Commission had actually tried to discourage re-enactments because "very few local groups" could handle such programs, there was "little chance of such re-enactments causing any serious disturbance or reopening the old wound." [25]

To some the re-enactment at Manassas was a glorious affair. Others felt it possessed all the weaknesses inherent in such efforts. On July 22-23, 1961, the hottest days of the year, guns were literally drawn up the sides of the hills, and Civil War buffs staged their version of the original drama. Though the participants sought authenticity, they caught only a small part of the realism of the actual day of combat. Weary observers and participants recalled crowded hotels, sleeping in an open field on the hot, sultry night, and trying to make sense out of smoke, cannon fire, rebel yells, dashing horses, and sanitary problems. Strong criticism, including remarks by President Kennedy and Chairman Allan Nevins, followed the pageant. Nevins stated his own position emphatically when taking charge of the Commission, "If the National Commission tries to reenact the battle, my dead body will be the first found on the field." These and other criticisms were enough to divert emphasis from re-enactments during the second phase of the Civil War Centennial.

Other re-enactments did follow, however; and Civil War buffs all over the country sought them out and devoted time, effort, and resources. One person even pulled a privately owned caisson with cannon from an Ohio city to a Virginia battlefield. A note in the bulletin of the North Carolina commission for April 1963 contended that "North Carolina's Sixth Regiment . . . has already seen almost as much action as did the original Sixth during the entire course of the Civil War." At the re-enactment of the third day at Gettysburg, 40,000 people, including eight governors, viewed 500 "Yankees" protecting the old

---

25. *Ibid.*

stone wall from 600 charging "Confederates," all narrated dramatically over a loudspeaker by actor Walter Abel. The final battle re-enactment took place in Harnette County, North Carolina, in April 1965, as more than 700 participants from fifteen states commemorated the state's last Civil War action.

All re-enactments were not battlefield scenes. Less spectacular were Clara Barton's activities at First Antietam, the inaugurations of both Lincoln and Davis, and the Virginia Peace Conventions. Re-enactments are traditionally part of a centennial and will continue to be. If properly researched, kept within manageable proportions, and truly representative of the spirit of a particular historical event, they can be proper forms of centennial expression. My own observations, however, point to the fact that they are usually expensive, often divisive, and capture little of the real meaning of history. Planners will do well to look at alternatives for releasing man's festive spirit.

The Civil War Centennial closed during the early months of 1965 with a series of memorable activities. On Lincoln's birthday, President and Mrs. Lyndon B. Johnson entertained Centennial officials and dignitaries at a luncheon. At Appomattox, on April 9, a quiet and dignified ceremony commemorated the Confederate surrender. General Grant re-entered the picture briefly to greet Robert E. Lee, IV, the great-grandson of the Confederate leader. On April 25, Vice President Hubert H. Humphrey spoke to a large gathering commemorating the surrender of General Joseph E. Johnston at the Bennett House in North Carolina. It was at Springfield, Illinois, however, at the Eighth National Assembly, that the Civil War Centennial reached its dramatic conclusion. Hotels and motels in the Illinois capital strained to accommodate the more than 650 registered officials, historians, members of Civil War Roundtables, students, and guests who were meeting with other workers to share the achievements and frustrations of their four years of Centennial labor. Amidst kudos and commiserations, they listened to Senator Paul H. Douglas' address, "Lincoln: World

Symbol of Freedom," and Bruce Catton's talk, "The End of the Centennial." These planners had had failures and triumphs. Crisis had been their lot, but they had weathered most of the crises and kept their enthsuiasm.

I personally wish that Centennial planners had involved more young people in their planning sessions, and they might well have given greater play to the role of women and Indians in the war years. And as the Commission itself finally admitted: "The Negro had every right to share in the Centennial on equal terms with the white man." [26] But he never did. I also regret that projects involving painters, poets, sculptors, musicians, and philosophers never made much impact. The fine arts, with the exception of drama, were not made a vital part of the Centennial, at least in the forms which could have conveyed new meaning and understanding.

While there were several art exhibitions—the most noteworthy being a Currier and Ives display arranged by Nationwide Insurance Company which included war photographs of the famous artists and an explanatory booklet and film for schools, churches, and civic groups—and art teachers sponsored some contests, little art emerged. Music faced the same dilemma. Music was part of many of the commemorations, but there was little original composition, nor was there great concern for the creative musician. Ulysses Kay's presentation at the Emancipation commemoration in 1962 was probably the highlight of creative production, but this was hardly enough. Some symphony orchestras became involved, and one produced two excellent albums of Confederate and Union music, but the *great* production never materialized.

Several good productions, like *John Brown's Body* as presented at the Old Museum Village at Monroe, New York, and

---

26. *Civil War Centennial Report*, 6.

The Andersonville Trials, a Broadway success which toured the country during the Centennial days, showed effective use of drama. And, of course, there were many locally written pageants and theater productions which included the stories of heroes, spies, courageous men and women, and other incidents peculiar to the communities roundabout.

Despite failures and frustrations, the Civil War Centennial remains a significant commemoration in our nation's history. It made its mark in several new museums, libraries, and other structures that stressed the academic approach to an understanding of our heritage. Library shelves now house many volumes of well-written works which provide the student with better tools for research and understanding. Many people remember their visits to battlefields, museums, and historic sites during the course of those four years, where they learned first-hand of the experiences of other Americans in another generation. In the course of new research and study, the Civil War became the leading thrust in the story of our nation's growth and development. Robertson has suggested that the Centennial was instrumental in bringing about significant basic changes in the teaching of American history. Emphasis turned from the teaching of tactics and strategy to the deeper meanings of men at war and the impact of this war upon American thought—past and present. New questions were probed, new answers were found, and doors opened to new perspectives.

Allan Nevins summarized the kaleidoscopic nature of the Centennial in his summary remarks to Congress: "The National Commission is well aware that, like all such bodies, it must confess to its share of failures and shortcomings . . . it offers no excuses. It begs merely to state that some of them proceeded from an excess of good intentions, from a zealous attempt to do too much with too little—too little in time, for time is always short; too little in money, for although Congress was generous, it was natural to depend heavily upon unpaid services; too little in trained personnel, for experts are often hard to find; and too little in thoughtful planning." Bicentennial planners across the country, looking to another national commemoration less than two decades after the Civil War Centennial, will read Nevins' words with sympathetic understanding.

The New Jersey Tercentenary

F EW commemorations have generated the enthusiasm that marked New Jersey's 1964 observance of the three-hundredth anniversary of its founding. Though the Tercentenary was tied closely to New York's World's Fair, New Jersey planners put on a good show within the state. Their efforts in appealing to citizens, selecting leadership, planning programs, and providing funding solicited responses which brought many of their goals to reality.[1]

The idea of a Tercentenary originated early in 1950 in the conversations of three Jerseymen—John T. Cunningham, a newspaper writer interested in history; Richard P. McCormick, professor of history at Rutgers; and Roger H. McDonough, director of the State Library—but not until 1958 did they gain approval for the venture from Governor Robert B. Mayner. Their proposal to the Governor is a statement of objectives and themes that could be commendable in any centennial:

---

1. Material in this chapter was obtained primarily from interviews, notes in the extensive Tercentenary Papers in the New Jersey State Archives and History, and Bernard Bush, *The New Jersey Tercentenary 1664–1964* (Trenton: New Jersey Stahe Archives and History, 1966) .

We see the Tercentenary as a rare opportunity for New Jerseyans to look with pride upon a notable history, to re-emphasize the strong economic and intellectual role of the state in·modern times and to look to the future of New Jersey.

Basic in the celebration, of course, must be a philosophy, a motif. This, we believe, must not be a "backward-looking" spirit, focusing only on 1664. Rather, the approach should be from the past to the present—and thence to the future.

We especially urge that the observance be designed for enduring rather than temporary impact. Surely there is a need for spectacular observance in the form of pageants and special events—all traditional parts of an anniversary—but the Tercentenary should serve also as an occasion for contributions to the preservation and interpretation of New Jersey's heritage.[2]

Three men and a co-operative governor gave impetus to proceedings in New Jersey, but the final celebration was the result of much concerted effort among many people within the state.

On July 2, 1958, legislation provided for a state commission to begin work preparing a celebration for 1964, the three-hundredth anniversary of the naming of the state. An appropriation of $25,000 heralded tangible support. On May 2, 1959, an eleven-man commission was appointed. The real leaders emerged three years later, when businessman Paul Troast was named the permanent chairman and David S. Davies, from the Department of Conservation and Economic Development, became executive director.

How could a commission, a director, and a small staff impose a statewide celebration upon six million people? And this was a state divided within itself, a state that Benjamin Franklin had once called "a barrel tapped at both ends," by New York City to the northeast and Philadelphia to the southwest. Get people committed, said Davies. "Men and women and children, Jersey-

---

2. Bush, *The New Jersey Tercentenary, 1664–1964*, 8.

men all, would have to make the Tercentenary their own before anything substantial could be accomplished." [3]

Existing records in New Jersey point to creative leadership and planning at the top. With Troast and Davies directing affairs, there were few days of inactivity. Troast spoke with authority to business interests and solicited their funds and resources for Tercentenary needs. His was also the calm voice in committee meetings that stilled the winds of dissent when they blew too hard. His role as chairman usually meant intervening between strong personalities and vested interests, and he appeared at his best in situations fraught with possibilities for total disruption.

Davies' leadership was different. He was a hard driver who labored at his job full time and expected the same of his associates. Plotting a state celebration was a compelling thing to him. "Doing this kind of thing is like falling down stairs," he said, "there's nothing you can do until you reach the bottom." His personality was stamped strongly on all the Tercentenary activities, and his record of achievement speaks for itself.

Early letters from the commission to official leaders in each county and many cities urged appointment of local planning committees to broaden the base of participation from the counties and municipalities. Share programs and ideas for a better celebration, the commission urged. When a local committee was formed, the Governor and Troast sent congratulations, and the commission continued the encouragement with additional mailings of materials as they became available. The response to the commission's plea was encouraging: "some five thousand" Jerseymen eventually formed 368 municipal and 21 county committees.

In addition to local committees, the commission created and staffed a series of state Advisory Program Committees: Arbor and Garden, Design, Education, Fine Arts, History, History-

---

3. Correspondence, Tercentenary Papers.

mobile, Interfaith, Licensing and Marketing, Performing Arts, Public Information, Sports, Transportation, and Ways and Means. These committees provided recommendations that formed a framework for the year of celebration.

Though New Jersey developed a commendable committee structure, appointments to committees caused more than their share of difficulties in the planning stages. Generally, appointive policy was highly selective, as the membership of the Ways and Means Committee indicates. The chairman was Lee H. Bristol of Bristol-Myers Company of New Jersey. Committee members included the presidents of New Jersey Bell, Suburban Propane Gas Corporation, National Newark and Essex Bank, Kresge-Newark, Inc., the Public Service Gas and Electric Company, Esso Standard, Trenton Trust Company, DeLaval Steam Turbine Company, Grand Union Company, Merck and Company, Inc., New Jersey Manufacturers Association, and several other prominent businessmen, chairmen of industrial boards, and state officials.

Pitfalls always occur in the American political system when large numbers of appointments must be made, however, and New Jersey made her mistakes. Efforts to include the wider spectrum of society seldom succeeded. Representation on the important committees was weighted with upper middle class white men, thus discriminating against social elements that might have added their cultural impact to a larger program. Sometimes appointments did not live up to expectations. Several committeemen used their positions to personal advantage, or served only as names on a roster. Others worked for programs that offered little but entertainment or community self-gratification. In spite of these failures, however, New Jersey's committee did well. They solicited widespread participation, raised over a quarter of a million dollars, and inspired local programs of variety and quality.

To attract attention to a celebration of some magnitude, New Jersey planners realized the need for good public relations.

Here commission publications played an important role, covering virtually every facet of the celebration. *New Jersey Heritage,* the Tercentenary newsletter, financed by state funds, was noteworthy. Ten issues appeared, circulating widely and bringing firsthand information to local committees—sharing ideas, identifying personnel, describing programs, and establishing "a firm identity for the Commission" and a good reputation for the Tercentenary.

The major barrage of publicity came with the beginning of the Tercentenary year itself. News media collaborated on descriptions of every aspect of the celebration. New Jersey newspapers showed creativity, imagination, and enthusiasm in their articles, Sunday specials with color pictures, and editorial comments. Periodicals of historical societies, business journals, magazines, and tabloids offered articles on New Jersey history as their contribution to the birthday year. High school and college editors wrote feature articles and covered news events in school papers. Radio and television stations publicized the Tercentenary. E. G. Marshall narrated on television *The Three Hundredth Harvest,* a summary of early New Jersey history. Educational television had a field day of special programs. Radio had short spot programs with Tercentenary themes.

Local newsletters constantly reminded New Jersey editors of the developments along the celebrating front, constantly solicited newspaper space to publicize programs and seek support. Tercentenary spokesmen conducted press conferences. Tercentenary authorities listed their names with speakers' bureaus, wrote feature articles for the press and radio, produced calendars, slogans, and symbols, and designed movie riders for New Jersey theaters. Public relations teams publicized their state to companies, organizations, and political groups as the ideal meeting place for a 1964 convention. They placed announcements of coming programs in bus and railway terminals, on taxis, on billboards along well-traveled highways, in libraries, museums, parks, and other places of public interest. The official

Tercentenary design appeared on buildings, in shop windows, in schools, on cigarette lighters, even on the covers of telephone books and match folders.

Contests in photography, song writing, stamp design, flower raising, and painting were also popular public relations gimmicks. Jerseymen still treasure plaques, certificates, and other awards received as contest winners in 1964.

In the midst of celebration, a sort of Tercentenary "spirit" engulfed the state, and many responded enthusiastically. Protestant leaders joined with Catholic, Eastern Orthodox, and Jewish clergymen to radiate a spirit of religious harmony. North Jerseymen sometimes sat with South Jerseymen in attempts to iron out complex intra-state difficulties. Several joint sessions of the Tercentenary Commission, meeting with the New Jersey Civil War Committee, eventually led to the integration of some aspects of what might well have been competing programs. Throughout the state there was an air of congeniality and goodwill that related directly to Tercentenary activities.

Governor and Mrs. Richard J. Hughes officially opened the Tercentenary year at the State House in Trenton on December 31, 1963, with a party to which the public was invited. Guests of honor included Boy Scouts, high school students, several Delaware Indians from Oklahoma, and a deputy bailiff from the Isle of Jersey. At midnight Governor Hughes threw a switch. A bright light beamed, from the lighthouse at Atlantic City, a signal for the grand opening of the Tercentenary year. The Tercentenary had begun!

Programs and projects in New Jersey's Tercentenary showed an unusual blend of the traditional with the innovative, the historical with the futuristic, the serious with the lighter side. Everywhere there was action; few municipalities or counties sat on the sidelines. The commission continued to set the tone of celebration, and history appeared prominently in many programs—reminding men of past achievements, warning the over-optimistic with tales of hopes deferred. A look at even an in-

complete list of projects shows history's mark on the Tercentenary:

Type of Project	Number of Localities Involved
Writing some kind of local history	88
A historical exhibition	75
Erecting historical markers	43
Historical tour	29
Restoration	17
New Museum	17
New Library	16
Map-making	13
Creating a historical society	12
Setting up a new junior history chapter	11
Program on Indians	10

Other actions often stole the spotlight and demanded the
talents of celebrants. Though these projects are similar to those
in most centennials, one can still be impressed with the large
numbers recorded in New Jersey:

Type of Project	Number of Localities Involved
Contests of various kinds	86
Parade	60
Pageant	55
Band or choral contest	38
Tree-planting	34
Tercentenary dinner or picnic	30
Special church services	28
Art exhibit	17
Program for Senior Citizens	16
Park built or created	16
Re-enactment of the past	11
Flower show or fashion tea	10

These figures are only as accurate as the records compiled and submitted.[4] Many programs ended when the curtain fell or the last whistle blew, never to be logged or compiled in any permanent record. What *is* on record shows the Tercentenary as a time of motion—of citizens sharing the moment of celebration together, each with his own direction, tempered by the goals of men and women who did their homework—the state commission and the local committees.

Few state centennials have matched New Jersey's activities. The serious blended with the ludicrous, men and women marched for causes and for fun, senior citizens shared the spotlight with the younger generation, professional talent vied with amateurs for center stage; programs ranged from the cutting of a three-hundred-egg birthday cake to the dedication of the new library in Trenton.

Several New Jersey communities, selected for diversity, the hallmark of that state's Tercentenary year, illustrate the variety of activities. In Little Silver, there was dancing in the streets during celebration days—a community square dance and a block party in the center of the town, with carnations pinned on the first thousand women who appeared. While the town danced, high school folk singers strolled through the streets singing old ballads. Shoppers were served by clerks dressed in costumes of the city's early days, and customers arriving at the stores received documents reprinted from seventeenth-century originals. In quaintly decorated shops, colorful vendors made and sold old-fashioned homemade candy. Outside their doors a town crier detailed the news as he might have done in 1664. The town library exhibited Little Silver's historical documents, and a special newsletter, distributed free through the community, told of the beginnings, legends, and changes that marked the town's history.

Cedar Grove placed its energies on the "establishment of a

4. Figures taken from county summaries in Bush, *The New Jersey Tercentenary, 1664–1964,* 115–186.

free public library." Its citizens dedicated themselves to arousing public interest, promoting participation in the celebration, better acquainting neighbors with their past, and bequeathing that past to generations yet unborn.

Sayersville citizens converted part of their library into a museum where impressive exhibits drew enthusiastic audiences. The community awarded a plaque to its oldest citizen, gave prizes in an essay contest for high school students, held a parade, an outdoor band concert, and a massive fireworks display.

At Florham Park the interest was on a lecture series, the film *A Land Called New Jersey*, and historical exhibitions under the sponsorship of Boy and Girl Scouts.

Tenafly had a successful clean-paint-fix-up campaign and reflected a bit on current social change by renaming a street in honor of Elizabeth Cady Stanton, an early women's rights crusader. The townspeople of Old Nottingham donned merry costumes of Robin Hood and his men and marched through the downtown streets in a ceremony that "attracted a good deal of public attention." In Willingboro the bloodmobile requested three hundred pints of blood in the name of the Tercentenary, an order quickly oversubscribed.

These are but a few patterns from among many communities celebrating, each involved in "doing its own thing," sharp in contrast of style and goals. A look beyond these, into the welter of activities throughout the state, further illustrates the scope of planning and performance set off by the Tercentenary. Originators and sponsors of local programs include every type of local arrangement: individuals, business and civic clubs, religious and ethnic groups, garden clubs, historical societies, Scouts—organizations intent on having fun or promoting fellowship, and those with more serious purposes. Their programs, inspired, written, produced, acted, managed, even financed by local groups using their own talents and resources, show sound community leadership and extensive participation. Some of the programs were trivial and of parochial interest. Others were profound and illustrated the goals of the planners, revealing their hard work and sensitive creativity.

One town expressed its Tercentenary spirit by planting a community flower bed with Dutch tulip bulbs in the shape of the Tercentenary symbol. Another sponsored a treasure hunt with hopes of getting the historically minded into attics and basements to ferret out books, clothes, letters, and papers—anything that would throw light on the past. Several communities made Christmas cards, using Tercentenary symbols, historical pictures, and reprinted documents. Many planted trees in special ceremonies.

One group of high school students prepared a map of their town's history, with all important sites at the time of incorporation clearly marked. Another group prepared a map marked with the names of the original town property-owners, their acreages, and the dates of each land grant. Enterprising planners later used these maps as the format for table menus at a local Tercentenary dinner. In another community a woman assembled a twenty-four-page brochure, a statistical analysis of the town which included everything that the average citizen would need to know about taxes, income, banks, churches, history, and other local activities and statistics. From a smaller community came an impressive one-page history, prepared for distribution to all newcomers and visitors.

Exhibitions were prominent on the local scenes and showed initiative and an occasional artistic flair. One high school had a history fair in the cafeteria with posters, dioramas, models, collages, and photographs—all blending into an impressive and well-attended exhibition. Glassboro State College chose an exhibition series with such diverse items as a piece of slag from an old furnace, an Indian hatchet, two pieces of original South Jersey glass, a 1733 marriage certificate, the minutes of a women's club from 1680 to 1762, a letter written by General Washington in 1777, deeds, letters freeing slaves, bills of sale and stock, and many others.

Some Jerseymen preferred to re-create their history. The Colonial Debs displayed teen-aged girls in colonial costumes, spinning yarn, making lace, and discussing their work with passers-by. One woman dressed dolls in period clothing which she made from original designs and patterns. Later, in proper ceremony, she presented two of these dolls, clad in early colonial costume, to Governor and Mrs. Hughes.

Well-organized tours introduced visitors to a larger arena of history. For those who could not tour directly, there were simulated tours, with slides and tape recordings—ideal for senior citizens, class presentations, or as preliminaries for actual tours.

Few citizens and groups in New Jersey remained untouched by the Tercentenary. Menus in restaurants reflected its influence, as did window displays and sales advertising programs. Even the military felt the Tercentenary, and McGuire Air Force Base opened tours of its facilities on a regular monthly basis. Significantly, the tour began at a display board which exhibited the post's historical background. A more spectacular military involvement was a special swearing-in of a large number of inductees in a pre-Tercentenary affair in which military "brass" mingled freely with politicians and the man in the street.

Across the state there were parades, pageants, hootenannies, beauty contests, dances, jazz festivals, bridge tournaments, fairs, and hoopla that defies description—all to the glory of New Jersey's three hundred years. Kings and queens reigned over local celebrations with the blessings of the Sons and Daughters of the American Revolution, the PTA, or civic clubs. Scantily clad bathing beauties passed in review. High school students ground out essays on the history of their state or town. Singing waiters, attired in early twentieth-century costumes, complete with arm garters, mustaches, and straw hats, served at an old-fashioned picnic. A Boy Scout Indian dance team entertained the PTA with a "Pageant of History." As a Tercentenary feat, sixteen members of the Paramus Slimmers Club collectively lost 300 pounds. Catholics ate meat at an Early Settlers' Dinner on Friday: "After all," said the Bishop, "this only happens once every 300 years!"

In the midst of frivolity, the enduring also sought its place. Franklin established a mineral museum, a library, and a municipal park. Ventnor City found resources for a new library, a municipal park, and a sea aquarium. Outdoor concerts in Paterson and Rutherford exposed youth to good music. Roxbury experimented in drama; Glassboro State College had an art show; Bordentown, a youth government day; and Tenafly, a children's ballet.

The sheer number and diversity of activities during Tercentenary days clearly demonstrate the enthusiasm and creativity of New Jersey citizens, but some of the larger programs left a more permanent legacy. Publications rank high among them. The New Jersey Historical Series, edited by Richard M. Huber and Wheaton J. Lane, comprised 31 volumes of state history written by some of New Jersey's most prominent scholars. Though some were of high caliber, some critics felt that the project was too expensive or unscholarly, while others criticized the lack of uniformity. One critic felt that Madison Avenue writers could have done better. The commission weathered this criticism and finally secured a publisher, D. Van Nostrand Company of Princeton. Publication was a losing proposition for Van Nostrand, and the remaindered copies, bought up for new distribution at a very low price, are now the property of Rutgers University. Despite the criticisms and financial difficulties, observers agree that these books fill a void in New Jersey history writing, and a reviewer in the *American Historical Review* suggested that the series might "provide a model unique in historical conception and execution." [5] Planners will do well, however, to note pitfalls as well as opportunities when projecting such a series.

---

5. *American Historical Review*, 70 (April 1965), 804.

"Tercentenary Tales," eighty-three sketches written and published in newspapers by John Cunningham over a period of two years, began in 1962. The tales popularized local history, communicating with people who would not ordinarily be reading historical material. They touched all parts of the state, represented all the people, including those who seldom make the history books. They related people to their own world, the joy of being and creating, the depressions or frustrations spawned by changing times, the excitement of unusual experiences common to all men. Fifty of the tales have been published as a book, which continues to circulate widely.[6]

The historymobile, a traveling exhibition modeled after similar units in Wisconsin and other states, was not as elaborate as the Canadian caravans—but very effective. Through the good offices of Ford Motor Company and the Bell Telephone Company, the commission obtained a large tractor-trailer, which it converted into a rolling museum. Three exhibits, designed by historians and tastefully mounted by museum personnel, traced the history of state growth and development—its beginnings, its growth from a colony to a state, and its coming of age after 1850. The historymobile made a strong impact on young and old, its success attributed "to the quality of its exhibits and to the intelligent efforts of those who were responsible for the three exhibitions." Its personable driver-narrator also did much to sell his unit to the public. The historymobile sometimes confronted scheduling difficulties and once was accused of playing politics,[7] but it nevertheless attracted large crowds as it traveled to almost all the state's municipalities. In 1962 it made a 3,539-mile round trip to represent the state in Seattle's World's Fair, and it appeared at the New Jersey booth at the New York World's Fair of 1964-65. It served its best function at

---

6. John T. Cunningham, *The New Jersey Sampler* (Upper Montclair: The New Jersey Almanac, Inc., 1964).

7. One woman repeatedly accused the commission of using the historymobile to promote a bond issue.

home, however—moving about from community to community, exhibiting state history to long lines of curious visitors.

At least one community also experimented with a local historymobile. Cumberland County converted a school bus it had borrowed for a year into a small unit to illustrate its own history. Together teachers and students assembled a display of local materials which became popular throughout the county.

The Jerseymen Junior Historians' program particularly appealed to the state's younger citizens and, in the minds of some, was the most important single contribution of Tercentenary days.[8] Under the direction of Joan Hull, the Junior Historians became one of the most active groups in state historical activities. Their magazine, *The Cockpit,* and their bulletin, *The Crossroads,* were impressive publications, showing "what an exciting and meaningful experience it can be to discover history in one's own backyard."

The Young Jerseymen, still very active in the state, are now hard at work planning for the 1976 Bicentennial. They have agreed that this should be a serious time, and they have set up meetings and workshop to implement their concerns. Their publications will devote special issues to Bicentennial subjects, and the impress of these young historians during the several years of national and state celebration will be well worth watching.

Other state history projects included such publications as the *New Jersey Almanac* and *New Jersey Roadmaps of the Eighteenth Century,* the "Colonial Records Project," in which Professor McCormick located and microfilmed in Great Britain many "bodies of important source material" closely related to New Jersey's history; a $20,000 contribution toward the publication of the Woodrow Wilson papers; and a college lecture series, with four lecturers making a total of twenty-five pre-

8. Dr. Frank B. Stover, an assistant superintendent of schools in a New Jersey community, enthusiastically predicted that "this will be the greatest achievement of the Tercentenary."

sentations in sixteen institutions. Interest in the lecture series never reached expectations, as people seemed to prefer activities which involved them more directly in the proceedings.

Several movie and television films appeared. The most ambitious was a thirty-minute 16mm sound-color film entitled *The Land Called New Jersey*. Financed by the Humble Oil Refining Company, this film presented a panorama of "three centuries . . . of New Jersey." A "model of authentic and skillful historical interpretation," it received a special award for excellence from the American Association for State and Local History. This film is still being shown in movie houses, schools, civic clubs, and on television as a valuable source for students interested in New Jersey's history. While other television and film productions were not always of such high caliber, some were good examples of enthusiastic planning and creative imagination—especially some of those shown on educational TV.

New Jersey, like many others, discovered real problems in using music, art, and drama as avenues to celebration. There was great potential in all areas, but it seldom materialized. The state commissioned two large musical works: a cantata for orchestra and chorus by Ulysses Kay of Englewood and a symphony by Roger Sessions of Princeton. Critics described Kay's composition, performed by the New Jersey Symphony Orchestra in 1964, as too advanced for the occasion, and Session's Sixth Symphony, performed in 1966, received similar reviews—and poor attendance. Between April 26 and May 7, 1964, five Tercentenary concerts by Metropolitan soprano Dorothy Kirsten were attended by such limited audiences that the commission had to pay part of the bill.

The New Jersey Festival of Music also had its difficulties. Focusing on an orchestra that the critics acclaimed as magnificent, with a program that was "one of the cultural high-water marks of New Jersey's Tercentenary year," it too failed to attract a large audience. Even with a $75,000 grant from the commission, it still ran a $30,000 deficit. Again the commission had to pick up the tab.

All of this music was of highest quality as art, but it spoke to only a limited section of New Jersey citizens. The offer of a thousand free tickets to local students in Atlantic City for a New Jersey Symphony Orchestra concert received an enthusiastic response, suggesting that less expensive tickets and better publicity might have opened these musical programs up to larger and broader audiences. Other musical programs in the Tercentenary year attracted larger audiences, with community concerts and summer musical festivals proving quite popular. The dilemma of centennial planners in using music seems to be constant—how to plan a sophisticated and dignified commemorative work or program and still appeal to the larger audiences.

Though New Jersey was the home of many American artists, art planners faced similar disenchantment. Nine regional art contests held throughout the state were popular, but, as in music, the art works carried little mass appeal. Largest involvement was always on the local level where programs and exhibitions including both national and state art works did show to sizable audiences.

Drama, too, faced severe challenges as a celebration medium. New Jersey's dramatic productions appeared mainly on the college campuses, while communities often substituted pageants for serious drama.

Several lesser projects rounded out the major state-centered programs. There were photography contests, a re-enactment of George Washington's retreat across New Jersey in 1776, a historical pageant of early New Jersey history presented to a group of three thousand teachers of speech and drama, a publication featuring songs composed by Jerseymen, the official planting of the state tree, and the Boy Scouts' visit to the Governor to present a special letter of greeting from the governors of the other forty-nine states. The annual Miss America Pageant and the

1964 Democratic National Convention were also considered Centennial observances.

Though not a Tercentenary project *per se,* the Education and Culture Center at Trenton became closely associated with Tercentenary activities, as throughout the planning the commission co-operated totally to make this great complex possible. The first of the buildings was not completed until 1965, but the center, which now consists of the State Library and three State Museum buildings, is still a reminder of the more significant activities that occurred during New Jersey's year of history.

In the middle of successful celebration, Director Davies listed other projects conceived but never realized. He lamented the commission's unwillingness to support his "Camera on New Jersey" project which he had hoped would leave a permanent photographic record of the state in its three-hundredth year. He regretted the shortage of funds which precluded the possibilities of an artmobile, a project which would have taken New Jersey's culture into parts of the state less endowed than the urban areas. Finally, he was unable to organize a "Forum for the Future," a study by the best minds of New Jersey of what the state could expect in the years ahead. All of these programs appear as commendable but expensive possibilities. Other disappointments were less pronounced. Davies hoped in vain that his state would continue a historic buildings survey, a project that had originated in the days of the New Deal and accumulated much documentary material in the interim years. He also regretted that the commission would not sponsor a book of experiences, letters, and papers of New Jersey's most prominent citizens. Before the collapse of this project, the director did obtain some letters which became part of a special file in the State Archives. One, a hand-written letter from John Masefield, the Poet Laureate of England, was a beautiful expression of warmth and praise for a state he had once visited.

Other frustrations for the imaginative director and his staff included the failure to develop a Trenton battlefield project like Gettysburg, the unwillingness of the commission to set up a national film festival, a shortage in financial support which prevented the transfer of the USS *New Jersey* from the mothball fleet to a permanent residence as a museum in New Jersey, and the failure of a heritage tour to materialize.

Enthusiasm wanes rapidly after commemorative events reach their peaks. In late 1964, with the leaves changing to fall colors and thoughts of winter ahead, many Jerseymen were back at old routines, the Tercentenary a pleasant memory; others had little noticed the celebration. Yet enthusiasm still bubbled for some special programs. New energies were mustered as late as November 21, when the Leonia Tercentenary Committee successfully re-enacted George Washington's 1776 bloody retreat across New Jersey, part of a greater effort to create a state park at Bluff Point, one of the historical spots along the retreat.

For most Jerseymen, however, the celebration had ended by late November, and its leaders could reflect upon a year of commemoration at their final dinner. From the banquet table they looked back at thousands of events to weigh both successes and failures. New Jersey's Year of History had run its mad pace through many days and across many miles. There was rejoicing that the Tercentenary ended with harmony and good will still prevailing—even though some unsolved crises added a sober note. When things had run smoothly, people were lifted up from the dull routines of daily living; at other times performance had been little more than sound and fury. Sometimes problems frustrated and discouraged planners. One local dignitary spoke his mind, and probably the minds of many, in a letter criticizing Tercentenary costs in both time and money. "I am at a loss," he wrote, "as to who is responsible for selling our great governor this idea of a birthday party that will take three or four years when we celebrate the birth of Christ in one day— the birth of our nation is celebrated in one day."

Ultimately the smaller problems took the heaviest toll, harassing the various committees and complicating their work. Thousands of requests for free literature and free tickets to the various programs cluttered planners' days. People ordered "free" Tercentenary materials in unusual quantities—lapel buttons, handout brochures, calendars, folders, and other promotional material—and complained about shortages. Rarely did anyone consider the difficulties of the small staff, operating on a limited budget.

Continuous solicitation by salesmen further complicated the lives of the director and his staff. Salesmen filled hours of busy staff days trying to sell products ranging from necessities to worthless gadgets. Advertising often capitalized flagrantly on Tercentenary symbols and issues. Though some sports figures and events provided good publicity with their halftime ceremonies, others were guilty of exploiting serious themes in flying Tercentenary flags, sewing on patches, and titling important sports events in Tercentenary language.

Sectional and regional problems occasionally lent notes of disharmony. "We [South Jersey] are very jealous of our position down this way," read a statement in late 1963, "because in most cases we have been left out in the cold making us a defensive people." This problem may seem inconsequential to Bicentennial planners, but many states and local units already have backgrounds of conflicts of interest. Planners must accept the realities of the possibilities of schism and discord, and work constantly toward resolving them. A centennial should be an occasion for binding up sectional and local wounds, not opening them!

New Jersey always had problems, just as others will have, but planners were seldom deterred. Plans that had long been on the drawing board, in the shadowy limbo of a committee, or ideas in some imaginative mind suddenly emerged as reality— as programs that covered the face of the state, always gravitating toward the common goal of celebrating the state's three-hundredth birthday.

What can one learn from the New Jersey Tercentenary?

Davies predicted accurately that the Tercentenary influence would continue to pay dividends to the state in years to come, as the continuing interest in history evident in New Jersey today reveals. Because of 1964 more museums and libraries, facilities better used and better appreciated, exist throughout the state. The educational and cultural complex in Trenton is used by growing numbers. "There is scarcely a single institution associated with the study of New Jersey history that did not emerge stronger for its participation in the Tercentenary celebration," wrote Bernard Bush in his book summary. Because of the Tercentenary, Jerseymen now "see themselves within the flow of human history," said Davies. Governor Richard Hughes, concluding what Governor Meyner had begun, echoed these sentiments. The Tercentenary program, he felt, helped to give the people a sense of history in a state that formerly had not been as enthusiastic as it might have been. According to John Cunningham, the people in the state became conscious of their history for the first time during 1964, especially on the local level. History previously had been too much a story of the first families of the state, of whites, of people who had already made their marks. But the new history that came out of the Tercentenary had a deeper base, a more personal point of reference for many people who had never before advanced beyond the first stages of understanding. One individual even suggested that the Tercentenary had given New Jersey "a soul."

Not counting local funds, the total income on the state level of the Tercentenary Commission reached $2,670,308.48, more than half of which went into the New Jersey Pavilion in the World's Fair. Of this sum, $1,430,000 was appropriated by the state legislature and $1,189,095 was contributed by New Jersey's industrial firms. Spread over a five-year period, this is not a large sum, but coupled with large local appropriations, it is a significant amount to be devoted to history.

1964! New Jersey celebrated a birthday. Men and women,

boys and girls—New Jersey citizens all—were involved in a celebration. Hopes and frustrations blended in an outpouring of action that made 1964 a small Golden Age in the state's history.

VI

Illinois

IN many ways the Illinois Sesquicentennial of 1968 was an extension of the state's successful Civil War Centennial program. Staff members of its central commission were much the same; they operated along similar lines; and they even extended some of the same themes into the new commemoration. This commission, the chief architect of the two celebrations, was made up of permanent members. The Sesquicentennial Commission consisted of seven state senators and seven representatives appointed by the speakers of each House, ten appointees of the Governor, the Secretary of State, and the Director of Business and Economic Development. Ralph Newman, the proprietor of the Abraham Lincoln Bookstore in Chicago, a prominent historian in his own right, remained the commission chairman, and V. Lynn Sprague, formerly a consultant on tourism in Illinois, became its executive director.

Encouraged by a $500,000 initial appropriation from the state's agricultural premium fund, a fund raised from pari-mutuel betting instead of personal taxes, the commission held its first official meeting, an exploratory session, on January 1, 1966. A second meeting followed in April in Champaign, this time in conjunction with the annual meeting of the Illinois

Historical Society. The Society extended its annual program two days to discuss how to plan a Sesquicentennial with the business and civic leaders who joined them.

More than seven hundred concerned professors and businessmen sat together, probing possibilities for celebration—in a sort of "Let's Talk Sesquicentennial" confrontation. Their ideas ranged from the serious to those with little more than circus implications. There were suggestions of Sesquicentennial golf balls, license plates with special centennial themes engraved on them, trade fairs, business window displays, containers of all sorts made distinctive with Sesquicentennial markings, covered wagons driving through the state, T-shirts with state emblems stamped upon them, Sesquicentennial liquor bottles, and Christmas tree ornaments shaped as Sesquicentennial decorations. Someone suggested a placemat for use in restaurants throughout the country, while another spoke of preparing a drama on state history for presentation on university campuses. Moved by growing environmental problems, ecologists suggested "Clean up the state in '68" as the best course of action. Historians, archivists, and librarians, among others, spoke of research programs, library acquisitions, and publications.

From this discussion seven different interest groups emerged, each with an assignment to research a specific dimension of celebration. Later these groups issued official reports, which became the blueprints for many of the commission's later actions. Three points received common emphasis: maintaining ties with the business community, promoting Illinois as an important state in American economic life, and seeing that commercialism did not run rampant.

Other goals appeared in formal presentations at the meeting. Governor Otto Kerner commented that the Sesquicentennial had all the marks of being a "milestone," not only helping to mark the progress of the state, but giving Illinois "an opportunity and incentive" to see how far they had come in a century and a half and where they were going.[1] According to Kerner, "every Illinois agency . . . , community . . . , and citizen" should use the Sesquicentennial to help make Illinois first "in enterprise, imagination, opportunity, progress, and achievement." Chairman Newman echoed these sentiments, calling for the presentation of the best of his state's cultural, historical, recreational, educational, and industrial virtues "with dramatic effect, and in the best of taste," not only throughout Illinois, but "to the rest of the nation and to many places beyond our country's borders."

Speeches faded quickly as the commission assumed burdens of leadership and set patterns of operation. Deliberations and reports resulted in decisions on a Sesquicentennial objective—dramatizing Illinois "as a great place to live, to work, to raise families, and to visit"; a state slogan—"Make '68 the target date!"; and Sesquicentennial beginning and ending dates—December 4, 1967, to December 3, 1968.

Theories and dreams were important to Illinois planners, but they also needed an elaborate and workable committee structure to extend activities to local fronts. To facilitate planning and communications, the commission divided the state's counties into four sections, centering them around Northern, Eastern, Southern, and Western Illinois Universities, with a field representative appointed directly by the commission in each section. The representative was responsible for canvassing his section, encouraging local communities to celebrate, assisting them in the organization of planning committees, and serving as liaison officer between the local units and the commission. Though field representatives traveled widely, using state funds, and did much personal counseling with local officials, on their own time, major decision-making remained

---

1. Copies of the speeches and minutes of the meeting are filed under Illinois Sesquicentennial Proceedings, Illinois State Archives and History, Springfield, Illinois.

at the state level. Power usually concentrates where the purse strings tie.

Firm outlines of the Sesquicentennial took shape slowly. Illinois was not unfamiliar with commemorations; the state had celebrated its Centennial in 1918 with projects that included an important building in Springfield and a six-volume state history. More intent upon pageants and parades in a day when popular entertainment was live, however, the Centennial's main attractions were circuses, wild west shows, and silent movies. The Sesquicentennial demanded more sophisticated action.

To assure an assortment of programs and to guarantee maximum local participation, the commission called directly on each of the state's 102 counties and 48 of its urban communities to prepare and present their own local celebration programs—a celebration for each year of state history. To assist in such planning, and to involve all elements of the state's organization, the commission issued a model of a local planning chart which concentrated on three specific areas—activities, emphasizing programs and events; research, related to historical publications; and operations, including all the other details of planning. (See Figure 1.) The suggestion of fourteen subcommittees staffed with local citizens under both the activities and research divisions was meant to involve a cross-section of county economic, social, and intellectual interests, in an attempt to extend the celebration to every level of society.

Of the fourteen subcommittees, it is interesting to note that the first two were industry and labor, another indication of the importance of the business community in Illinois' celebration schemes. History and education were important foundations of New Jersey's Tercentenary, and they appeared prominently in Illinois's Sesquicentennial, but business interests dominated the scene in Illinois's final preparations. Representatives from the commission worked long hours so-

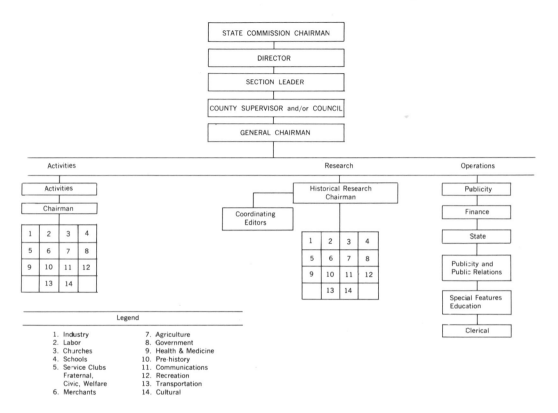

STATE COMMISSION CHAIRMAN

DIRECTOR

SECTION LEADER

COUNTY SUPERVISOR and/or COUNCIL

GENERAL CHAIRMAN

Activities

Activities

Chairman

1	2	3	4
5	6	7	8
9	10	11	12
	13	14	

Research

Historical Research
Chairman

Coordinating
Editors

1	2	3	4
5	6	7	8
9	10	11	12
	13	14	

Operations

Publicity

Finance

State

Publicity and
Public Relations

Special Features
Education

Clerical

Legend

1. Industry
2. Labor
3. Churches
4. Schools
5. Service Clubs
   Fraternal,
   Civic, Welfare
6. Merchants

7. Agriculture
8. Government
9. Health & Medicine
10. Pre-history
11. Communications
12. Recreation
13. Transportation
14. Cultural

FIG. 1

ILLINOIS SESQUICENTENNIAL COMMITTEE STRUCTURE

liciting businesses and industrial co-operation, not only for funds but also to prevail upon businesses to initiate appropriate projects and activities. "Good business is the name of the game," declared Chairman Newman. "To become successful, the Sesquicentennial celebration must have the help of business." Appeals went out to chambers of commerce, associations of commerce and industry, the Retail Merchants' Association, farm organizations, labor groups, and large industrial concerns. Newman felt that these groups would "best know how to exploit the promotional advantages of the state's anniversary to its maximum benefit without conflicting with existing programs."

Many Illinois businessmen got on the Sesquicentennial bandwagon, and some invested money and talent wisely in programs. Companies put out illustrated bulletins, articles, or brochures that publicized the state's beauty, progress, and economic opportunities. They sponsored banquets, prepared projects, contributed money, and lent facilities and personnel for Sesquicentennial planning. Some appealing and profitable suggestions and projects came out of the business community. Creative merchandisers prepared a historical map of the state, made available to visitors and travelers by local Chambers of Commerce. The Caterpillar Tractor Company brought in representatives from overseas companies during the Susquicentennial year to inspect their facilities in the Peoria area and then to tour the Lincoln Museum. The Moorman Manufacturing Company of Quincy sponsored a historymobile that toured several nearby counties. The Illinois Railway Association prepared a popular fifteen-minute film entitled *Illinois Railroads,* which related Illinois's growth to the development of the railroad. The National Bank of Chicago underwrote a Sesquicentennial stamp design contest.

Carson Pirie Scott and Company responded to the commission's request for the unusual by appointing Eugene Kubjack to design fifteen miniature rooms that illustrated periods of

Illinois history. In some cases they represented rooms in the lives of men and women prominently associated with Illinois: Abraham Lincoln, Ulysses S. Grant, Carl Sandburg, and Jane Addams. Other rooms illustrating the history of a developing state included a room from an early Carson and Pirie firm, a farm kitchen, a general store, a railroad depot, a schoolroom, a corner drugstore, and a livery stable and garage. Among the most popular and attractive exhibitions of the Sesquicentennial, these little rooms helped to recreate "eras, events, places, and old friends." They were first exhibited by their sponsors in December 1967 at a $100-a-plate benefit in Chicago. Carson Pirie Scott then shipped them widely through the state, showing them in museums and at their own outlets. They are now part of the permanent collection of the Illinois State Museum in Springfield.

The Illinois Bell Telephone Company also chose as its Sesquicentennial project a traveling exhibit—twelve paintings by Robert Thom which create a panorama of Illinois's past, beginning with the visit of Joliet and Marquette to an Indian village over three hundred years ago and proceeding in chronological order to show the British taking over Fort Chartres, George Rogers Clark in his Illinois campaign, the British at Fort Dearborn, and Shadrack Bond in his inauguration as first Governor of the state. The viewer witnessed the unveiling of the first John Deere plow, the opening of the Illinois Central Railroad, the last Lincoln-Douglas debate, and the repeal of the Black Laws. He gazed at the towering new structure of the first skyscraper and participated in the opening of Hull House and the first demonstration of nuclear fission at the University of Chicago. The paintings were shipped throughout the state as a special collection during the year of celebration, and afterwards were distributed to museums and libraries where the subject matter of each had special appeal. Individual paintings are now housed in the Illinois Historical Library, the Chicago Historical Society Library, the John

Deere Company Library, the Illinois Central Railroad central office, and the office of the Illinois Afro-American Society.

Business interests alone would not carry the celebration, and planners rejoiced when counties and communities began to enter into the swing of Sesquicentennial enthusiasm by late 1966. Nearly every county had its committee, and many of their program suggestions revealed substantive creative planning. Suggestions from these local committees varied from writing up-to-date local histories to organizing plays, pageants, and programs in churches, schools, park districts, and the local clubs.

Twilight zones appeared at times in the relations between the commission and the local committees. From the beginning there was some disagreement as to the use of funds. The commission felt that the state allotment was for larger programs and for administrative purposes, with counties responsible for most of their own financing. Many of the counties, however, inferred that the commission would help them financially. Although the remaining records do not show just how much appropriation the commission promised to each county, some counties apparently expected more than they received. The flurry of programs that emerged indicates that the problem was soon resolved—at least to the satisfaction of many planners.

To provide a central structure for the Sesquicentennial, the central commission set aside twelve dates for major events. Each event related to a specific issue of celebration; each had its own particular meaning for the communities which celebrated. The dates included:

December 4, 1967. The first day of the Sesquicentennial year, marked by a state celebration.

February 12, 1968. Issuing of the commemorative postage stamp at Shawneetown, site of the oldest Illinois post office. The Commission suggested the wide use of the lecture "Lincoln, the Postmaster," for this day.

March 4, 1968. Charter Day— a time to honor all those cities and towns chartered by the Illinois state legislature when it was in session at Vandalia.

April 18, 1968. Territorial Day—commemorating the Congressional act which enabled Illinois to prepare its constitution.

April 19–22, 1968. Sesquicentennial Sabbath Weekend, marked by special church services throughout the state.

May 30, 1968. Memorial Day—Arthur Godfrey was the main speaker at a special commemoration in Carbondale.

July 4, 1968. Independence Day—Special celebration at Kaskaskia State Park, the site of Illinois's first capital, highlighted by the presentation of a pageant, orations, and a fireworks display.

August 9, 1968. Opening of the Sesquicentennial State Fair in Springfield.

August 26, 1968. Constitution Day—commemorative action of the first Constitutional Convention.

October 5–6, 1968. Inauguration Days—major celebration in Springfield, marking the first meeting of Illinois State Legislature.

November 11, 1968. Veteran's Day—Parades and special ceremonies tying in the fiftieth anniversary of World I with the Sesquicentennial.

December 3, 1968. Statehood Day—Special convocations and banquets mark the Sesquicentennial closing.

To challenge public apathy and encourage maximum participation in Sesquicentennial activities, planners on every level always gave a high priority to publicity. From the beginning, newspapers, television and radio, and industrial publications heard entreaties from Sesquicentennial leadership to tell the Illinois story in the months preceding the celebration years. The commission wisely chose Larry Wolters, formerly of the Chicago *Tribune,* as its director of publicity, and called on Walter Schwimmer, a television expert from Chicago, to produce a Sesquicentennial film, which the commission hoped that Illinois industry would finance. With his experience, know-how, and contacts, Wolters soon brought the Sesquicentennial to life throughout the state, and Schwimmer contributed his own special expertise in numerous television specials.

No one was more active in selling the Sesquicentennial, however, than its magnetic and energetic chairman, Ralph Newman. His robust form and vibrant personality seemed to appear on every speaker's platform, between the lines of every letter, and in the debates of every committee. Newman was the idea man who set up plans for programs of which other men only dream. Some say the Sesquicentennial was "his baby." An honest man, dedicated to a worthy task, Newman may have indeed literally run the show. He instilled the spirit of celebration, he related the program to the business community, he radiated action, and others moved to his beat. And, somehow, he usually managed to weave history into the fabric of celebration. Some resented his brusque manner of operation and his glib promises of funds and services. Some felt he expected too much of his staff and others across the state, and there was a feeling that in too many crucial decisions, when the buck should have stopped at his desk, it passed on to other state agencies, where it was finally lost in the shuffle. Sometimes Newman's methods offended spirits and bruised feelings, but workers usually had the stage set in time for the scheduled performance. Newman put his own feelings on record when he said: "I once said humorously if I thought a striptease would work, I'd do it, if I thought a "Steal-a-Book Campaign" would work, I'd do it because a youngster can't stab or shoot anyone with a book, all he can do is to read it."

Newman was blessed with an excellent assistant, Joyce Warshaw, whose voice and presence were in so many of the proceedings of '67 and '68. She was one of the most informed sources of Sesquicentennial information and authority, and she played a major role in keeping harmony among the members of the Sesquicentennial team. The services of two other men, John A. Koten, lent by Illinois Bell, and Malvin K. Hoffman, a Chicago merchandising expert, were part of the dividend of the commission's close working tie with the business community.

These leaders and others prepared well for the Illinois Sesquicentennial. When the season of celebration began, a newsletter was already in wide circulation. Communications media were giving remarkable coverage to all activities. National magazines and newspapers had picked up Sesquicentennial themes and were giving them broad publicity. The moment was at hand for the grand opening. The official beginning was on Monday, December 4, 1967, but the first events took place on the preceding Sunday afternoon when the Chicago Historical Society entertained with a reception. The Old Town School of Folk Music followed with an open house, including refreshments and music. That evening the University of Chicago Symphony Orchestra ended the initial celebration with a gala performance.

It was not a spectacular beginning, but a substantial one, and the Sesquicentennial was underway. Soon other programs exploded across the state. On the lighter side were rodeos, tree planting, crow calling, coon squalling, rail splitting, and pony pulling. Folk festivals, a sidewalk sale of almost every type of goods, a parade of early fire-fighting equipment, an antique car show, and an arts and crafts event which included dulcimer playing, chair caning, tatting, wool spinning, rope making, stone polishing, flower pressing, and hair weaving were included in the celebration. There were displays of antique clocks and wood carvings, a buffalo barbecue, and a rifle shoot. A timberjack contest demonstrated tree-cutting with axes and crosscut saws, flower arrangers used the natural grasses and flowers of Illinois exclusively; and at a farm exhibit near Geneseo visitors could chop wood or wash clothes on an old-fashioned scrub board.

Under the banner of the Sesquicentennial, Illinois sponsored the National Coon Dog Trials, an outboard motorboat championship, and a flatboat race on the Sangamon River. The

Huck Finn, a forty-foot paddleboat, made the 1,462-mile river trip to New Orleans to commemorate both the Sesquicentennial and New Orleans' 250th anniversary. Ham operators received special cards for communicating news of the Sesquicentennial around the world. The Chicago Playing Card Collectors saluted Illinois with a two-day meeting at the Sheraton Chicago Hotel, at which time out-of-town collectors and visitors joined local members and guests for a weekend of activity and a display of playing cards that depicted the history and the heritage of Illinois. Each person who registered received two decks of playing cards especially printed in red on black backgrounds, with a blue border to commerorate the 150th anniversary of the state.

Sesquicentennial programs popped in Illinois like corks from champagne bottles. Excited people clinging to a happier past seemed dedicated to the confusion of noisy parades, ethnocentric pageantry, and erratic exhibitions. Strange sounds, past, present, and future, blended in the noise of ringing cymbals, exploding fireworks, honking horns, and flashing signs. Bathing-suited models shivered before their judges, Sesquicentennial magazines lay unread in dentists' waiting rooms, low-intensity television specials manged low viewer ratings, and tinny-sounding high school bands and symphony orchestras played to half-filled houses. But abundance and materialism marked Illinois's celebration.

Yet to this frivolity other planners added notes of serious purpose, a renewal of spirit, and an exciting appreciation of what had been—with new hopes and concerns for what was yet to come. Constructive and innovative actions often are much less spectacular than the sights and sounds of more festive celebration, but they do cite firmer and longer-lasting goals. Many programs showed their concern for more serious issues, as planners sought new guideposts to replace the shopworn and out of date.

Contests for new writers of fiction, non-fiction, poetry, and journalism searched for talent hidden in native stock. Contests in art and music uncovered new artists and gave hope to an aspiring few. Essay contests introduced exciting interests and broke new ground in the continuing dialogue between teachers and students. Informed tour guides introduced Illinoisans and their visitors to the beauties and the mysteries of the state. Some followed the trails that Lincoln had followed on the old Eighth Circuit. Here the more sensitive touched directly the heritage of a great man, and for a moment, shared his world. Here also was the heritage of the circuit-rider, the lawyer, or minister who had helped shape the state's moral and legal codes. With their anecdotes, stories, and descriptions, tour guides opened new vistas to those who followed important trails through Illinois.

As a Sesquicentennial project to preserve part of Illinois's natural heritage, a group of ecology-minded citizens attempted, with some success, to clean up Goose Lake Prairie at the Illinois and Michigan Canal. Other citizens followed this lead and attacked ecological problems in other parts of the state.

One project deserves special attention. On July 20, at Chicago's Soldier Field, children from twenty-four states and Canada—retarded children who had never known such an experience—were guests of the city, participants in a most unusual Olympics program. Under the direction of Bob Mathias, Jesse Owen, and others, a thousand youngsters ran, jumped, swam, and won medals just as the Olympic athletes do. Every boy and every girl who participated was a winner—as was the State of Illinois for initiating such a project.

In the programs and projects dealing with the arts, Helen Tieken Geraghty, chief of the arts program, deserves special kudos. Under her direction, painting, sculpture, architecture, music, and drama portrayed many dimensions of life—the energy of the people; their creativity, intelligence, and mobility; the public or private ethic by which they live; and the pragmatic spirit that drove them on. Mrs. Geraghty's division directed a groundswell of activities, including exhibitions of works of the past as well as contemporary art. Exhibitions included both the works of the masters and those of "a free market of ideas." Her official report tells of 1,274 art programs during the year, with 480 continuing beyond the Sesquicentennial's closing date. Exhibitions of fine paintings, sculpture, and crafts toured the state, while others were shown in museums, libraries, and art galleries on a more permanent basis. The 52 paintings and 14 sculptures by Illinois artists shown at the Art Institute of Chicago formed a popular exhibit with the Thom paintings a highlight.

The year of re-examination and new expression in music is hardly as clearly defined in its objectives, but the state wasted little effort or time getting programs underway. A symphony was commissioned for Ulysses Kay, who also wrote one for the New Jersey Tercentenary. Norman Luboff did a cantata called "Freedom Country"; Will Earl Robinson, a ballad, "Illinois People"; and Luboff, Harold Walters, and Everett Kessinger wrote specially commissioned band numbers. Roger Nixon and Ray West put together a chamber opera entitled *The Bride Comes to Yellow Sky* after the Stephen Crane short story. Eastern Illinois University commissioned a band number and De-Paul, four original compositions.

Musical performances sounded popular notes of celebration. Chicago audiences applauded the American Ballet, the Chicago Jazz Festival, and Marian Anderson in a special production of Aaron Copland's "A Preamble for a Solemn Occasion." Luboff's "Freedom Country," the story of the never-ending fight for freedom in Illinois, played to large audiences across the state. A children's musical based on the life of Mike Fink was popular. Ulysses Kay's symphony was not so popular, for in Illinois as well as New Jersey people found the music ahead of its time.

The best of the dramatic productions, if judged by the turnstiles, was the official Sesquicentennial play, *Make Her Wilderness Like Eden,* by Professor Christian Moe. Three versions of this drama of Illinois history appeared during the Sesquicentennial; a pageant version for communities, an indoor chamber theater version, and a summer tour version. Six of the state universities produced this play, which performed in more communities than any other dramatic work.

State history was prominent in other dramatic presentations. As its Sesquicentennial project, the University of Illinois Theater Department produced *Taste for Violence*, by Webster Smalley, a story of Elijah P. Lovejoy's assassination. Millikin University produced a play about Lincoln, and Springfield's Theater Guild dramatized the Lincoln-Douglas debates in *The Rivalry*. A new production of Robert Sherwood's *Abe Lincoln in Illinois* also appeared. Sesquicentennial audiences applauded all these plays as well as the home-produced pageants, the traveling productions by church, college, and professional groups, and the successful one-act local play contests.

Radio and television effectively extended the role of theater to even larger audiences. Radio saluted the Sesquicentennial with a series of four taped one-hour plays on Illinois history themes. Television excelled in smaller productions, especially on the education-oriented channels, but there were also important spectaculars. Walter Schwimmer's magic touch appeared in *I Remember Illinois*, a fine mosaic of sound, color, and historical events which utilized nationally known television talent including Jack Benny and Bob Hope—"sixty jam packed minutes of sights and sounds . . . a glittering and electronic birthday greeting to Illinois from itself and illustrious friends." The cost of this program reached $470,000, which was paid by sponsors since the program rated high enough for network showing. Although *The Giants and the Common Man* was not as popular a television program, it did give an interesting account of Chicago's history through the lives of people now buried in that city's Graceland Cemetery.

The labors of the research committee did not produce as spectacular results as some of the other committees, but this group provided an important academic dimension to the celebration. "Sesquicentennial Month" in many of the state's libraries hardly brought rave notices, but hundreds of new readers found open library doors and appeared before exhibits, in browsing rooms, and in close conversation with librarians on the latest developments in a world they should know better. Sesquicentennial enthusiasm was a boon for historical interests. While an oral history project will not still the noise of fireworks and racing cars, the Illinois State Historical Society's innovations in this area of research and study carried far into the months beyond the celebration. This society also converted the basement of the Old Capitol into an attractive library in the name of the Sesquicentennial. The Evanston Historical Society recalled war's tragedy and meaning in the exhibit of World War I newspapers and posters. A historymobile visited more than 88,000 school children. New historical societies appeared, to probe deeper into local backgrounds and preserve community records. New museums in Jasper, Boone, and Iroquois counties also attribute their being to interest in the Sesquicentennial.

Publications on many levels recounted the story of the past in Sesquicentennial trappings and offered new interpretations to self-styled historians as well as to the professionals. The University of Chicago Press published Paul Angle's *Prairie State* and Frederick Koeper's *Illinois Architecture from Territorial Times to the Present, A Selected Guide.* The latter was a well-written narrative that told the story of people of Illinois—their "strength and dignity, ingenuity and craftsmanship, ambitions, and vitality . . . through their architecture of a century and a half." Southern Illinois Press published John Clayton's *Illinois Fact Book.* Rand McNally Company published an *Illinois Guide and Gazetteer.* Other historical works included a new release of Solon J. Buck's Centennial publication, *Illinois in 1818;* Margaret Flint's *Narrative Chronology of Illinois History;* and Clyde C. Walton's anthology, *An Illinois Reader,* published in 1970. The reprinting of *Illinois Intelligencia* combined history with current publicity and descriptions of centennial activity.

Other publications included the revision and reissuing of the Illinois Centennial history, many county histories, a book suggesting various roles of the churches in the Sesquicentennial, well-prepared newspaper supplements, and articles in the various journals of business companies. Some of the latter were of high quality, like the ones in *Highlines,* the magazine of the Illinois Power Company, which included articles on "Prehistoric Illinois," and "The Valley of Illinois." The Spring issue of the *Journal of the Illinois Historical Society* inaugurated a year of issues paying tribute to the Sesquicentennial with a continuing series of special articles on Illinois's past. The State Historical Library and Historical Society provided valuable staff time and assistance to the commission in their effort to maintain historical authenticity throughout the celebration.

Illinois planners were not always so successful in providing programs and stimulating interest for ethnic groups, the underprivileged, the young, and senior citizens. Problems in these areas crop up regularly as centennial planners ponder the deeper meanings of celebration, and Illinois had its uncomfortable moments. To its credit, however, the commission did encourage participation of all of its citizens, offering suggestions and material help for ceremonial parades, cultural festivals, national dances, and proper music and dress to meet almost any occasion. As a result of far-sighted planning young people played special roles in school fairs, community pageants, and musical concerts. The city of Sycamore turned a Hallowe'en celebration, long a despair to parents, into a youth festival with pumpkin sculpture, dancing, musical activities, and assorted programs which involved both young and old. Sesquicentennial activities gave young people a chance to learn about their heritage in song and poetry, essays, dramatic productions, art exhibitions, dioramas, murals, models, and other related media.

Historical tours introduced many of the younger generation to parts of the state they had never known before. A youth summer music festival attracted many participants. Tours and exhibitions appealed to senior citizens, and many of them enjoyed the musical and dramatic works that were offered in behalf of the Sesquicentennial. The problem of how to extend a centennial to all ages, however, remained, and Illinois struggled with it throughout the entire year.

Solutions to how to promote ethnic involvement came harder. Some groups lost their identity in celebration, though some of the larger ones put on exciting culture shows. Sometimes only music and drama seemed to be the common ingredients that gave universal meaning to ethnic participation. The Indians had their brief moments of triumph in special dramatic productions at the local level and in exhibitions, but they were usually on the periphery of involvement. Some groups complicated matters for planners with troubles in their own ranks. The Armenians, for instance, divided into two separate groups and never agreed among themselves on a common course of action.

Involvement of the Blacks sputtered as planners attempted to involve them in significant programs. There were special commemorations for the first non-Indian citizen of Chicago, a Black man—Jean Baptiste Point du Sable. Many young Blacks pointed to the fact that this Haiti-born Negro was in Chicago before the whites and contended that the whites did not show the proper spirit of appreciation for du Sable. Several projects attempted to encourage Black participation; the commission sponsored the research and publication of "A Study of Nationality Groups in Illinois and their Contribution to the State During the One Hundred and Fifty Year History . . ." and supported what became the Blacks' finest hour in the Sesquicentennial—a Chicago jazz festival with outstanding Black artists from all over the country participating. At least one parade in Chicago stressed Black history, and the *Journal of the Illinois*

State Historical Society produced a special issue on Black history in the state.

Illinois faced ethnic participation as a real Sesquicentennial issue and encouraged involvement of all its citizens. There is always a terrible frustration in planning a celebration in finding ways to involve *all* the people. Too often committees cater to people already interested in this sort of thing. The Illinois Central Committee recognized this dilemma and made sincere efforts to extend its programs more widely. Nevertheless, the author of a long and labored letter of criticism to the commission struck a sensitive point when he wrote: "That Cantata could be magnificent to be sung to Black children from the Chicago slums. . . ." While a centennial cannot bind up all the wounds of an exploding society, it is a time to try to open lines of communications.

Illinois recorded about 3,000 separate events, with more than 8,000 "event days" during its celebration year. These figures do not include many other unreported programs. Though one perceives a touch of Madison Avenue in any statement summarizing the year, Illinoisans attained genuine achievements. The state can be proud of some of its rehabilitation programs and its school for handicapped children, and each community that developed a social service center or neighborhood house could take special pride in its project. Lauren A. Wollen, a unit leader from Springfield, suggested that the Sesquicentennial was also successful in alerting the people of Illinois to new state pride and appreciation, while stressing a due concern for larger human issues.

Observers must finally raise serious questions, however. Why were there no Blacks on the major committees? Why was participation by colleges and universities generally perfunctory? Was there not just a bit too much commercialism in the fundraising and publicity? Were local historical societies given due consideration in planning the Sesquicentennial program? Were the committees too highly structured to promote maximum individual initiative? Was the business community too dominant a force in determining direction? Was the leadership too sharply focused in a single man?

Though such questions must be raised, it is apparent that Illinois grew during its experience. There were no cigarette lighters playing "Illinois, Illinois," like those that played "Dixie" during the Civil War Centennial.[2] A resurgence of interest in history occurred throughout the state, and many historical programs, projects, events, and publications provided "intangible proof . . . that, indeed, history can be fun." [3] A close look at this Sesquicentennial should give planners for the Bicentennial some idea of what they, too, will face in their planning if their celebrations are to be more than just "fife-and-drum" affairs and commercialism is to be held within bounds.

---

2. William K. Alderfer, "Introduction," *Journal of the Illinois State Historical Society*, 61 (Spring 1968) , 7.

3. *Ibid.*

VII

Four Centennials and a
Philosophy of Celebration:
Virginia, Minnesota, Oregon,
and North Carolina

Despite striking similarities in centennial celebrations, different locales often show sharp differences—in underlying philosophies and themes, in organizational patterns, and in types of programs. Brief case studies of Virginia, Minnesota, Oregon, and North Carolina reveal both similarities and differences in their patterns of celebration.

The Jamestown Festival of Virginia in 1957 was distinctive in its unusual federal government involvement, its strong scholarly thrust, sustained interest in a specified historical period, and concentration upon a single geographic area. The Minnesota Centennial of 1958 was for its own people rather than for outsiders, a celebration of a hundred years rather than of a single event, with an appreciation of the past underlying its basic themes and *joie de vivre* apparent in nearly every scene. The Oregon Centennial of 1959 emphasized the arts, especially the performing arts, in a state exposition and local celebrations, and music and drama lured crowds to Centennial programs. The North Carolina Tercentenary of 1963 concentrated on historical events within the state, worked closely with the State Historical Society, and celebrated North Carolina's entire first century rather than just its founding.

In my opinion, these four centennials present to a marked degree some of the best qualities of celebration. Each capitalized on regional, philosophical, and topical differences, copying techniques, devices, and even programs of other centennials, adapting them to the time, the place, and the circumstances of celebration. Each educated its citizens in the history of their state while also instilling a deeper consciousness of national unity. All supported continuing social, intellectual, and material goals. No program achieved all it set out to accomplish. All planners recalled moments of frustration, futility, and failure. Still planners in each state found ways to encourage people in their search for identity and perspective, at the same time fulfilling festive and creative needs. Each centennial had its strengths, and participants remember their days of celebration with pride. Collectively, these centennials embody many of the suggestions I have already associated with productive seasons of celebration.

THE JAMESTOWN FESTIVAL

Virginia began early to plan the 350th anniversary of the first permanent English settlement in America. In 1952 the General Assembly appointed a temporary commission to study possibilities for a 1957 commemoration. After a two-year delay, this commission recommended a permanent state anniversary commission, staffed with seventeen prominent Virginians, and an appropriation of $200,000, earmarked for planning and development. Because of the national importance of Jamestown, its members successfully solicited Congress for appointment of a federal commission to assist in the planning.

Under the critical eyes of the press and the public, these newly appointed commissioners went to work, conducting research and study not only on the history of the first English settlement in America but on the physical facilities in the Jamestown area—highways, motels, eating places, and parking.

From these studies the commission determined its permanent guidelines. It would be a celebration for the entire nation, concentrating on the triangle formed by the important historic communities of Jamestown, Williamsburg, and Yorktown. It would be a program of living events to highlight the anniversary year while affording "daily entertainment and instruction for the entire eight months of celebration." Finally, all Virginians would be hosts to the celebration, participating when possible.[1]

On the more practical side were other considerations: temporary buildings would be kept to a minimum, highest priority in physical planning would go to the repayment of operating costs, and Virginia's business community would be prominently included in the leadership.

If the Virginia Festival had any single over-all theme it was its emphasis on the importance of the Jamestown settlement in American history, with special attention on the newly built Visitor Center there. This unique facility, which remains today as testimony to the planners' ingenuity, was an elaborate structure, supported by funds, land, labor, and expertise from government and business working closely with the citizenry. Practical solutions were provided for such problems as "the circulation of many people, shelter in foul weather, air conditioning, volume food dispensing [and] unbroken interior wall space for exhibits."[2] Every effort was made to avoid gaudiness, commercialism, and overpricing.

Equally fine facilities at Glasshouse Point, Williamsburg, and Yorktown, as well as completion of several other historical projects in the area by the National Park Service, added attractions to increase visitor interest. A new parkway connecting the

---

1. Summarized from seven principles outlined in *Report of the Virginia 350th Anniversary Commission,* House Document No. 32 (Richmond: Commonwealth of Virginia Division of Purchase and Printing, 1958), 16. [Hereinafter referred to as *Report of the Virginia Commission.*]

2. *Ibid.,* 25.

three historical communities became the route for a continuing tour.

History blended with the artistic in Festival Park, the attractive center of the Jamestown Festival. Inside the park the visitor passed through a large parking lot into a Court of Welcome, often used for important ceremonies. Beyond this was a landscaped Festival Mall, for special programs; an information center; a gift shop; the Mermaid Tavern, a dining terrace modeled after a seventeenth-century London hostelry; the Old World Pavilion for exhibits of national interest; and a Gallery of the States with flags of the original thirteen colonies. A short distance away Powhatan's Lodge recalled Indian culture in the early colony, and a recreated Fort James portrayed colonial English life. Watching over this scene from the basin nearby were replicas of the three ships which carried the first permanent settlers.

The Centennial, more than just a festival around Jamestown, however, required a complex organization to maintain it and extend it into other parts of the state. The commission worked to this end through six departments: Special Projects, Finances, Programs, Planning and Pageantry, Park Management, Exhibitions, and Visitors' Services. Supporting and implementing their endeavors as well as adding their own ideas was a vast network of subcommittees which included archives and history, religious functions and observances, finances, educational functions and observances, agricultural, commercial and industrial expositions, arts, highway beautification, and international naval review. An even more intricate network of local committees, mainly county and municipal, tied the communities to the larger structure. In addition to these committees, several other agencies involved in the Festival also reported to the state commission: the Centennial Corporation, a reservations bureau, a guide service, and those members of the Virginia State Police, health department, highway department, and conservation department whose services the Festival required. The appointment of a member of the finance committee of the state legislature to the commission chairmanship assured rapport with an important agency.

A team of professionals and amateurs worked together on public relations to bring maximum exposure to commemoration events. The first target was Virginia. Throughout 1954 and 1955 the state was blanketed with publicity emphasizing a common theme, "Celebrate America's 350th Birthday," an insignia or symbol which portrayed the three ships of the original settlers, a Festival flag which prominently displayed the symbol, and a musical theme by seventeenth-century composer Jeremiah Clarke entitled *Trumpet Voluntary*.[3]

Turning to wider horizons, Centennial publicists poured a steady stream of Festival specials and news to the national wire services. Columnists wrote colorful accounts of daily developments. Features appeared in newspapers, professional journals, and popular magazines. National television was the last source tapped, but by curtain time, this medium was in the action. Unfortunately, eight educational films on state history failed to appear in time for the Festival, but other promotional material filled the gap.

Travel agencies and carriers worked out package tours to promote interest. Designers, manufacturers, and outlet stores used the Jamestown theme in their merchandising. Automobile tags, window stickers, airline publicity, special stamp issues, festive travel literature, brochures on selected Festival events, monthly calendars of affairs, and elaborate programs testified to the extensive circulation of news and views about this significant year of Virginia history.

Three unusual tours by some of Virginia's prominent citizens publicized the Festival. The first, a 1956 visit to the British Isles limited to 114 persons, the governor, and their private chaplain, toured prominent English shrines, including the

---

3. Often attributed erroneously to Clarke's more famous contemporary Henry Purcell.

graves of John Smith and Pocahontas. After England they moved to the Continent, stopping in Holland, Belgium, and France. Two other tours covered the Caribbean Islands and the Mediterranean countries, and gave "notice to the world of the approaching American celebration." The news media responded to all these tours with extensive coverage.

A celebration can hardly be better than its programs, and Virginia's varied and balanced programs and projects fell generally into eight categories: festive events, centered in the Triangle; special programs sponsored by sections of the state; visits to selected Tidewater communities by the *Discovery,* one of the three reconstructed sailing ships of the first immigration to Virginia; the arts; scholarly activities; participation by groups, societies, and other organizations; commemorations of counties and cities; and programs of colleges and universities.

Triangle events attracted large crowds. They included the grand opening of the Festival, several important visitations highlighted by the appearance of Queen Elizabeth, the commemoration of the meeting of the First Assembly at Jamestown in 1619, and the christening of the immigration ship models. Though the visit of the Queen was the real spectacular, the commemoration of the meeting of the First Assembly in July drew large crowds. Representatives from Congress, state and local governments, and England provided an element of realism as delegates met in Jamestown Church to re-enact the first representative government in America.

Less-publicized programs continued the variety. A three-day affair, climaxed by a historical pageant, celebrated the first Virginia landing at Cape Henry. Special ceremonies honored landings at Old Point Comfort, Hampton, Newport News, and Jamestown. Hampton Roads had an international naval review. Virginia Ruritan Clubs conducted a series of nine regional days at the Festival Center in July and August, with a different region responsible for each day's program. Along the coastline the visits of the *Discovery* aroused enthusiasm from people who flocked to the docks to view the craft and participate in the ceremonies that accompanied the docking.

The arts appeared in many Festival programs, and art devotees, their eyes on the aesthetic, commissioned poetry, drama, and music for special presentations. With this encouragement Ulrich Troubetzkoy of Richmond wrote a prize-winning poem about Jamestown; and England's poet laureate, John Masefield, offered original verse entitled "The Virginia Adventure." Many American writers also wrote poetry for the occasion.

Under a special commission the distinguished American composer Randall Thompson wrote "a choral-symphonic setting" for Michael Drayton's "Ode to the Virginia Voyage." In describing its world premiere at the Festival in April the New York *Times* commented that "it would be hard to imagine a more felicitous beginning for all this than the premiere of Mr. Thompson's Ode." [4] There was also a musical performance of Richard Bales' patriotic cantata, *The Republic,* whose themes of the American Revolution and early national interest hold possibilities for the Bicentennial.

Drama brought back Shakespeare and other artists of the seventeenth century, but pageantry written by local citizens dominated the community stages. In the visual arts, several works, commissioned especially for the anniversary, appeared, including a canvas of the three original ships, a mural of the park area, a statuette of Sir Walter Raleigh, and a portrait of Queen Elizabeth II.

Academic interests took their turn when the commission opened opportunities to scholars for new research and writing on colonial Virginia. A group of consultants screened written proposals for grants. Important projects approved and produced included the publication of twenty-three historical booklets whose varied titles presented a cumulative history of early Virginia, an important symposium on seventeenth-century colonial

---

4. Quoted in *Report of the Virginia Commission,* 86.

history, and the microfilming from both American and British depositories of a large number of early state records—the Virginia *Colonial Records* Project. Historian Julian P. Boyd later called *Colonial Records* one of the Festival's "most inspiring, most useful, and most enduring accomplishments . . . that will help us to understand as well as to commemorate." [5]

The symposium brought together some of the most renowned colonial scholars in the country, who produced eight essays, later edited by James Morton Smith and published by the Institute of Early American History and Culture at Williamsburg and the University of North Carolina Press under the title *The Seventeenth Century: Essays on American Colonial History.* Special issues of historical magazines, archaeological publications, and newspapers played up Virginia history, as did exhibits in libraries and museums of books, pictures, documents, and other materials dealing with Colonial Virginia.

From the beginning, groups of many persuasions, including patriotic societies, religious, civic, and ethnic groups, engaged in celebration. Their programs featured lectures; re-enactments, like the marriage of Pocahontas and John Rolfe; restorations; special days, such as cherry tree planting or American Dairying; the arrival of the first Blacks on the continent; ladies' days; and even a Malayan Independence Day on August 30, related to the entrance of Malaya into the British Commonwealth of Nations on that date.

Religion as a factor in early American settlements stimulated church interest in the celebration. A resident chaplain held daily devotions at Old Jamestown Church under the joint sponsorship of the leading denominations, and many churches observed a "Jamestown Sunday." The Episcopal Church proclaimed 1957 as "Jamestown Year" and encouraged special programs in Episcopal churches across the nation. With a film strip, a color film, and such specially prepared folders as the

5. Quoted, *ibid.,* 72.

Centennial star and lighting ushers in Canadian Centennial on New Year's Eve, 1966. Home of Mr. and Mrs. C. F. Prevey, Ottawa, Ontario. Dominion Wide photograph.

The Provincial Museum and Archives of Alberta was a Canadian centennial project.
Photo courtesy of Department of Industry & Tourism, Edmonton, Alberta.

Regimental band recreates the past in Civil War Centennial.
Photo courtesy of State Department of Archives and History, Raleigh, N.C.

Civil War medicine exhibition in North Carolina.
Photo courtesy of State Department of Archives and History, Raleigh, N.C.

CSS *Neuse* salvage operations at Kinston, North Carolina.
Photo courtesy of State Department of Archives and History, Raleigh, N.C.

North Carolina folk singers sing the old songs in the Civil War Centennial. Photo courtesy of State Department of Archives and History, Raleigh, N.C.

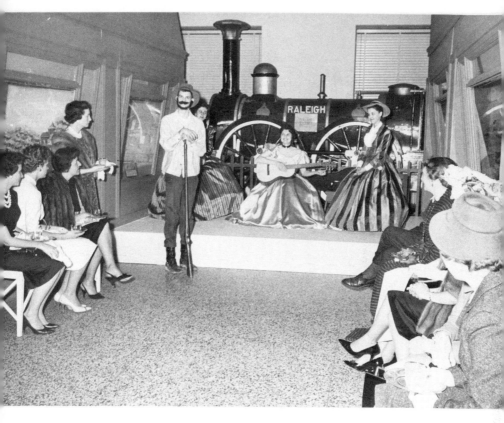

Reception for legislators in North Carolina Museum of History during Civil War Centennial Commemoration.
Photo courtesy of State Department of Archives and History, Raleigh, N.C.

"Old Glory" flies above the official New Jersey Tercentenary flag.
Photo courtesy of New Jersey Historical Commission.

Governor Hughes greets Tercentenary composers Ulysses Kay and Roger
Sessions.
Photo courtesy of New Jersey Historical Commission.

New Jersey dignitaries officially begin Tercentenary celebration.
Photo courtesy of New Jersey Historical Commission.

Citizens of Pompton Lakes, N.J., erect Tercentenary sign at start of the celebration.
Photo courtesy of New Jersey Historical Commission.

Boy Scout Camporee honors New Jersey Tercentenary.
Photo courtesy of New Jersey Historical Commission.

Astronaut Walter Schirra and his family appear in New Jersey Tercentenary Parade.
Photo courtesy of New Jersey Historical Commission.

Tercentenary scenes inside New Jersey's historymobile.
Photo courtesy of New Jersey Historical Commission.

Diorama inside New Jersey historymobile.
Photo courtesy of New Jersey Historical Commission.

New Jersey turns back the clock.
Photo courtesy of New Jersey Historical Commission.

Professor Richard McCormick chats with Tercentenary participants.
Photo courtesy of New Jersey Historical Commission.

Precious Galinthia, prize calf presented to New Jersey by the Isle of Jersey,
celebrates Tercentenary.
Photo courtesy of New Jersey Historical Commission.

Distinguished Illinoisans raise the colors at the Sesquicentennial opening.
Photo courtesy of the Illinois State Historical Library.

Beards, banners, and bowlers in Illinois Sesquicentennial.
Photo courtesy of the Illinois State Historical Library.

Governor Terry Sanford (right) and Secretary of State Thad Eure (left) celebrate the 300th birthday of North Carolina with Chief Osley Saunooke. Photo courtesy of State Department of Archives and History, Raleigh, N.C.

North Carolinians dedicate a Tercentenary mobile museum.
Photo courtesy of State Department of Archives and History, Raleigh, N.C.

Demonstration of native weaving at San Diego's 200th anniversary celebration.
Photo courtesy of Charles E. Cordell (former president, San Diego 200th Anniversary Celebration Corporation).

Los Voladores—re-creation of the ancient religious ritual of Indians of Papantla at San Diego centennial celebration.
Photo courtesy of Charles E. Cordell (former president, San Diego 200th Anniversary Celebration Corporation).

The Ballet Folklorico at Fiesta Two Hundred, San Diego, 1969.
Photo courtesy of Charles E. Cordell (former president, San Diego 200th
Anniversary Celebration Corporation).

Young visitor views historical objects in historymobile.
Photo courtesy of New Jersey Historical Commission.
Reprinted with permission of Newark *Evening News*.

"Colonial belles" sit one out at a North Carolina Tercentenary ball.
Photo courtesy of State Department of Archives and History, Raleigh, N.C.

Founding of Jamestown and the Church and *The Church Comes to America,* its leaders played up their church's role in Early Virginia history. They also publicized the Festival in bulletins, magazines, and radio programs.

Celebration in the counties, cities, and towns varied with the leadership and the interests of the local planners. To encourage participation of local groups, the state commission, in February 1957, brought together representatives from thirty-two of Virginia's counties to share the commission's studies, hear its general plans, and exchange ideas. The usual hodgepodge of appropriate and inappropriate programs resulted. String quartets performed before regally dressed audiences, fiddlers played for toe-tapping crowds, band music echoed in hollows and auditoriums, school choirs polished up colonial tunes to sing to PTAs and garden clubs, and dance bands varied their beats from the sounds of the 1920s to modern "rock."

While the music swelled, librarians rearranged their shelves to give prominent display to colonial literature, museums replaced dusty exhibits with artifacts of the colonial season, local historical societies published books and tracts with early Virginia themes, patriotic societies searched out and recorded genealogies, and newspapers put together special articles on local personalities and obscure historical events. Visitors toured churches, homes, and historical sites, sat through pageants with early Virginia themes, then dined in the atmosphere of another century. They studied exhibitions of local pictures, maps, early codes, colonial paintings, costumes, and furnishings. They handled materials whose usefulness extended back across 350 years, reliving the past in the museums. They attended special church services and civic improvement days, and they viewed flower shows, parades, and fashion fairs that illustrated the color and the affluence of their frontier forefathers.

Some counties celebrated with more·enthusiasm than others. Norfolk County provided a variety of programs for its school children in Jamestown Week. The county publicized the event with leaflets which enumerated its assets, described its early history, and listed the events of the celebration. Hanover County converted an old stone jail into a museum where it displayed documents, prints, engravings, firearms, and other early materials. Amherst County had a special day at Sweetbriar College, which included a pet show, a farm tour, cattle-judging, movies, a home demonstration program, a parade of bands, a fly-casting contest, a flower show, and an exhibit.

On the urban front, Roanoke combined its 75th anniversary with the Jamestown Festival in nine days of varied activities beginning with Premiere Day and running through Governors' Day, Agriculture and Good Neighbor Day, and finally American Heritage Day. Exhibitions, music, pageantry, speakers, drama, and athletic contests highlighted these days of celebration.

Richmond's celebration was sedate. A central committee composed of a former president of the Virginia Confederation of Garden Clubs, the executive manager of the city's Chamber of Commerce, a museum curator, the state librarian, the public relations director of a utilities company, a landscape architect, the district manager of a life insurance company, the passenger-traffic manager of a railway, a local historian, the executive vice president of a restaurant association, and the mayor involved the city's academic community, local historians, and others interested in the city's past in a year-long program. Besides lecture series there were exhibits, a festival of the arts, important museum displays, pageants, and "special day" programs.

Other communities on the Lower Peninsula combined their talents in a two-day program in early May, while Fredericksburg celebrated with an elegant ball, a candlelight tour of certain shrines, an exhibition of colonial materials, and colorful pageantry.

When the state commission called upon the colleges and universities to participate, six responded. The College of William and Mary was the most active. Besides using its library facilities for developing the "Old World Heritage" exhibit, one of the most widely acclaimed of the Festival, the college also sponsored musical concerts, professional meetings, a commemoration of the First Legislative Assembly, and an important series of historical publications, including five by members of its own faculty. The college commissioned its alumnus Christian Moe to write the pageant *Hark, Upon the Gale,* which portrayed the history of the college. Washington and Lee gave two scholarships in commemoration of the anniversary, and several college newspapers featured colonial themes. Colleges usually emphasized the aesthetic in much that they sponsored, including fine music, lectures, concerts, exhibitions, pageantry, convocations, and extensive recreations of early Virginia history.

Elementary and high school children fared poorly in the division of centennial resources. Special programs of the Virginia State Department of Education focused upon "Jamestown: A Place of Beginnings," utilizing a film of the same name in the high schools throughout the school system; but most school programs were in-school affairs, products of teachers' and students' initiative.

Over-all, Virginia put extensive effort into celebrating its 350th anniversary, accomplishing it, in the words of its director, "on schedule, within its budget and without recourse to commercialization." Like many other celebrations, it appeared to be white-oriented, although Indians and Blacks were honored on occasion. Much was made over the initial contact between the Indians and the first settlers, and Indian activities appeared prominently in pageants and exhibits. While a celebration of the arrival of the first Blacks at Jamestown commanded some attention, generally Blacks remained on the periphery.

Despite this somewhat elitist approach, the Virginians put on a dignified show. Aided extensively by the federal government, planners also spent state and local money to promote this celebration of history. In an Alpha-to-Omega approach, planners placed the colonial beside the modern, involved many of the state's citizens, and maintained a serious note throughout the commemoration while concentrating on projects which would have meaning and appreciation beyond the days of celebration. The Festival's executive director, Parke Rouse, Jr., summed up his achievements, saying "We bore in mind the desirability of projects that would be of permanent benefit to Virginia and also a diverse program which would interest all age groups, socio-economic levels, and regions of Virginia." [6]

The excellence of the Festival may be judged by its publications alone, and one only has to visit the Peninsula today to share some of its other successes. Virginia can look back upon its 350th birthday as one of the most constructive and prosperous years in its history.

THE MINNESOTA CENTENNIAL

In preparation for its Centennial, the 1955 Minnesota Legislature appointed sixteen prominent citizens to the Statehood Centennial Commission to direct operations. Supported by a $100,000 appropriation from the legislature, this commission proclaimed a twofold task: preparing a statewide celebration and assisting local communities to prepare programs.[7]

Minnesota's Centennial was a pageant of the people of the state: men and women from every walk of life and from many national backgrounds joined together in celebrating themselves and their past. Her history was that of a farm state, recalling people planting their first crops as the sounds and smoke of the Industrial Revolution moved in upon them; of a frontier state, settled by dynamic people with unbridled enthusiasms for growing crops, cutting timber, mining the minerals, and settling more land; of a contested state, where blood had flowed as Indians and whites defended two different cultures and land pol-

---

6. Letter of Parke Rouse, Jr., to the author, July 21, 1971.

7. *Final Report of the Minnesota Statehood Centennial Commission* (Minneapolis, 1959), I. [Hereinafter cited as *Minnesota Report.*]

icies. Minnesota's admission to statehood in 1858 came in the nation's darkening hour. Its maturity occurred in an age fraught with frustration and conflict.

In 1958 Minnesota's citizens commemorated this past and attempted to understand this history. She celebrated reconciliation, with citizens of different backgrounds living together in harmony; adaptation, with citizens realistically facing the challenges of a rapidly changing world; and resolution, with citizens actively promoting social change in the midst of economic growth. The Centennial radiated the pride of a people who had made their way through severe crises past, and it unveiled an inventory of vast resources present and a promising future.

Unlike many other centennials, Minnesota beamed hers primarily to her own citizens rather than to a larger audience. Hoping to substitute programs with lasting benefits for baby contests, wooden currency, and beard growing, planners first studied and then recommended and prepared for a celebration with emphases on Minnesota's political history, the contrast between pre-agricultural life and rapid urbanization, the life of the fur trader, the assimilation of minority immigrant groups, the amalgamation of cultures, and the state's economic activities.

Planning rested primarily with the strong central commission, which co-ordinated most of the programs. Its subcommittees concentrated on familiar areas: arts, education, history, library, military, religion, and sports.

The commission also added other subcommittees: agriculture, business-industry-labor, society, hospitality, health, commemorative stamps, territorial pioneers, women's affairs, and youth.

If a good centennial depends upon extensive public relations, Minnesota should have excelled. Every committee and commission member assumed public relations duties. More formally, a publicity and promotion department under the central commission worked closely with a New York public relations firm to broadcast the Minnesota story through every communications medium. News releases by the hundreds were mailed to industries, small businesses, schools, and trade and professional organizations, soliciting support and counsel and urging special Centennial projects. Universities were asked to use their unusual resources to develop their own programs. Public relations teams distributed brochures, souvenirs, maps, and program guides. Commission members traveled widely over the state, entreating local committees and individuals to dream new dreams. They mailed letters and brochures to national groups and organizations urging the selection of Minnesota as a convention site. Visitors to the state in 1957 received "Honored Guest" scrolls, inviting them to return the following year. A hospitality manual provided food and shelter industries with a handbook of Centennial suggestions. Sports programs carried Centennial themes to their special audiences. Hundreds of voluntary speakers channeled the flow of ideas into clubs and organizations of every description.

Newspapers discovered in the Centennial "a yearlong source of news and feature material," and they mined its rich veins with editorials, special editions, picture stories, creative magazine sections, unusual features, and paid advertising. A broad selection of magazines also treated the subject. Radio and television lent their efforts with spot announcements, daily presentations of plans and events, an occasional "special" that gave in-depth coverage to specific events or personalities, educational programs,[8] interviews, and tapes of special events. On the national networks, *Today* and *Queen for a Day* publicized the Centennial.

The programs of the Centennial varied with the tide of people's emotions, the distinctive nature of each community, and the special bent of local leadership. Over-all the stress was educational, with even pageants, parades, and fairs emphasizing

8. "Minnesota Milestones" won an American Association for State and Local History Award of Merit.

history. On the state level, programs appeared as responses to the actions of the central commission's varied committees. The unusual agriculture committee concentrated on three projects: a film, *An Agricultural Portrait,* which depicted the rapid changes in Minnesota's farm history; a series of contests among the state and local fairs which highlighted Centennial themes in their programs; and farm exhibitions which included machinery, general farm equipment, household furnishings, and other items of interest to farm families past and present.

A subcommittee of the arts committee, architecture and visual arts, sponsored two traveling exhibitions—"Water-Colors of Minnesota Homes" and "Works of Minnesota Artists"—and produced a popular publication that chronicled early state art achievements. Other subcommittees kept pace. Arts concentrated on exhibitions, one which featured Minnesota artists. Literature financed the publication of a checklist of Minnesota authors and their works, produced and distributed television and radio tapes and films of several local authors, and sponsored an "authors' roundtable." The music subcommittee concentrated on festivals, symphony concerts, and orchestral, choral, religious, band, and folk music presentations. It sponsored the publication of an important catalogue of Minnesota composers and a short history of Minnesota music and arranged for performances of many out-of-state musical dignitaries. The theater and dance subcommittee, working with the liaison group to colleges and theater companies throughout the state, sponsored the Centennial Showboat, along with a folk and square dance festival, a modern dance review, and a ballet.

Elementary and high school programs received more attention in Minnesota than in Virginia. The Centennial education committee produced a film strip called *Pioneers of Minnesota* and a cartoon sequence entitled *Makers of Minnesota* for the students; for teachers, they edited a resource guide on state history and arranged a state conference on problems of education in the century ahead.

If any one agency set the pace of celebration, it was the Minnesota Historical Society, as it extended its influence into Centennial planning with ideas, material, and historical perspective. To television, the society made available important programs, exhibitions, publications, historical photographs, paintings, and drawings. Its journal stressed Centennial subject matter, and its meetings were Centennial-oriented. The society also issued several ethnic-oriented publications, including *The Negro in Minnesota History*. It was active in the restoration of Old Fort Snelling and in the promotion of a series of eight popular tours which explored almost every facet of Minnesota history and geography, combining scenery and history with the joys of adventure and travel. Tourists entered old mines, stopped at reconstructed forts, followed Indian trails, and visited reservations, then skirted the scenic shores of rivers and lakes and gazed at the beauties of waterfalls as they carried their own canoes over the portages.

Other committees did their part. The library committee sponsored the usual book displays and exhibitions, but it also won an Award of Merit from the American Association for State and Local History for its publication *The Gopher Reader,* an anthology of Minnesota stories, articles, plays and biographies. The military committee provided color and honor guards where needed and furnished equipment for exhibitions. The religious committee encouraged statewide commemorations and suggested worship patterns in several new publications. The sports committee sponsored water events, gymnastics, and winter activities.

The women's division sponsored a Centennial breakfast for visiting European nobility, participated in a Mothers' Day program which promoted special church services honoring the pioneer mothers, set up an international gifts project which exchanged mementoes of friendship with South American and European countries, and prepared and hosted a state fair display contrasting pioneer and modern kitchens. Other projects included a cookbook—*100 Years of Good Cooking*—that is still popular today. Women engaged in art shows, flower shows, pageants, choral activities, style shows, and writing projects, and one women's group presented a drama entitled *Hiawatha's Wedding Feast.*

When young people appeared in the Centennial, it was generally in parades, field days, sports events, and in menial labor that they contributed to many of the projects. Most youth activities were under the guidance of counselors, but if more emphasis had been placed on youth participation and creativity, there might have been more stimulating results. Although there was a Youth Day in the week of celebration, too often young people and women appeared throughout this Centennial in the subdued roles they have played in so many other commemorations. In too many instances theirs has been a role of implementation on every level, though special programs have sometimes related to particular interests of each.

The Centennial Showboat and the Centennial Train, projects supported only in part by state funds, deserve mention, if for no other reason than because of the large audiences they attracted. At the cost of about $50,000, part of which was contributed by the University of Minnesota Theater, an old Mississippi craft was converted into a floating auditorium. Its performances became headliners in the river towns. During the summers it continues to tie into ports before admiring riverfront spectators who look out at its cumbersome shell and relive "the good old days."

The Centennial Train's six exhibit cars featured six special display themes: history, resources, agriculture and food products, industry, social progress, and the future. Very popular in a region where the railroad is so much a part of history, the train crisscrossed the state, eventually visiting all counties but one. Some credit it with triggering other Centennial activities along its route of travel. Only the memories of the train exist today, for it was dismantled and many of its parts turned over to county historical societies.

The Centennial climaxed in Statehood Week, which dedicated each day to a specific theme—sports and pioneer recognition, education, youth, heritage and cultural arts, military, parade of the century, and finally Statehood Day on Sunday. This was a week of gala events, speeches, pageants, visiting dignitaries, a variety of programs, and a giant Parade of the Century—a three-and-a-half-hour spectacle that extended 2.3 miles and was watched by more than 200,000 cheering spectators.

If Minnesota's state programs seem diverse, the many local activities take on the appearance of a collage. To stimulate county organizations toward specific goals, the central commission initiated a series of monthly bulletins for regular mailing. These bulletins not only offered suggestions but served as a forum for exchange of ideas and information. Other commission aids included a film strip entitled *Everybody Ready? Let's Go!*, a set of slides accompanied by a high fidelity record which told the story of the state, a speaker's kit, a two-day clinic for county chairmen in St. Paul, the special consulting services of two field representatives, and a series of regional meetings where planners could share ideas and co-ordinate actions.

By Centennial time some communities were living and breathing the birthday. Over and above school, service club, and annual civic events, more than 1,600 major programs appeared in the name of the Centennial. Rough statistics gathered from unofficial county reports reveal the wide scope of Centennial action, the similarities of interest, and something of the different types of programs: [9]

Event	Counties Participating
Honoring of pioneers	63
Pageants	56 (33 major ones)
Antique exhibitions	51

9. *Minnesota Report,* 40–61; "Majestic Minnesota," a supplement to Minnesota newspapers, May 5, 1958.

Special church services	41
Museum improvement	34
Flower shows, style shows, and teas	33
Dinners, picnics, and banquets	30
Writing of county history	24
Contests of various sorts	23
Band concerts	24
(Many musicals have no record in the statistics)	
Art exhibits	15
Restorations	12
Programs with special Indian themes	8

A more complete listing would include the inevitable speakers and lecturers, the designating of historical sites and the placing of markers, library book and research projects, musical programs featuring works from Beethoven to modern pop, trade days, historical re-enactments, tree-plantings, treasure hunts, photographic displays; and two communities even dedicated time capsules. In Minnesota commemoration was a rifle shoot, a polka festival, a water carnival on one of the state's beautiful lakes, an Indian powwow, a canoe derby, a farm machinery exhibit, a ski jump, a threshing bee, a good neighbor program, a queen contest, and a night street dance. Special Centennial events included a Halloween festival, a courtesy clinic, Steamboat Day, Paul Bunyan ice-fishing derby, big corncob smoker, young America's *stiftungfest,* a "Timbertennial," and a chess tournament. Agricultural interests dedicated special days to potatoes, popcorn, sugar beets, soy beans, turkeys, and dairying.

For Big Stone County the Centennial was a time to place a 110-ton granite rock, with an anchor chain welded through it, atop four pedestals at the intersection of two highways to symbolize Paul Bunyan's boat anchor. Carlton County dedicated a Centennial forest. Goodhue and Sibley Counties ran Pony Expresses which actually carried the mail. Itasca County featured a musical band pageant with historical narrations for an audience of more than 4,000. Kanabec County effected a summer exchange of young people. Marshall County attracted nationwide interest with an oxcart trek—a rebuilt oxcart bouncing over a 450-mile trail for forty-five days, its riders dressed authentically in costumes of a century ago, their day-to-day regimen patterned after that of the pioneers.

In good humor, Nicollet County celebrated a cheerful disdain for Joe Rolette—the notorious gentleman who at one time hid the bill that would have made St. Peter the state capital—by hanging him in effigy on the courthouse lawn. Homestead County initiated a new course of study in Minnesota history for all of its schools. Winona County dry-docked an old lake steamer and made it into a Museum of Upper Mississippi River Lore. Yellow Medicine produced one of the most exciting historical pageants of the Centennial, written locally and performed by more than four hundred of its citizens.

Much that happened in Minnesota in 1958 had Centennial overtones. "Miss Minnesota" became "Miss Centennial Minnesota," a new state building became the Minnesota Centennial Building, state educational television stressed early historical events, and annual events heralded Centennial themes. In the excitement of celebration, but with limited imagination, the state legislature authorized two statutes for display near the state capitol and the repainting of a box car of World War I fame that the French government had earlier presented to the state.

Minnesota's galaxy of events officially began with elaborate bell-ringings in Cook and Rock Counties. It ended in a saturation of programs and near exhaustion for performers. Some events hewed closely to history; some were little more than frivolity. Some were products of sensitive creativity; others were little more than mundane. Some emphasized national patriotism; some stressed local pride. Some seized upon specific themes and searched for understanding; others never got outside the local fairground. But at the end of the year few Minnesotans were unaware that something unusual had happened in their state.

In 1955 the Oregon State Legislature created a nine-man centennial commission to supervise the planning for commemoration of that state's one-hundredth birthday in 1959. To this commission the legislature delegated the usual centennial responsibilities: co-operating with other agencies, publicity, county and city assistance, appointing advisory committees, receiving gifts of property or money, and doing everything possible to make the celebration a memorable one.[10]

The legislature made no fiscal appropriation in its original act, so the new commission faced its tasks with the severe limitation that too often plagues those who engage in centennial preparation—a shortage of funds. To fill the gap, the commissioners effectively buttonholed many of Oregon's "first citizens," a move which prompted the creation of the Citizen Committee of One Hundred. As with the Canadian Centenary the private sector rose to the challenge, pumping life into sagging spirits by raising a $17,000 nest egg.

With this money the centennial commission engaged the Stanford Research Institute to help chart a course of action. The Institute studied the situation and recommended basic procedures and promotion activities, suggesting that the commission consider a regional exposition emphasizing Oregon's unique role in the settling of the West.

Again a shortage of funds limited follow-up. Finally, two years later, the legislature appropriated $830,000 to put Centennial planning wheels into motion. Proceeding with new enthusiasm, the commission put together a firm committee

---

10. *Final Fiscal Officer's Report to the State of Oregon Centennial Commission* (Portland, 1960), 5. [Hereinafter cited as *Oregon Report.*]

structure from citizens all across the state, their specific areas designated to concessions, finance and budget, fine arts, entertainment, insurance, fire protection, first aid, labor, and publicity. Assuming unusual individual responsibility, each commissioner served on three or four of these subcommittees.

The task facing the commission was a monumental one: in less than a year they had to plan a fair and a statewide celebration. Like many double-barreled programs, this one held exciting prospects for a fuller interpretation of Oregon history, but it also faced the possibilities of becoming a two-headed monster.

Planning, promoting, and publicizing a fair is a topic that extends beyond the scope of this study, but the 1959 Oregon Exposition was so much a part of the state's Centennial that any discussion of that Centennial must consider it. Even though the central commission delegated its authority to a special management committee, these fair officials considered themselves part of the Centennial and publicized accordingly.

Centennial planners shared in the big crowds the fair attracted. The Exposition became the Centennial money-maker and crowd-pleaser—the basic objective stressed in its public relations was simply to "develop paid admissions to the grounds." [11] To bring people through its turnstiles, fair-planners depended upon big-name stars. Popular artists—Roy Rogers, Lawrence Welk, Harry Belafonte, Art Linkletter, Ricky Nelson, and Spike Jones, along with the larger traveling companies such as the Thakrazuka Ballet and the Ice Capades—stimulated interest. During its fifteen-week stand, the fair recorded 1,335,082 paid admissions, an indication of its crowd-pleasing aspects.

Festive though it was, the fair made other appeals to Centennial-minded visitors. A cultural highlight was its International Trade Fair, the first of its kind in the state. This program

---

11. *Oregon Report,* 64.

displayed the exhibits of twenty-three countries which had been personally solicited for the occasion. Another fair attraction with Centennial overtones was the International Garden of Tomorrow—a display of plants, bulbs, trees, shrubs, flowers, and other vegetation, loaned or donated by nurserymen, growers, dealers, garden clubs, and interested citizens. A large floral clock, a Japanese garden, a teahouse, a holly farm, a Swiss garden and chalet, a fuschia garden, and a tower of chimes set off this display and gave it unusual color. This display was not only beautiful but presented an excellent panorama of the state's natural life; it could be adapted to other centennials.

The fair was the most spectacular Centennial event in Oregon, engendering enthusiasm and setting the pace for other Centennial projects and programs. Some of its historical exhibitions also made important contributions to the Centennial. Unfortunately, some of its expensive acts did not pay their way and the fair also diverted enthusiasm and resources from other commemorative fetes. Though a close association between fair and Centennial activities continued, the transfer of fair responsibilities to the special management committee relieved the central commission of a heavy responsibility and allowed them to concentrate more on cultural interests, especially the arts. Supported by a budget of more than a quarter-million dollars, the fine arts subcommittee arranged a variety of programs with Portland and the hub of much of the activity. There the subcommittee financed much of the cost of six performances of the San Francisco Opera and covered almost all the costs of the "Oregon Scene," a Centennial exhibition of 92 paintings eventually seen by 82,000 people. Also in Portland, the subcommittee sponsored an art contest, a Gilbert and Sullivan opera festival, a print-makers' fair, and a "changing exhibition with daily demonstrations of print-making processes" by Oregon artists. It also participated in the planning and funding of a "Century of Oregon Architecture" exhibition, showing state architecture and its changes since the earliest days; and an exhibition of sculpture at the fairgrounds. Fine arts subcommittee money aided in the Portland Civic Theater's production of *No Time for Sergeants,* starring actor William Holden, which traveled to eleven Oregon communities in June, and in the production of the Portland Junior and Senior Symphonic Choirs that played in several Oregon communities.

The planning of many local communities emphasized the arts. In Marion County an art workshop attracted hopeful artists. Its curriculum included poetry, sculpture, weaving, writing, painting, and drawing instruction and inspired the formation of a special fine arts committee for the entire Willamette Valley. Local funds combined with matching grants from the central commission helped build an art gallery in Klamath, set up an arts and crafts museum at the National Indian Encampment in Umatilla County, and financed a Children's Art Festival in Benton County, a special performance by the Eugene Wind Ensemble, and special concerts by other orchestras, ensembles, and choristers.

Funding for programs in the fields of literature, art, photography, and music concentrated on creativity as against performance. One popular statewide high school photography contest awarded college scholarships as prizes for individual success. From this contest came photographs that eventually provided materials for "This Land—This Oregon," one of the most popular traveling exhibitions of the Centennial. Poetry and short story contests with prizes ranging from $150 to $250 also attracted many young people.

Other state subcommittees depended heavily upon cultural programs for their expressions of celebration. The colleges and universities committee filmed and showed documents on all of Oregon's colleges and provided a lecture series by important Oregon college graduates. With funds from the commission, several colleges underwrote a series of programs which included Centennial costume teas, musical performances, plays, art exhibits, history lectures, campus tours, and even an all-college rodeo.

The elementary and secondary education advisory committee worked to increase "the student's knowledge of Oregon history, resources, geography, and economy," distributing packets of materials containing a map of Oregon, a chronological list of historic dates, a brief history of the state, special topics of state history, a bibliography, and a list of audio-visual aids for teaching Oregon history. The subcommittee co-operated with a local television station that kinescoped *With Her Own Wings,* fourteen programs of Oregon history that were available for school distribution.

The history subcommittee focused on projects to acquaint the citizens of the state with the first hundred years of Oregon's history. These included an Oregon Centennial album; a popular cartoon series depicting the lives of famous Oregonians; a series of strip maps that marked historic sites along the major highways; an Oregon history exhibition at the Exposition; and regular distribution to many newspapers of "This Day in Oregon History," a column that daily recounted Oregon history from the year of statehood. Under the creative leadership of Thomas Vaughan, the director of the Oregon Historical Society, the committee participated in equipping a history van, which eventually visited 86 towns and attracted approximately 200,000 people.

Other projects attracted special attention. The Oregon Centennial religious advisory committee, representing most denominations, set up at the Exposition an impressive display of nine large murals by Carl Morris "depicting the coming of the spirit of God to the people of the state." [12] These are now a part of the permanent art display at the University of Oregon. The centennial commission also promoted and helped finance the Centennial Pony Express—a promotion venture with real mail

---

12. *Ibid.,* 40.

carriers; a national Indian encampment in Pendleton; and a natural resources display at the Exposition, a scale-model relief map. A real spectacular was the Wagon Train, several wagons re-creating the original wagon-train trek from Independence, Missouri, to Independence, Oregon, which the commission supported with $28,000.

Oregon's Centennial was overshadowed by its Exposition, but the people celebrated their important year with programs that extended to the villages and hamlets that lay beyond the Exposition grounds. The Centennial was an important occasion for the state, as it made a "cultural and commercial impact upon . . . [the] economy, institutions and people," [13] revitalizing their museums, libraries, and archives, but more particularly extending their funds and taxes to new and better programs in the arts.

THE NORTH CAROLINA TERCENTENARY

North Carolina's seventeenth-century beginnings hardly accommodated planners searching for an exciting theme for celebration. What kind of interest does the granting of a charter by the King of England to eight Lords Proprietor rouse? In 1963 planners answered this question by enlarging the perspective of celebration to include the entire first century, 1663 to 1763, "as the chronological basis for its planning." [14] Since settlement patterns of North Carolina's first hundred years extended to its western border, this decision increased sharply the number of communities which could celebrate beginnings.

The first rumblings of a Tercentenary sounded in 1958, swelling into action a year later with official authorization by the General Assembly. In the enlarged perspective of celebra-

---

13. *Ibid.,* 1.

14. *Report of the Carolina Charter Tercentenary Commission* (Raleigh, North Carolina: State Department of Archives and History, 1964) , 5. [Hereinafter referred to as *North Carolina Report.*]

tion, planners chose to emphasize education and to instruct the public, especially the young, on the facts and meanings of the past. Thus they hoped that citizens would understand and appreciate an entire century of North Carolina history.

The superintendent of public instruction, the director of the state department of archives and history, and the director of the departments of conservation and development joined twenty-two other prominent citizens to form the North Carolina Charter Tercentenary Commission. An elaborate committee structure gave wide state representation in the central planning. (See Figure 1.) Five committees functioned from the beginning—scholarly activities, concerned with historical exhibition, microfilming, and identifying and publishing scholarly materials; arts, which covered fine arts, music, and literature; religious activities; commemorative events, which scheduled observances of special occasions both in state and local affairs; and programs in schools, colleges, and universities. Later added were finance and building, public information activities, and tourist activities. Appropriate subcommittees under these larger committees completed the organization picture.

North Carolina's Tercentenary leadership focused sharply on four strong-willed men—the Honorable Francis E. Winslow of Rocky Mount, the commission chairman; Brigadier General John D. F. Phillips, U.S. Army (Ret.), executive secretary; Dr. Christopher Crittenden, director of the state department of archives and history; and Governor Terry Sanford. The first three gave the Centennial its direction, selected the personnel who served on its various committees, inspired enthusiasm among the many small communities of the state, and solicited financial support. Governor Sanford strongly supported the Tercentenary and participated in many of its programs. Wearing full colonial dress, he and Mrs. Sanford inaugurated the year of celebration with an elaborate ball at the executive mansion, where the Governor cut a birthday cake sporting three hundred candles.

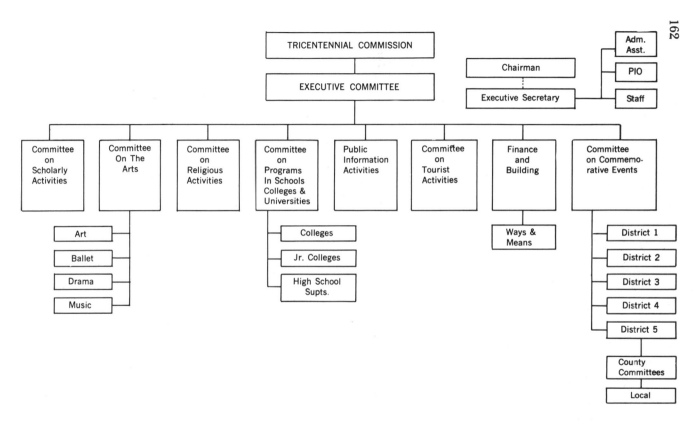

FIG. 1

COMMITTEE STRUCTURE FOR NORTH CAROLINA TERCENTENARY

Chairman Winslow, a successful North Carolina politician and businessman, gave dignified professional leadership to the commission. General Phillips brought qualities of firm leadership, administrative talent, and tireless energy. Dr. Crittenden held closely to historical perspective and cemented the relationship between the commission and the state historical society. This association was a productive one because of the society's long-standing role in the state.[15] The society not only held a firm hand in the activities of local history organizations, but it had often interceded between state legislators and their local constituency in situations involving historical interests. Dr. Crittenden was also instrumental in translating the strong academic interests of the historical society into local community planning.

Sometimes these men worked together smoothly. Sometimes there was tension between them. General Phillips was a hard worker, military-crisp and well-organized in his daily regimen, and he was present at every committee meeting. Dr. Crittenden, imaginative and creative, concerned with the academic standards of his profession, sometimes severely limited by failing health, was not so well-organized; often he was too interested in the political scene and in his own organization. Fortunately, Chairman Winslow, the commander, like Paul Troast in New Jersey, was usually able to iron out difficulties. Personal interests wax strong in Centennial planning, and the presence of patient and informed leaders is indispensable to success.

For the most part North Carolina followed traditional patterns in publicizing its Tricentennial—news releases, colorful radio programs, television specials, and billboard displays. Speakers alerted clubs, organizations, schools, and churches with detailed lectures of heritage. *Tercentenary News*, a newsletter, chronicled and circulated the events of the Centennial as they happened and provided a forum for an exchange of ideas. A

---

15. Interview with H. G. Jones, State Historian and Administrator, Office of Archives and History, Raleigh, North Carolina.

Tercentenary symbol circulated widely, appearing often in ten-second slots on television programs, on the mastheads of news-papers, and on posters in shop windows. Reproductions of this symbol were common in letterheads, on envelopes, and in pub-lications that circulated within the state.[16]

Perhaps the primary emphasis in public relations was to localize and personalize the news release. The commission made a special effort to appeal to local schools and churches, provid-ing them with materials, booklets, and suggestions of what to do. It encouraged school libraries to post reading lists and set up exhibitions of North Carolina materials; urged English de-partments to encourage students to write historical plays, skits, essays, and short stories; appealed to home economics depart-ments to plan programs to illustrate colonial needlework, quilt-ing, and cooking; and requested that art, physical education, history, and science departments use their disciplines in similar creativity. In a less academic move, Winslow urged schools to inject Tercentenary themes into half-time ceremonies at ath-letic contests during the Centennial year.

Financing the Tercentenary year was at first a tedious job. A first-year grant of $9,330 was the initial resource for planning. Public funds for the celebration eventually increased to a quarter-million dollars, but much of it was earmarked for spe-cial projects. Funds from private sources added approximately $85,000 to this account, a sum which included a mobile museum of history tractor.

State level programs appear to have been more scholarly than local activities. A new large State Archives and History Build-ing and a colonial records project [17] commanded much of the commission's attention. The state finally dedicated the archives building in 1968 as part of the Tercentenary. The colonial

---

16. Chronicled in the meetings of the Centennial Commission, in State De-partment of Archives and History, Raleigh, North Carolina. [Hereinafter cited as Centennial Archives File.]

17. Modeled after the Virginia project from the Jamestown Festival.

records project, which continues today under the auspices of the state historical society, succeeded in its objective of publishing the first volume of early colonial North Carolina records during the Centennial year—*North Carolina Charters and Constitution 1578 to 1698,* edited by Mattie Irma Edwards Parker.[18]

The committee on the schools, colleges, and universities initiated the Historical Pamphlet Series, seven popularly written monographs dealing with the particulars of colonial life during the state's first hundred years, materials valuable in teaching state history at the junior high school level. Supplementing this pamphlet series were "less elaborate brochures and leaflets which dealt with colonial subjects." [19]

Two grants—an automotive tractor from an automobile company, and money for a trailer from a tobacco firm—made possible the historymobile museum. Thousands of North Carolinians eventually viewed the traveling trailer's twelve exhibits which illustrated highlights of the state's first hundred years— dioramic exhibits, sound-and-light presentation, and assorted displays of artifacts. In the van were an electrically operated terrain map of the Albemarle region, a panel showing early church life, a series of paintings depicting the beginning of education in the state, pictures of the Lords Proprietor and other historical personages of the first century, and pictorial panels of a typical North Carolina town, farm, and wagon road. One of the most impressive displays was the Shiloh Indian diorama illustrating the role Indians played in early North Carolina.

History was important in the state's production of *The Road to Carolina,* a motion picture employing modern methods and techniques "to create in the audience's mind a sense of the presence of historical past." [20]

---

18. Interview with Mrs. Mattie Irma Edwards Parker.

19. *North Carolina Reports,* 14.

20. Description in Tercentenary Archives File, Raleigh, North Carolina.

North Carolina concentrated on the arts but hardly to the extent that Oregon did. A forty-day display of paintings, sculpture, silverware, and furniture appeared as a Centennial exhibition at the North Carolina Museum of Art in Raleigh. This display utilized local resources, materials borrowed from over the state—and from England. Through the entreaties of Secretary of State Dean Rusk, the National Portrait Gallery of London lent four portraits of the Lords Proprietor to the North Carolina Museum.

Hunter Johnson's musical composition "North State," a full symphonic work in three parts, depicted North Carolina's early history. The North Carolina Symphony Orchestra performed this work several times durng the year in different communities. Composers combined music, drama, and dance in the folk opera *The Sojourner and Mollie Sinclair,* one of the most heralded programs of the year. With professional singers in the lead roles supported by local talent and the state symphony orchestra, this epic of North Carolina's rich folk traditions appeared first on the stage and then as a videotaped television production. Centennial music publications—*A Selective Music Bibliography from the Period 1663 to 1763* by James Pruett and Lee Rigsby, and *Songs of the Carolina Charter Colonists 1663 to 1763* by Arthur Palmer Hudson—were helpful to historians and musicians.

The influence of the state religious interest committee appeared in the success of its call to all churches to prepare sermons and lessons that had historical reference points. Churches responded with tracts, special lectures, sermons, and brochures on religious themes. Many of the denominations set a Dedication Sunday for concerted worship and thanksgiving.

North Carolina's state Tercentenary programs were generally low-key but well planned, well presented, and up to the standards demanded by the planners. Local programs could claim no such consistency. Some were exciting, scholarly, entertaining—representative of the talent and resources of the particular community involved; others were shallow or flashy, showing little creative effort. Sometimes a college dominated the planning in a single community; at other times it was the DAR, the American Legion, or the Sons of the American Revolution. Occasionally a club or an organization, the mayor, or maybe a group of local citizens working with a county historical society or school officials took over. They had music—string ensembles, piano concerts, folk dances, organ recitals, and orchestra performances; drama—pageantry whose quality varied with the performance and the script; exhibitions; carnivals; folk festivals; contests; and lectures—all heavily weighted with local talent.

Merchants decorated their store windows with historical themes, serving their customers dressed in colonial costume. Citizens celebrated with costume balls, tours, pilgrimages, craft displays, colonial teas, special exhibitions, hand-painted decorations and handwoven clothing, and colonial flower shows. There were slide programs for the clubs, folk sings and choir presentations for the musically oriented, breakfasts and dinners for the gourmets, and tree plantings for almost anyone who cared to participate. Bands played in city squares, garden clubs conducted beautification programs, PTA groups emphasized "Know Your State" themes in their monthly programs, and civic clubs chose speakers with historical topics. There were restorations, re-enactments, art programs, antique displays, and the inevitable parades.

County programs were similar to local programs in the tenor and variety of planning and in vacillating enthusiasm. One county settled on such a simple action as acquiring a new edition of the North Carolina *Colonial Records* for their library. The governor opened Bertie County festivities by cutting the ribbon of an exhibit of a local artist's work, followed by a show of colonial relics in an information center. There were tours of famous homes highlighting colonial furnishings, social hours, luncheons, a ball, and a parade featuring Miss North Carolina.

The Curricuck County Centennial summer reading program awarded certificates to anyone reading fifteen books from an approved list. Boone County's exciting three-day wagon train trek followed Daniel Boone's original route across the Blue Ridge as part of an annual outdoor drama, *Horn in the West.* The library was the center of attention in Wilson County as its citizens dedicated a new building and celebrated with the special library week. Its bookmobiles also exhibited colonial artifacts along with special book collections. Boy Scouts in Tyrrell County recreated Indian scenes, using war paint, feathers, and relics. Martin County had an elaborate colonial tea party served by high school girls in colonial costumes. While drinking tea, guests admired a display of antiques, original land grants, diaries, and colonial records.

Cumberland County had an art gallery lecture series, a painting exhibition, several interesting photograph exhibits, and a Little Theater production, *The Night of January 14th,* played several nights to receptive audiences. Bath County's elaborate program included an outdoor concert featuring classical music by Bach, Handel, and other seventeenth-century musicians, folk sings, exhibitions, a tour, and a special church service.

Buford County emphasized local geography with a shrimp-boat parade along the waterfront, an address by an admiral, boat trips, and exhibitions of maritime objects. Boat racing, a boat show, a water-skiing exhibition, a re-enactment of the capture of Beaufort by Spanish pirates, and a giant clambake used the state's water resources. In the midst of a simultaneous Civil War Centennial, Tarboro combined Civil War and Revolutionary themes in a program that featured a giant cake-cutting and a pageant with performers wearing Revolutionary and nineteenth-century uniforms.

Citizens of North Carolina celebrated their Centennial enthusiastically but simply in 1963. General Phillips later lamented the dearth of fine arts in the Centennial, especially regretting that few native artists lent their names and work to the program. He was pleased with the publication of the *Colonial Records,* the special commemoration stamp, and the meetings of three historical associations in the state during the Centennial year. He expressed some concern at the cost involved in putting a historymobile on the road, though he felt that "history on wheels was necessary for any large centennial program." His one cautioning remark was that a historymobile is very much like a yacht—"if you have to ask how much it costs to run it, don't buy it." [21]

Like most centennials, the Tercentenary had its moments of simple drama. General Phillips recalled one of those moments. The second prize in one of the writing contests went to a young Black student in a predominantly Black school in a small town. When the general called the school principal to announce the prize, the principal responded: "Glory hallelujah!" Then excitedly he said to the general, "I'm sorry, I have to hang up now; school is almost over and I want to tell everybody." And off he went to the public address system to make the announcement.

North Carolina celebrated its Tercentenary during the high tide of the Civil War Centennial. Unfortunately, the North Carolina planning commission for the Civil War Centennial operated a separate office and generally explored themes and avenues of celebration different from those of the Tercentenary. While the Tercentenary commission looked toward educating people of the state to their past, the other commission stressed re-enactments, recording military history, and the more festive means of celebrating—parades, costumes, and pageants. Sometimes these commissions overlapped in their efforts, and their programs dovetailed. Too often each went its own way, one a drain on the energy and enthusiasm of the other. Overlapping leadership might well have prevented confusion and brought the two programs into closer harmony.

---

21. Interview with Brigadier General John D. F. Phillips.

North Carolina celebrated with consistent themes of growth
and development for citizens to ponder. Although planners
performed a Herculean task to bring about this celebration, the
state went a long way to "revive and refresh interest" in its
heritage.[22] The editor of the Goldsboro *News Argus* recognized
this accomplishment with these words: "It aroused a rare appreciation of our early history . . . but it has given this state
substantial projects and accomplishments which will be of
service to the scholar and the interested layman for years to
come." [23]

---

22. Sanford *Herald,* January 9, 1963.
23. Goldsboro *News Argus,* October 25, 1963.

VIII

Two Vignettes from the Provinces: British Columbia and Manitoba

C ANADIANS, as we saw earlier, celebrated a national birthday with enthusiasm. In addition, most provinces have been successful with their own commemorations. Two provincial examples, representing different cultures and contrasting leadership, provide excellent illustration of the localized Canadian spirit of celebration.

British Columbia has had four centennials since 1958—commemorating the establishment of mainland British Columbia as a Crown Colony in 1958, the union of British Columbia and Vancouver Island in 1966, the Centennial of Canadian Confederation in 1967, and the province's entrance into the Confederation in 1971. Her celebration patterns demonstrate a continuity of interest and philosophy from one centennial to another; her people celebrated for nearly fifteen years without losing sight of the basic objectives decided upon in the first planning sessions. Sensitive leadership, a well-defined historical perspective, superb planning, fine organization, and varied projects and programs marked their endeavors.

Manitobans sustained celebration excitement for the full year of celebration, and many persons still recall the exhilaration of being alive during those crowded days. The variety of events, the enthusiasm of the leaders and the participants, and the money raised and spent to promote various activities show the impact a centennial can make and the excitement it can stimulate. The leaders in both of these provinces were recruited from the government, the academic world, and the people. Men and women traveled the length and breadth of the provinces to promote centennial programs. No region, no group remained outside, as Indians and other groups prominent in western Canada participated on equal terms with the more dominant cultures. These celebrations left tangible reminders and wistful memories of action-packed days.

BRITISH COLUMBIA'S CENTENNIALS

"God forbid that we would ever have another centennial in my lifetime in British Columbia," emphatically stated Provincial Librarian and Archivist Willard E. Ireland shortly after the conclusion of his province's 1958 Centennial celebration in which he had served as a member of the Central Planning Commission.[1] In 1971, in the midst of planning his fourth provincial centennial in thirteen years, he wiped his forehead with his handkerchief and commented even more forcefully: "No more centennials for me!"[2] Despite such reservations, Ireland and hundreds of British Columbians maintained their enthusiasm and sustained their creativity through the four centennials, ending each on a note of harmony. Most of the planners agree that the 1971 affair should do it for a while, but in spite of exhaustion after long labors they spoke with confidence that their efforts had been worthwhile.

Where did this all begin? Ireland remarked frankly that he

---

1. *History News,* 15 (December 1959) , 22.
2. Actually this was the fifth centennial in a quarter of a century, as British Columbia mildly observed Vancouver Island's hundred years of being a Crown Colony in 1949.

just didn't know.[3] Certainly British Columbians made no spontaneous outcry for a celebration. Perhaps the celebration spirit came from "a very simple thing," suggested Ireland. In trying to reach a decision on whether to restore a prominent landmark, Fort Langley, the provincial government set up a small committee to investigate and make recommendations as to the feasibility of such a project. Ireland was a member of this committee. "I wrote into the report one, I thought, most innocuous sentence," he stated, "which simply said that if the government was planning to commemorate the year 1858, Fort Langley would be an integral and significant part of that commemoration." [4] This action was hardly spectacular, but it did set wheels in motion. In less than a year a cabinet committee was working out possibilities for a celebration. The long years of planning and celebrating had begun.

This two-man cabinet committee set 1958 as the year of celebration and appointed a Committee of Co-ordination to begin planning the centennial of the province's status as a Crown Colony. The new committee was a strong one, including two cabinet members, the executive secretary of the Union of British Columbia Municipalities, a business man and an alderman from Vancouver, a senior public relations man from the British Columbia Electric Company, the head of the Department of Classics at the University of British Columbia ("a wonderful arrangement," later said Ireland, "in that we have learned more about English grammar and the meaning of words than we ever knew before.") [5], and two civil servants—L. J. Wallace of the Provincial Department of Education, chairman, and Ireland, secretary.

The new appointees went to work immediately in what Ireland described as "a fantastic experience." Through all provincial communications media, the committee conducted a sur-

---

3. *History News, loc. cit.*
4. *Ibid.*
5. *Ibid.*

vey to see how British Columbians wanted to celebrate. They studied former celebrations of neighboring provinces and then planned their own centennial. When the Centennial Celebration Act was passed in March 1956, the original central committee was appointed as an eight-man board of directors of a new organization. Seventeen provincial committees emerged under this board, and these committees set the patterns for celebration. (See Figure 1).

For several weeks these committees worked in almost complete secrecy. Only when they were ready to talk about programs, financing, and publicity did they begin to leak news to the media. First, they identified their objectives: to put on a party for the people of British Columbia, not ignoring tourist trade but not catering to it, and to extend the Centennial to the smallest communities. Then they began extending their organization into the communities through an elaborate local committee structure which eventually included 333 communities. Local committees remained completely autonomous, receiving suggestions and projects from the Centennial committee, but using only those that they chose to identify with their own programs.

The central commission successfully solicited a Centennial commemorative postage stamp and a commemorative coin, selected Centennial colors, approved a Centennial song, Centennial license plates, photograph albums, and even Centennial textiles—special decorative bunting prepared in the Centennial motif. They sponsored Centennial publications, editions of newspapers, television and radio programs, and a large Centennial wood-carved mural of a hundred years of British Columbia history—placed appropriately in the new Government House in Victoria. They chose a Centennial slogan, "1858–1958—A Century to Celebrate," and official Centennial souvenirs, which attempted to provide visitors and participants with worthwhile mementos of their British Columbia adventure.

To assist local committees, the Centennial commission concentrated on three areas. The first, *Projects '58,* was a series of

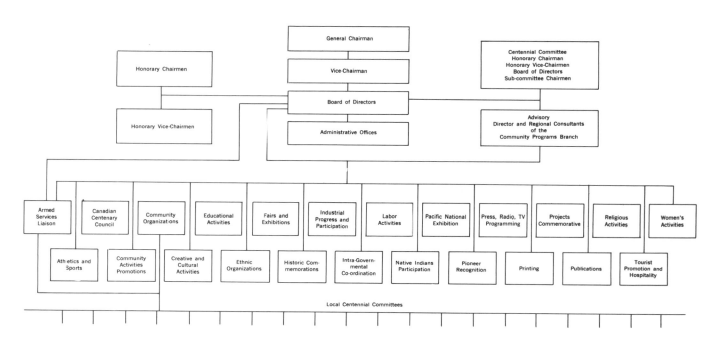

FIG. 1

THE BRITISH COLUMBIA CENTENNIAL COMMITTEE

government-supported programs, projects, and events that could be transported throughout the province—programs that would bring culture and entertainment to people usually far removed from such fare. The second granted forty cents per capita to each community whose committee submitted an acceptable proposal for local celebration to the Board of Directors. The third, a matching grant, awarded sixty cents per capita toward a specific project approved by the provincial Centennial Commission and required dollar-for-dollar participation by the community receiving it.

"Celebrations Everywhere," the title that planners bestowed upon *Projects '58,* eventually touched nearly every community in the nation, reached into almost every individual's life, interrupted individual and community routines alike, and brought excitement and changes to schools, businesses, workers, men in uniform, and local government officials. These programs produced festivity, entertainment, educational growth, and cultural awakening. They opened the Centennial with a special New Year's Day spectacular and filled the year with a steady stream of programs. Among them were the "fun-provoking" stagecoach run, a rebuilt stagecoach dashing across the country with mock holdups, hangings, and all the action which history attributes to those romantic episodes of the past. A vintage automobile run pitted ancient vehicles against each other. More than 100,000 people viewed a Centennial air show—with sky diving, flying circuses, and other aerial exhibitions. Two mountain-climbing clubs made a Centennial conquest of Mt. Fairweather, a 15,300-foot peak in the northern part of the province. Her Royal Highness the Princess Margaret visited British Columbia and traveled extensively in the province.

Ethnic groups capitalized on "Celebrations Everywhere" with programs identifying their cultural traits, skills, and history. Included was a commemoration of the Queen's Totem Pole, carved by Henry Hunt, one of the province's ranking Indian artists; a Chinese opera sponsored by the Chinatown Lions

Club of Vancouver and Victoria, and "Caribou Chorus," songs of different cultures by the Prince George Choral Society. A drama group toured many communities with its three-act play entitled *The World of the Wonderful Dark,* a tale of early Indian life. The *Salute to the Sockeye,* an unusual program of tribal pageantry, singing, games, fishing contests, and cookery exhibits staged on an Indian reservation, told of the spawning of the salmon.

Music, drama, and pageantry appeared in many forms during *Projects '58.* The Vancouver and Victoria symphony orchestras toured the larger cities of British Columbia. The conductor of the Vancouver orchestra enlivened children's concerts with stories about the composers, an introduction to the instruments, illustrations of how music is created, and examples of how classical music can be fun. Holiday Theatre, a non-profit organization devoted to bringing good drama to children, presented *Magic Nugget,* a play about early British Columbia written especially for the Centennial, to more than 90,000 children in seventy-seven different communities. Though not an official Centennial project, a drama group, Theatre Under the Stars, also performed to record crowds and attracted Centennial visitors. The "British Columbia Centurama" toured twenty-five communities, depicting the flow of Canadian life for a hundred years with a variety program of music, dancing, and historical drama. There were concerts and dances for young people, square-dance jamborees with both "live" and "canned" callers available, as people danced round the Centennial clock. For those who did not care for fiddle music, a prominent band leader, Mart Kenney, and his Western Gentlemen also toured for eleven weeks.

As a part of *Projects '58,* the Central Committee officially encouraged local pageantry by making available standard and expanded scripts of *From Wilderness to Wonderland,* a pageant about British Columbia from its earliest days to the time of the Centennial. Pageantry also combined with important exhibitions in the first International Trade Fair ever held in the province, which provided displays both foreign and domestic. Ceremony was also integral to *Projects '58* activity. Beginning and ending the Centennial year offered occasions to wave the flag, sing the Canadian anthem, and dedicate lives to another century of achievement and growth. The church commemorated more transcendent values with special days of prayer and thanksgiving. Firelighting services across the province in April created an opportunity for all citizens to note in a quiet way the nation's passing into its second century.

The historical perspective of *Projects '58* added the important dimension of understanding the past. A history caravan, two 34-foot vans towed by a tractor, toured the province, exhibiting relics, paintings, photographs, and original manuscripts to nearly 150,000 persons. A Canadian national railway museum train toured the rail lines of the province, bringing back "the gas-lit glory of early railroading in Canada." An attempt to tell the early history of boating in a traveling exhibit did not come off so well, but there was an important "Fleet Week" in Vancouver where ships of both ancient and modern vintage opened their decks to visitors. History also appeared in re-enactments and reconstructions. A great water spectacle, the Fraser Brigade, re-enacted the historic journey of one of the early pioneers down the Fraser River. Reconstructed Fort Langley, dedicated as part of a Centennial program by Princess Margaret on her visit to the province, became a focal point for much of the activity in the Centennial year.

Several significant historical publications marked the Centennial celebration. An attractive *Record Book* presented the background of the province, describing its agriculture, education, energy and power, fisheries, forestry and logging, government, mining, and recreational activities. An education committee distributed *Land of Shining Mountains,* a Centennial history of British Columbia, to elementary school children of the province. *British Columbia Centennial Cook Book* recalled recipes from a hundred years back, retaining their spontaneity, charm, and regional expressions. The central committee commissioned the publication and distribution of a revised Centennial picture map and helped to produce an important historical film entitled *The Tall Country.*

Projects '58 only scratched the surface of the celebrating energies of more than 300 communities in British Columbia. When left to devise their own programs in the "40¢ per capita" grants, the number of projects, events, programs, and festivals that developed staggers the imagination. Some towns extended their activities over the entire year. Others celebrated for only a day. "The success of our day surprised and delighted us all," said the chairman of a community of 116.[6] "Our celebrations, while perhaps not being on a large enough scale to attract a great deal of outside interest, did create interest in our own community and helped us to bring about the 100 percent cooperation" said the chairman of a seventy-person community.[7] Other community leaders testified to moments equally exciting. People throughout British Columbia danced, laughed, and sang; they put on their best clothes, and they modeled clothes of an earlier period. They watched spectacles, sporting events, and worshiped—all because they were assisted by this grant.

Beyond the festivity and pageantry were the more serious moments highlighted by the "60¢ per capita" grant, which provided inspiration and funds for more lasting projects. In return for grants of $820,000, local communities raised approximately $3.2 million for 344 such projects, including new city buildings, additions and improvements to community halls, new parks, playgrounds, recreational areas, health and civic centers, libraries, museums, band shells, senior citizens' homes, curling rinks, and fire halls. Centennial grants also provided for the purchase of an operating table for a hospital, X-ray equipment,

---

6. *Report of the British Columbia Centennial Committee* (Victoria, 1959), 261.

7. *Ibid.,* 262.

an ambulance, the restoration of a stone church, and the construction of a special ski lift.

In 1958 British Columbians put time, money, and energy into a year of celebration. The provincial government alone spent nearly $3,000,000. (See Figure 2.) For what? A renewal of a sense of history, a feeling of what the province and the nation really were and what they meant to every citizen, a new awareness of a "fair land"? Yes, these and more—a new interest in fine arts, new acceptance of change, and encouragement to continue the province's growth with a willingness to look to the past for inspiration and meaning. At least this is what the British Columbians thought, for they had hardly relaxed from the rigors of '58 when they began two more centennials—'66 and '67—sometimes simultaneous celebrations, sometimes separate.

Centennial celebrations do not just grow—they must have careful planning and hard work. British Columbians could not rest on the laurels of '58 in later celebrations, but they could build upon their experiences. Veterans turn to veterans in time of crisis, and a centennial is a crisis. Experienced men lead troops into battle better than untried giants, though eventually both can work together to achieve victory—so it was in British Columbia's continuing centennial experiences.

The Centennial Commission of 1966–67 showed a marked resemblance to the one of '58, with the names of Wallace and Ireland again on the marquee. Some new faces appeared, but the planners repeated many of the procedures of their first experience, adding a few new twists but always stressing the large participation of community and individuals. The Centennial commission instituted the regional meeting to keep in touch with local communities and funnel ideas and programs to them more effectively. Additional subcommittees, including native Indian participation, pioneer recognition, and women's activities, provided better services and tapped new resources for celebration. (See Figure 3.)

A major innovation in planning consisted of publicizing the

THE BRITISH COLUMBIA CENTENNIAL DOLLAR

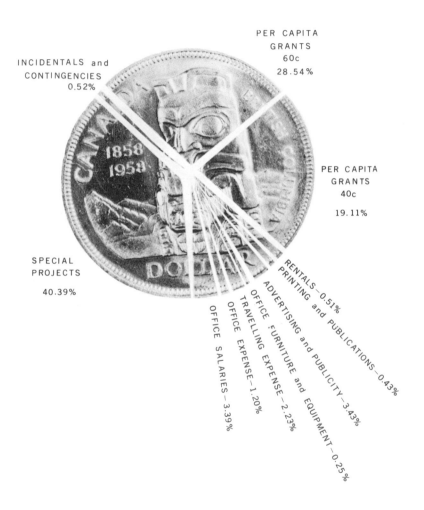

PER CAPITA
GRANTS
60c
28.54%

INCIDENTALS and
CONTINGENCIES
0.52%

PER CAPITA
GRANTS
40c

19.11%

SPECIAL
PROJECTS

40.39%

RENTALS—0.51%

PRINTING and PUBLICATIONS—0.43%

ADVERTISING and PUBLICITY—3.43%

OFFICE FURNITURE and EQUIPMENT—0.25%

TRAVELLING EXPENSE—2.23%

OFFICE EXPENSE—1.20%

OFFICE SALARIES—3.39%

FIG. 2

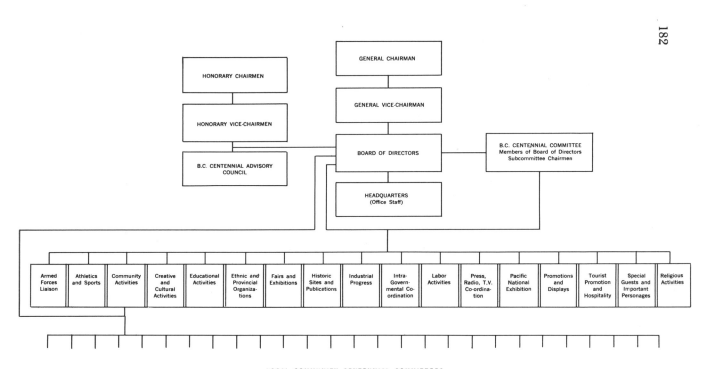

FIG. 3

CANADIAN CONFEDERATION CENTENNIAL COMMITTEE OF BRITISH COLUMBIA

program to broader interests—soliciting support and participation from outside British Columbia. One novel idea in this new thrust included entering an elaborate float in the Rose Bowl Parade to attract Americans to western Canada. Following the patterns of '58, the Centennial commission also initiated what they termed an "All-In" effort—an appeal to citizens to spread the news throughout the province for months prior to '66. This contributed to the formation of nearly a hundred more local committees than had existed in 1958.

In this renewed excitement, British Columbians again celebrated—and for two years—with such an outburst of Centennial happenings as to dismay the chronicler of such events. Five editions of "A Calendar of Events" barely kept up with the flow of activities. Public relations teams worked hard to keep up with the furious pace. Several of their publications attracted attention—"100 Founders of British Columbia," a biographical series; "Backward Glances," twenty-four features for newspapers dealing with the Centennial; *The Spokesman,* a monthly publication for provincial committees; and more than 250 general news releases to stress the variety of the Centennial. A series of three-to-five-minute radio tapes entitled "Characters of the Century" deserves mention.

Programs exploded everywhere throughout the days of two centennials. The usual spectaculars—an air show at Abbott's Ford, an unusual presentation of flying events; hydroplane races; a large and gaudy International Trade Fair; and two festivals of forestry—attracted much attention but left little more than memories. The Nanaimo bathtub race was "an offbeat idea" that has since become an annual event. Queen Elizabeth, in an official appearance in March 1966, dedicated a building, and in 1967 Queen Juliana of the Netherlands laid the cornerstone of a carillon tower which now houses her country's Centennial gift—a forty-nine-bell carillon. Clerks in the provincial liquor stores wore Centennial tartan blazers issued especially for the occasion; a British Columbia plowing match commemorated the first such event about the time of Confederation; and an office building in Vancouver erected a large illuminated Centennial symbol on either side of the building. In more serious actions, a Red Cross youth program promoted understanding among the young people of the province; "Project 100" provided mobile classrooms for underprivileged communities; a fifty-one-day stagecoach run from Barkersville to Victoria in 1966 recreated a historic experience, and many new markers commemorated the past.

These were days when sporting matches took on Centennial designs, a time for the more prosperous to put on costumes for elaborate balls and dances and for new identities to be established, with ethnic groups identifying themselves in programs as varied and as real as their own cultural riches. The Chinese responded with traditional parades and festivals in Chinatown, Croations with a "Centennial of British Columbia Progress." A Netherlands Centennial Fair featured foods, crafts, and flowers; Danish, French, Finnish, and Icelandic programs had traditional themes; the Japanese donated a crocodile tank to the Vancouver Public Aquarium and set up funds for an academic scholarship; and Russian and Ukranian programs included food, music, and ballet.

Under the direction of their own special committee, the Indians set their own pace. Villages and isolated Indian bands concentrated on projects celebrating their pasts and their skills. Leaders encouraged Indian youth to special artistic endeavors— carving and painting—with emphasis on native creative work. Young Indians emerged from their isolated communities and participated in national sporting events, arts and crafts shows, and other Centennial contests of skill—benefiting both their people and those with whom they associated.

Moments of reconciliation and recognition occurred in Centennial days in 1966 and 1967: youth celebrated with parents, teachers, and government leaders, lending their exuberance and special spirit of discovery to festive scenes. Recognized were senior citizens—the Pioneers, many of whom traced their days into the early history of provincial growth and development; ethnic groups; outstanding Centennial leaders. The Order of the Dogwood, a special award of merit for service to the province was approved as a Centennial project. The first awards in this order went to members in the higher echelons of leadership, but someday others may receive them—clerks, postal carriers, teachers, archivists, plumbers, indigent lawyers, and others whose positions seldom command the center of national spotlight, but who celebrate with dignity.

Centennial days were as rich, as varied, and as unusual as their planners directed. There were moments of doubt, when the planners wondered if it was all worth the effort. There were occasions for lamenting as well as rejoicing. But the national memorial projects celebrating the Confederation stand as a reminder of exciting and productive days. The Museum and Archives Complex, an attractive showplace, is a product of the combined federal government-provincial Centennial grants, much like those of '58. The Confederation Gardens, flanking the British Columbia Parliamentary Buildings, the Centennial Fountain in Vancouver, and many other buildings throughout the province are reminders of Centennial days. Projects undertaken in 1958 were matched and surpassed by new ones of 1966 and 1967—parks, playgrounds, recreation areas, community halls, libraries, and museums are only a few. And the programs had greater meaning. One writer told it well: "Children who have had no safe swimming before now have swimming pools or improved beaches, and more people were able to take up golf, tennis, or lawn bowling, and enjoyed new facilities for cultural activities. New beauty spots have blossomed, historic sites have been restored, trails marked and history written." [8]

Two centennials ran out together in 1967, but another was in the wings. In 1971 familiar names reappeared to lead a

---

8. *A Tale of Two Centenaries* (Victoria: British Columbia Centennial Commission, 1967), 6.

fourth celebration—this time occasioned by the centennial of the province's entry into the Canadian Confederation. Wallace and Ireland were at it again, both a bit fatigued as a result of the prior action, yet as enthusiastic for creativity and residual benefits as ever.

The 1971 celebration was subdued, continuing projects begun in other centennials. Substantial works to recount the past were published; the many museums produced by earlier centennial endeavors were staffed and supported. The 1971 Centennial became a time for encouraging communities to support their museums and for museums to change displays and seek new themes. It was a time for all British Columbians to review the accomplishments of 1958, 1966, and 1967.

Still, the 1971 Centennial deserves its own special place in the annals of British Columbia's celebration. It had its own *Centennial Caravan,* a fully contained expensive road show "which probably said little about British Columbia that most of its citizens did not already know, but which apparently has reasonable popular appeal." [9] *Canada on the Pacific,* a historical exposition, was a special, generally academic, presentation of British Columbia's entry into the Confederation. Its appeal was somewhat limited, however, according to one authority, who suggested that the exposition was little more than an attempt to "explain to the population" what the earlier celebrations had been all about.[10]

Despite these criticisms, however, there was additional progress in 1971—more museums were built, interesting displays commemorated the Centennial across the country, important publications were issued, and interest continued in British Columbia history. Certainly, "The Legacy," an exhibition showing the history of the early British Columbian Indians, at the British Columbia museum at Victoria, is evidence of a worthwhile Centennial project. This display stimulated new interests

9. *Museum Round-Up,* 43 (July 1971), 33.
10. *Ibid.,* 34.

in Canada's past and new concerns for the Indians who were so much a part of this past. The appearance of ecological themes in exhibitions across British Columbia, including the museum at Victoria, indicates that interest in social problems went well beyond local interests.

The programs and projects of British Columbia's four centennials appear in the records like ghosts tramping across a distant land to the sounds of fiddle, horn, tom-tom, and bassoon. What brought so many people together to celebrate? Why did they respond with such fervor? Why did they build, dance, play, and worship with such frenzy? This intensity of celebration is really what a centennial is all about, and British Columbia planners took advantage of every opportunity, pulling all stops to achieve maximum participation. They created the initial media for expression, fanned enthusiasm as it grew, and extended the spirit of the moment to the largest number of citizens. From the official crest of the Centennial to the Centennial beards and bonnets, they publicized the special year to men and women suddenly possessed by an awareness of important moments in time. They called on "Century Sam," the pixie prospector created by a Vancouver artist, to tell a funny side of the province's past. "Century Sam" was joined later by "Centennial Sue," and these delightful characters, symbols of the joy and frivolity of the times, cavorted through the pages of newspapers, brochures, and on television screens to become symbols of the province's past as well known as the flag.

British Columbia celebrated four times with the energy and ardor that many places have trouble engendering for one celebration. Their festivals were fun, but they also produced a "crop of museums; restorations, galleries and other related institutions," [11] whose numbers grew from fourteen in 1952 to 124 in 1971. They produced books—including a study of meteorology by Thorne K. Won entitled *Meteorology in British Co-*

11. *Ibid.*, 18.

lumbia: A Centennial Review—and a series of folders and brochures produced by businesses, schools, and government, including *British Columbia,* an excellent survey of the history of the region, published by the Canadian Imperial Bank of Commerce.

British Columbians will probably not celebrate another centennial for some years to come. The pageantry, drama, and music have faded. People huffed and puffed to blow out the birthday candles as soon as they were lit, but in the process of celebrating, they drew themselves together as a province—and sometimes as Canadians—looked at their weaknesses and tried to shore them up, and found new strengths in co-operative ventures and in building efforts. One has only to follow the issues of *Museum Round-Up,* the periodical of the British Columbia Historical Society, to observe how often Centennial projects still make the news.

Whether a centennial is worth the effort or not is a question that every community has to answer. Mr. Wallace, Mr. Ireland, and a host of celebrants on the Canadian west coast feel that their efforts were fruitful. The traveler, wending his way across this broad and beautiful countryside, certainly takes notice of many of the accomplishments of Centennial days and may choose to agree.

THE MANITOBA CENTENNIAL

While Manitoba played a rip-roaring role in the Centennial of Canadian Confederation, her citizens pulled out all the stops in celebrating their own Centennial in 1970. Using the Canadian Centennial as their springboard, they initiated or continued projects and programs that set off another round of action. The serious blended with the comic. Science programs competed for attention with rodeos, historical projects, and building programs. On one day the tone of celebration was sublime: programs were dedicated to important long-range objectives, manifestations of the mysterious creative spirit so apparent among Canadians. The next day a giant carnival, a tubbing party, or a snowmobile expedition set the pace. And Bowsman, which had burned its biffies [privies] in 1967 to commemorate the installation of a new sewage system as a Centennial project, commemorated these same biffies—which "provided shelter from the stormy blasts and a place to read the latest catalogue"—in 1970 as a part of their history. In a special "Up, Up, and Away" ceremony on July first, they made a comic attempt to put a biffie on the moon.

During the celebration a giant cultural complex took shape in Winnipeg. Libraries opened Centennial wings, and Centennial parks appeared where open fields had been. Horses ran while men laid bricks; kites flew while historians researched the province's past—all in the name of a hundred years of membership in the Canadian Confederation. Enthusiasm never seemed to wane, whether the project built a modern building or merely freed a joyful spirit.

What happened to promote such enthusiasm for celebration? What stimulated such an outpouring of creative energy and physical action in two centennials? Premier Duff Roblin, in a commemorative statement, spoke of pattern and opportunity. "The pattern," he said, "is working together for common good. The opportunity is to provide the cultural and scientific facilities which our achievement in these areas deserves." Noble goals! And Centennial leaders fervently communicated them to the people. Manitobans translated these larger meanings into actions that produced long-range achievements. In a new spirit of the times they focused their celebration on ceremonies, centers, services, and smiles—ceremonies to commemorate the liturgies of historical reality; centers of learning for another century of growth; services to improve the state of mankind; and smiles of pride at the material growth of the builders or joy at the singing of the clowns.

Manitoba's 1971 Centennial cannot be separated from the

Centennial of Canadian Confederation. In 1963 the Manitoba Legislature answered John Fisher's call to participate in a period of commemoration by setting up the Manitoba Centennial Corporation with a fifteen-man board of trustees which retained its identity and responsibilities through two centennials, its leadership instrumental in promoting both affairs.

The board chairman was Maitland B. Steinkopf, whose enthusiasm, inspirational leadership, and devotion to his job have seldom been matched in centennial leadership. Few men have given so many hours, traveled so many miles, or sat through so many lengthy meetings. Testimonies to his service attribute the successes of two Centennials to his leadership, his imagination, and his hard work.

Few centennial commissions have met as regularly or employed as many standing committees as did Manitoba's in 1967 and 1970. The 1970 committees appear in two general categories, the more traditional ones—regional meetings, provincial Centennial grants, *Festival '70,* historical observances, school histories, historical publications, interfaith, *Youth '70,* children's programs, and the Centennial Citizens' Campaign—and some with special functions. Special committees dealt with school twinning, "Mom-Pop" Festivals, the "Athlete of the Century," car rallies, aquatic events, and centennial coins. In 1970 an important lottery committee, a building committee, and several other committees handled matters unique to Manitoba's needs.

To supplement the central committees, the board encouraged local communities by letter and personal visits to form their own planning committees. Eventually 216 of them did. To work more effectively with their local committees the board divided the province into thirteen regions, a geographical arrangement that permitted local committee members to meet together three times a year at public expense to discuss plans and share ideas. Regional committee meetings covered the face of Manitoba during the year before the 1970 Centennial.

Publicity was the responsibility of every individual participating in the Centennial of 1970. The board alerted Manitobans to their celebration in a variety of ways. They employed public relations firms, instituted a regular distribution of press releases to daily and weekly newspapers across the province, issued informative calendars of events, published and distributed Centennial brochures and tracts, established speakers' bureaus and information centers to improve local coverage, and published *Manitoba '70*—a Centennial monthly broadside whose eighteen issues now provide a historical record of the year of commemoration.

Newspapers in the province co-operated fully in publicizing the Centennial. They published the weekly briefs distributed to them by the board, and they found their own news. Radio also provided services, as eleven stations agreed to give daily news reports of Centennial happenings. To these stations and others, the board circulated special tapes, varying in length from 30 to 90 seconds, for periodic broadcasts. These tapes offered such features as a senior citizen's reminiscences, a youth's description of his exchange experience, a local Centennial leader's enumeration of plans to build an outdoor skating rink, and other Centennial happenings.

Television stations shaped many of their programs around Centennial themes and activities. All stations featured Centennial news programs, some regularly, while three stations presented weekly promotional programs. All stations made extensive use of the Centennial symbol, showing it often in special ten-second viewings. Extensive coverage was given to the opening exercises, a special program from the concert hall, the closing exercises, and exciting Canada Day. They presented four National Film Board clips produced especially for the province by the federal government, and one television station ran a special weekly children's program entitled *Archie and his Friends,* which featured Centennial corporation staff members talking with their children about the Centennial.

Sometimes the frivolous promoted the "spirit of '70." Flags, pins, stationery, and billboards kept the Centennial symbol constantly in the public eye. Centennial coins, medallions, and a special commemoration stamp appeared. Bobby Gimby, of Confederation Centennial fame, sang again to large, admiring crowds, heralding the Centennial as an important occasion.

Along city streets, stationary and revolving banners, plexiglass pole declarations, and polyhedron decorative balls flew high above the milling crowds, signaling the spirit of celebration. Overhead, at night, canopies of light and aluminum reflectors flashed in dazzling Centennial patterns. Large Centennial flags waved over schools and public buildings, and miniature Centennial flags decorated executive desks. There were Centennial decals, tie clasps, and balloons. When the federal government thinned out the Northern buffalo herds, the Centennial corporation gained distribution rights and sold several tons of this meat with the Centennial stamp marked on every package. Numerous sports events and an air show also adopted Centennial themes.

Revenue from Manitoba's two Centennials came primarily from four sources: the federal government, the provincial government, local resources, and the Centennial citizens' campaign. The federal government provided much of the big money by supplementing its matching grant of 1967 with two additional grants—five million dollars for capital funds and $500,000 for program assistance. Planning agencies channeled the new capital grants into five major projects, most of them continuations of earlier efforts. These five included the Keystone Center Auditorium at Brandon, the Manitoba Theatre Center, the Manitoba Museum of Man and Nature, the Winnipeg Art Centre, and the Saint Boniface Cultural Centre. Other federal matching grants went to promotional film projects, national exhibitions and displays, and cultural shows. Most other programs were eligible for consideration in joint federal-provincial action.

The Centennial Citizens' Campaign was also an important

breadwinner in the over-all financing. In 1964 this group set an initial goal of four and a half million dollars to match federal grants toward the major building projects then in construction. As the 1970 Centennial approached, they increased their goal to more than six million dollars, a figure which was finally surpassed. Much of their money came through the Manitoba Centennial Sweepstakes, a lottery specifically designated to raise Centennial money. The sweepstakes served several purposes: Besides publicizing the Centennial and raising money, it also stimulated the participation of a large percentage of the population, as approximately four hundred clubs and organizations received more than a million and a half dollars in compensation for their efforts in ticket sales that netted $3,750,000. The remainder went into the Centennial fund for large community projects. Canadian Sweepstakes proved even more popular than planners had imagined, and eleven different prize dates sustained interest. The highlight of the sweepstakes came when the planners combined the last of the drawings with the highly popular Manitoba Centennial Derby. In addition to sweepstakes funds, the citizens' campaign sold license plates, endowed seats in the concert hall in the Manitoba Theatre Centre, and solicited contributions from business firms.

Some communities supplemented federal and provincial grants with their own funds for local projects. The Agassiz School Board, for example, through a special assessment on taxpayers, obtained a special Centennial grant of fifty cents per student, for all schools in their division to use for Centennial improvement projects. Most communities raised money locally through individual solicitation and various sales projects.

As is the case in all Centennials, raising money in Manitoba was a complicated, sometimes frustrating job. Even the excitement of the sweepstakes did not solve the problems. This Centennial did illustrate, however, that by generating enthusiasm and properly employing matching grants, major projects and programs are possible.

Manitoba combined simple rusticity with urbane sophistication in celebrating two Centennials. Nowhere is this contrast better demonstrated than in the programs of 1970. Picture the isolated northern Manitoba community, Thomason, in July 1970, just after a "fly-in" stage show has landed. The shipment contains balloons, flags, a half-ton of candy, pioneer pins, participation medals, and much electrical equipment. In addition, the city has prepared a ton of birthday cake, and a live monkey is on display. Youngsters bask in the plentitude of the moment and later will remember seeing "a real live monkey for the first time." In sharp contrast, at the same time, workers in other cities were building a magnificent auditorium, a history caravan was showing its displays to thousands, and the Winnipeg Symphony Orchestra was preparing a program of classical music for performance outside the capital city.

Manitobans rapidly accelerated their programs toward maximum involvement. The first issue of *Manitoba '70,* the official newsletter of the Centennial corporation, listed a plethora of events that began with the dignified and serious "Light Up and Sing" program that launched the Centennial on December 31, 1969.[12] Initial commemoration events quickly turned to festivity: a bonfire of Christmas trees, moccasin dancing, torchlight processions, Centennial cake-cuttings, fireworks displays, indoor candlelight services, churchbell ringings, Centennial proclamation readings, one-minute greetings from government representatives, songs of local choirs, ethnic dances, skating parties, and family broomball games. And while Manitobans played Centennial games, "brew masters the Province over" were hard at work "preparing Centennial punch" for the thirsty celebrants.[13] Throughout the entire year activity never abated. As though someone had released a mainspring, every day brought a new call for activity from ingenious citizens taking cognizance of their birthday party.

---

12. *Manitoba '70,* I (Winnipeg: Manitoba Centennial Corporation, 1970), 1.
13. *Ibid.,* II, 1.

Official reports of the Manitoba Centennial Corporation catalogued their many events under six basic topics: *Festival '70, Sports '70, Heritage '70, Youth '70, Homecoming '70,* and *Recognition '70.* There were other programs on both state and local levels, but most fit this arrangement topically if not officially. A brief look at each reveals what another place did in another time to celebrate.

Festival '70

Arts dominated the action in *Festival '70,* which also ran the gamut from cultural programs to pure entertainment. Musical programs were popular, including concerts by the National Band of the Canadian Armed Forces, the U.S. Army Field Band, the English Chamber Mood, and popular artists Joan Sutherland, Guy Lombardo, and Charles Aznavour. There were folkloramas, youth orchestra presentations, quartets, and an appearance by the Royal Dutch Air Force Band. Presentations of *Orpheus and the Underworld* by the Canadian Opera Company; a "Beethoven-Bachman" Concert; and a traveling program, *Up With People*—youth singers entertained in nineteen different Manitoban communities—suggest the variety of musical presentations. Add to these, dance revues, public performances in the northern provinces by the Winnipeg Symphony Orchestra and the Royal Winnipeg Ballet, a Royal Canadian Mounted Police "Musical Ride" in nine different communities, and a choral festival of choirs from many countries. Popular music had its days in a "Man-Pop" festival and a "Mom-Pop" festival two months apart—the first a rock festival for the young at the Winnipeg Stadium, the other, music of the Glenn Miller big band variety for the over-40 group at a prominent Winnipeg hotel.

As a part of *Festival '70,* the Winnipeg Art Gallery exhibited "a hundred and fifty years of art in Manitoba." Le Cercle Moliere, a professional drama company, toured sixteen Canadian centers with its plays, and other theaters offered wide variety. Finally, an Omar Sharif Bridge Circus brought some of the best bridge players in the world for four days of furious play.

Sports '70

Canada, like the United States, is a sports-minded country, specializing in those sports that relate well to its climate and its terrain. Centennial sports enthusiasts followed five general patterns in celebration: emphasizing provincial, national, and international championship matches in Manitoba; honoring significant athletic achievements and personalities of the past century; developing "positive recreation programs"; encouraging "the use of athletic skills in retracing historical community routes on the water, on the land, and in the air"; and utilizing the unusual climate and terrain of the province in many of its sports activities.

The Centennial corporation supported championship matches with dollars, medallions, and special recognition. This encouragement, coupled with the province's natural zest for sporting events, brought eleven international, forty-one national, and twenty-eight provincial championship matches into Centennial Manitoba. More than 1,800 championship athletes performed in a staggering list of sports: badminton, baseball, basketball, bowling, boxing, canoeing, cricket, curling, cycling, darts, diving, dog shows, fencing, fistball, football, golf, gymnastics, handguns, ice and field hockey, horseracing, horseshoes, horse shows, judo, karate, lacrosse, water polo, rifle shoots, rodeos, rowing, sailing, ice and roller skating, skeet shooting, skiing, soaring, softball, soccer, squash, swimming, lawn and table tennis, tobogganing, track and field events, and volley ball.

Other sports activities opened participation to larger numbers of people. A "Fit for '70" plan stressed participation by all Manitobans in some sports or recreation activity. The Department of Youth and Education, working with the corporation, set up a popular special program based on the successful fitness performances of the 1967 Canadian Centennial. Over 200,000 students between the ages of six and eighteen participated, with about 30,000 receiving achievement certificates for physical proficiency. A Centennial sports caravan traveled through Manitoba and gave sports instruction, demonstrations, discussions, and in-service training, to students, teachers, and communities. Physical education instructors stressed such sports as lacrosse, soccer, and gymnastics for school in isolated districts.

Many sports activities were closely associated with three of Manitoba's leading physical assets—water, wind, and winter. *Sports '70* was a water derby and a "bathtub splash" on the Red River in August, a powerboat cruise for Manitoba families, a recreational and historical trip for 250 canoers, a Centennial fish derby that extended over nearly three months, with prizes for the best fish caught. Prominent personalities, including Prime Minister Pierre Trudeau, took part in a Centennial angling safari. The "bathtub splash" was a "light-hearted . . . high adventure," with genuine and fiberglass bathtubs, powered by wind, paddles, and six-horsepower engines, competing over a six-mile course. Air shows, including glider races, parachuting events, and air races, attracted as much attention in some localities as water events. Kites were popular, and several special Centennial kite flying contests drew much youth participation. Winter sports were predictably popular in Manitoba, as the Canadians used their snow and cold weather to good advantage in skiing events, snowshoe races, tobogganing, and figure skating. A six-hundred-mile snowmobile good will tour into the northern part of the province was exciting but failed to attract the attention expected by its planners.

Heritage '70

Heritage '70 recalled Manitoba's past. The more important

activities occurred in the field of publications, the school heritage programs, the interfaith activities, and the Centennial Caravan. Lighter programs included refurbishing an old locomotive, canoe trips over historic water routes, several Centennial year dedications, and a viewing of the Great Ring—a forty-inch ring with crystal plaques of the crests and flowers of all the provinces engraved therein, a special gift from the United States.

Public and private presses released several books with Centennial imprints which were financed in part by grants from the corporation. *Nor'Wester,* a sixty-four-page magazine-booklet, modeled after the first newspaper of the province, carried reproductions of articles, letters, and pictures of former days. The Manitoba Historical Society produced three official historical studies.

The school heritage program provided specialized training for youth groups all over Canada. Teachers and other specialists urged student participation in researching, writing, and dramatizing Manitoban history. Under their supervision students built models, stocked exhibitions, rummaged through attics and basements, interviewed senior citizens, and wrote and acted in plays.

Emphasis on history also appeared in other popular features. There were historymobiles—five 45-foot semi-trailers which traveled through the province, visiting most of the key cities with their multi-media presentations and experimental communications techniques. A "Gramps and Scamps" feature brought youth and older people together—breakfasting and conversing, then engaged in a history mystery hunt—a search for historical material wherein youngsters had to find not only hidden clues but something interesting about the historical area where the clue appeared.

Seven special days near the end of the Centennial also concentrated on historical themes. The legislation for Manitoba's entrance into the Confederation, the birthday of her entrance into the Confederation, a special Canada Day, and a Thanks-giving Day program all were celebrated during this week. These programs brought together men and women from all walks of life, who celebrated with food, music, speeches, and all that goes into a day of rejoicing for the legacy of the past.

The committee of religious leaders also operated under *Heritage '70*. This group, representing all of the faiths in Manitoba, provided the religious emphasis for the year. They prepared presentations for television and pulpits, and they sponsored Duke Ellington and the Neal Harris Singers in Centennial Concert Hall on Good Friday. In this concert the performers treated "songs of faith . . . in the traditional way, and through the jazz idiom." The committee held an interfaith breakfast for provincial legislators and the religious leaders, and they provided religious themes for other commemorative occasions.

Youth '70

Manitoba attempted to involve youth in the Centennial, but without total success. Besides contests and pageants to select Centennial princesses, "sing-songs," Bobby Gimby tours, and the honoring of Centennial babies, more serious youth programs included school-twinning, the young and intermediate voyageur programs, the International Youth Program, and "Platform '70."

School-twinning was based on a similar program in the Centennial of Canadian Confederation. It provided an exciting experience for many fifth- and sixth-graders by pairing schools in different parts of the province and giving the students an opportunity to live in a different community for a week. The voyageur programs took the exchange of students to the federal level and beyond. Students not only visited other provinces, but some journeyed to France, Great Britain, and the United States on special federal grants. Another look at the world beyond the province for Manitoba youth came in the International Youth

Program, a United Nations type of meeting held at Brandon University. Ninety-five young people from thirty-eight different UN countries participated in this program, discussing world problems and breaking down cultural barriers between nations.

One of the most exciting youth programs was "Platform '70," an affirmation of the role of the fine arts in the life of young Canadians. "Platform '70" revolved around a specially constructed stage in Winnipeg's Memorial Park, where drama groups performed their plays without cost to the audience. To attract other interests to the area, young instructors held open air classes in drama, ceramics, painting, and weaving for the young and for Senior Citizens.

July street festivals provided young people outlets for their energy and enthusiasm as well as an opportunity to join in celebration with older citizens. Cities roped off several blocks, making space available for diverse Centennial activities. There young and old danced to rock bands or popular orchestras—or stood by, watching and listening. They stopped at coffee shops to listen to folk groups sing, watched ballet performed on improvised stages, viewed art works that had been set up in the streets, attended plays, relaxed and drank beer in a German beer garden, and bought wares at hastily improvised flea markets. These street festivals attracted large and orderly crowds of Manitobans enjoying a unique experience.

Homecoming '70

To support a plan of inviting all former Manitobans back to the province for the celebration season, the corporation extended more than 5,500 invitations for them to return as individuals, with their families, or as members of a company or organization. Many did return, bringing with them friends and associates to swell the tide of tourists.

Recognition '70

Recognition '70 honored all those Canadians the corporation had singled out as special people in a Centennial year. Any person one hundred years old or older received greetings. The commission distributed anniversary pins to those citizens at least seventy-five years old who had spent most of their lives in the province. Two series of Centennial Farm Awards included one to farms that had been in the same family for at least a century, another going to a hundred and twenty-five farm families judged agricultural leaders. Finally, the 5,510 men and women who had worked so hard in the planning and execution of local Centennial activities were recognized with a special medallion.

The creative possibilities of people in a centennial are illustrated in few places more prominently than in Manitoba. Today the Royal Winnipeg Ballet and the Winnipeg Symphony Orchestra bring the world's great music to the people in a beautiful Centennial Concert Hall. This modern, acoustically perfect building, which seats 2,243 people, is available to all the citizens of the province. In a giant new Man and Nature Exhibit Hall, school children and adults share in the vast panorama of life throughout the world. With its 40,000 square feet and its 22-foot ceiling, this building is large enough to hold an unlimited variety of displays. In the planetarium, 315 people can stand in the luxury of a carpeted and air-conditioned room and study the complexities of space. Elaborate exhibits line the walls of four exhibition halls which surround the center area of this building, including four-color photo transparencies of the heavens at night. Two other halls in this building expand other themes, one on theory and the other on man's attempt to measure and explore the universe. Finally, in a last room, the visitor may follow in detail Manitoba's own achievements in the Space Age.

Audiences are also attracted to the new art gallery, whose 80,000 square feet show art from Tutankhamen to Van Gogh, with a specially sponsored children's arts exhibit, and a new theater nearby. Manitobans classify this last building as one designed for the next century but usable in this one.

To evaluate Manitoba's Centennial, one must think of the acquisition, construction, or restoration of libraries, museums, community halls, and other buildings of historical and aesthetic significance. In addition, the new parks and recreational facilities, the works of art, the Centennial books and plays, the composition of music, the many new paintings, and the acquisitions or improvements to collections of historical materials must be recalled. This Centennial had color, enthusiastic participants, and days filled with diversified events and programs. The prediction of the editor of *Manitoba '70* that the Centennial would mean something different to every person who participated touched the spirit of the times. His résumé summed up this spirit in these words: "It will be the laughter and the fun of our children; it will be the competition and excitement of our sporting events; it will be increasing participation in our enriched culture; it will be travel within our province's diversity and beauty; and it will be recognition of our pioneers as builders of Manitoba." [14]

Manitoba's Centennial was indeed all this for her citizens, present and future. Manitoba's strength as a relatively new province relates directly to her diversities—of race and religion; climate, terrain, and resources; occupations and interest. Her Centennial reveals this diversity—and this strength.

14. *Ibid.*

Bicentennial USA: Planning a Celebration

Though the Bicentennial of the American Revolution will be celebrated on three levels—national, state, and local—it is probably on the local level that the average citizen will be most intimately involved. It is also on this level that the sharpest disparities in planning will occur. A large community can hardly anticipate the same type of program as a small one. A community with a unique history or one with a direct association with the Revolutionary War will have a different point of view from those outside the original thirteen states. A community with extensive ethnic diversity will face problems different from a community of homogeneous population. An Eastern community may tend toward a perspective not shared in the West. Some communities will be in a position to share the creative efforts and resources of a historical society, a college, a library, a museum, or some other local cultural authority; others will not be so fortunate. Despite the many differences among communities, however, some of the initial questions will have a universal ring, some problems will have common solutions, and success or failure will depend upon established criteria. The common point of view may be found in the Bicentennial themes, which each community must identify in its own history. Local planners should look to national and state commissions for themes, programs, and support; but depending solely on plans originated elsewhere may restrict the possibilities for success and enjoyment. Those mysterious ingredients that give identity to a community also give meaning to its celebration, and it will be at the community level that the most appropriate and the most satisfying ideas will emerge.

Strategic planning usually centers around tangible problems: soliciting new and fresh leadership, getting large numbers of people involved, raising money, selecting and modifying themes, appeasing the discontented, and putting the machinery into action. Thus, even though little hitches may develop, the activity will continue unabated, the actors' enthusiasms undiminished, their paths toward predetermined goals marked with steady progress.

No planning committee will meet without raising questions of who and what should be included in the planning, what kind of organizational structure should be selected, what the cost will be, what resources should be utilized, who among the community's key leaders should be tapped, and what the objectives are. The struggles of communities which have faced similar problems in other centennials may provide some answers. Certainly some consideration of past actions by other people is important for any planner before he invests his time and resources. And yet, ultimately, each community must give its own answers. The suggestions of other communities and other sources may eliminate some of the tedium of planning, but in the final analysis each community must, within limits, set its own goals, face its own peculiar challenges, and work in concert with other communities in its own way. A long-needed library, a cultural center, a museum, or the preservation of a historic building may command immediate attention; some communities will work toward these ends in the name of the Bicentennial. In other communities the thrust may be more toward social issues, with people working together to eliminate problems that restrict the possibilities of celebration—a ghetto in a metropolitan complex, smog around an industrial center, and unwieldy local tax structure, a drug problem among the young, racial tensions in the local school system, a downtown traffic problem. Still others may see the parade, pageant, or local fair as their best or easiest means of expression and attempt litle else. And when one recalls the Yorktown, Virginia, Sesquicentennial of 1931, there is beauty even in the extravaganza of a fair. Historian Thomas Wood Stevens described the fair in *Yorktown Sesquicentennial Pageants:*

The Colonial fairgrounds, rich in the color of a pre-Revolutionary fair, attracted many thousands of visitors by the variety of offerings. Colonial figures walked the grounds hawking their wares; magicians and tumblers strolled about, followed by wide eyed children; Punch and Judy shows and marionettes vied with the attractions of the pageant field; the tepees of an Indian village, descendants of Virginia's aborigines, entertained by means of ceremonial and war dances. The livestock exhibits, jousting tourney, quoit pitching contest and old time Virginia fiddlers interested many.

Whatever its program of commemoration, a recommended first step is for a community to appoint a steering committee or a task force to set its course of action. Steering committees emerge in so many different ways that one is hard-pressed to find the right formula for their creation. Some receive mandates from local political authorities. Others spring up with no identifiable pattern of selection, the product of no particular planning or foresight, with one person seizing the initiative for getting people together to plan a celebration. Others represent uneasy factional compromises. Quite often, though, effective steering committees emerge from groups of people who have already demonstrated competence and ability to work together on another issue: a community planning or action group, a restoration committee, an intra-city church or fraternal grouping.

In 1966 Waterloo, New York, dramatically celebrated the fact that the first Memorial Day ceremony took place there a century earlier. The committee that directed the operations emerged under the leadership of two village trustees who reacted enthusiastically to a Memorial Day speech reminding them of such a heritage. This "Let's Do Something!" address led to the appointment of a committee and an impressive centennial observance. Minneapolis's 1936 commemoration of the hundredth anniversary of the arrival of the explorer Jean Nicollet seems to have been controlled by several local industries, which focused attention on their own industrial exposition and home appliance show. In Evanston, Illinois, city council action led to committee structure and planning in that city's Centennial in 1964. Kansas's 1961 celebration of its Centennial of admission into the Union as a state was largely in the capable hands of the state Historical Society, which offered leadership to the committees that emerged. As noted previously, North Carolina had two committees in action at the same time, in the early 1960s, one directing the state's Tercentenary, the other planning the North Carolina Civil War Centennial. The former committee held firm to a scholarly approach, stressing lectures, historical research and writing, and restoration. The latter sanctioned a more flamboyant affair, with re-enactments, parades, and elaborate pageants on both state and local levels. In both cases, however, the restraining voice of the state's historians was always there.

Some communities will not have such good fortune in the selection of committees; but to be successful, committees must carry weight in their communities, as well as within their own constituencies. They must be representative of significant community interests, diverse as they may be, and they must not be just figureheads to satisfy political and economic commitments. Leaders are always wise to seek out energetic, experienced and talented citizens, the "doers," as one planner has called them.[1] At the very least, each local steering committee should represent the following groups: municipal officials and leaders, service and social clubs, the Chamber of Commerce, the schools, staffs of local newspapers, the clergy, unions, youth organizations, prominent ethnic representatives, and historians. Every successful celebration will ultimately depend upon this little group of planners, working together in the best interests of the community.

The Connecticut Bicentennial Committee, which has been appointed to serve during our national celebration, shows good balance. It includes a novelist, a radio station executive, a historian, one banker interested in preservation, a state senator, an industrial engineer, an amateur genealogist, a librarian, the owner of a large amusement park, a retired teacher, and the leaders of two local professional societies.[2]

On any level it seems advisable to keep the steering committee small and manageable, possibly with no more than ten or twelve members. Smaller communities often choose larger numbers—to their detriment. Not only are large committees cumbersome, they are often ineffective because of erratic attendance, diffusive debate, and difficulty of consensus. On the other hand, the larger committee may be necessary to represent a diversity of community interests, even at the sacrifice of efficiency.

A dynamic chairman is essential to put the wheels into motion. Political power, personal magnetism, and diplomacy blend in a good committee leader; his program usually emerges in spite of even the most severe limitations. The ideal committee leader knows and loves his community, sympathizes with the general themes of the centennial program, and has already proven his leadership in other community projects which demanded tact, stamina, and initiative. In his manual for setting

---

1. Frank L. Wallace (Regional Officer, Nova Scotia), "Report: Canadian Centennial of Confederation." National Archives, Ottawa, Ontario, Canada.

2. *Connecticut Bicentennial Gazette*, 1 (Fall 1971), 2.

up arts committees, Joseph O. Fischer might have been outlining the qualities of good leadership when he wrote:

All that is required is hard work, courage, loyalty to objectives,
the inspiration of others to help, open-minded investigation,
analysis and planning, enlightened inquisitiveness, a balanced
point of view which appreciates people as well as facts, a
faith that people can improve their lives by improving their
communities, a faith in human values, a rather solid sense of how
to estimate hazards and some knack of raising funds. That's
all: Time, Energy, Ideas and Materializations.[3]

Ralph Newman, an important leader in Illinois's Sesquicentennial in 1968, supported the strong leader concept, suggesting emphatically that such an individual must give time and money and identify the projects he wishes to promote. Good leadership, he says, is more important than themes or objectives, for by the very nature of his personality a good leader will advance themes and ideals, while also serving as an ambassador of good will. Newman may overstate his case, for there is still something vital in democracy at work, even though personal antagonism may be involved, and many communities will thrive on concerted and diverse leadership. But he is right in implying that the need for enthusiastic leadership remains constant throughout and beyond the immediate commemoration.

The efforts of the steering committee should be supplemented by advisory committees and other subcommittes, which can not only deal with specifics, but also represent an even greater diversity of community elements. In 1963 Evanston, Illinois, counted 104 different organizations represented on its many Centennial subcommittees. Advisory committees should be carefully selected, and they should include talented people whose knowledge and experience relate directly to committee

3. Joseph O. Fischer, *Concepts for the Development of Local Arts Councils and Other Art Groups*, 2nd ed. (St. Louis: The Missouri State Council on the Arts, 1972) (hereafter cited as Fischer, *Concepts*).

responsibilities. Membership on a committee should depend primarily on what that member can contribute to the program.

Even the most basic advisory committee structure should include subcommittees on finance (ways and means), publicity, programs, history, and education. Arts, religious affairs, and publications involve other members of the community. British Columbia appointed a special committee on ethnic organizations in its 1958 Centennial, whose function was to encourage participation of the members of the various ethnic groups in the Centennial celebration of the province. Many American communities will find such a committee valuable. British Columbia also had an armed forces liaison subcommittee and an athletics and sports subcommittee. The subcommittees suggested by the excellent organizational structures in the case studies on the New Jersey Tercentenary and the Illinois Sesquicentennial, as well as the British Columbia Centennial, also offer suggestions.

Again, leadership is important. Time is always a factor in planning, and good leadership will encourage prompt and punctual attendance at meetings, the use of an agenda, and records to provide continuity of discussion and action. A good leader will prepare a calendar of events to alert community interests well in advance for specific involvement. Reserving "special days" provides opportunities for co-ordinating community efforts and highlighting local historic events.

Observations of various centennials on the national, state, and local levels reveal that the most effective steering committee goes to work immediately—beginning a dialogue among its members to determine direction. It is then that the committee members not only become acquainted but soon come to understand the nuances of each other's personalities. It is a time for educating the committee members, to research, study, and thresh out the general directions, objectives, and themes, as well as make necessary political contacts and prepare a responsible agenda. It is a time for planning the impossible, doing the possible.

One British Columbia committee spent about three productive months in this type of familiarization. Virginia had two important eight-month studies in planning her 350th anniversary for 1957. In New Jersey the many committees engaged in discussion over several weeks had such good results that John Cunningham later said that "Let's Talk Tercentenary" time was the most productive phase of New Jersey planning. Minnesota and North Carolina also were successful in similar periods of briefing. These were not times to pool ignorance but to determine directions, cement human relations, and focus on the significant issues that give the centennial meaning. Resolving differences, searching out new understanding, and learning to communicate in different languages will be real challenges in 1976. With rational men engaged in productive discussion, these challenges may indeed be opportunities. The preamble of the document that formed UNESCO in 1945 states that "wars begin in the minds of men." So also do misunderstandings and discrimination. "Let's Talk Bicentennial" is a preliminary action that committees on every level of planning will find productive as they approach 1976.

"Let's Talk Bicentennial" is also a good approach to extend into the community. It is a natural subject for forums, social action organizations, discussion groups, and speakers at weekly civic club luncheons and other club programs. It can also be extended to Scouts, historical societies, churches, the local ethnic organizations, schools, newspaper features, and radio and television programs. Stimulating citizen participation is usually a difficult task, whatever the occasion. "Let's Talk Bicentennial" offers a realistic approach for extending opportunities for participation in the crucial initial stages of planning.

During the give and take of discussion, steering committees will identify larger issues, patterns of action, and roadblocks; attract wide attention; and arouse enthusiasm. This is the point in planning when beard-growing, period costumes, and parades usually come in for serious consideration. This, then, is the time for decisive action, when committee members must set directions that emphasize the deeper meanings and responsibilities of celebration. If they offer only "diversion, entertainment and social outlets," they have not done their jobs well.[4] The committee misses an opportunity if, at this time, it does not channel creativity toward projects and programs that raise the quality of life in the community. Participation must ultimately involve the total person, and this involvement must begin early.

Life seldom runs a smooth course for planners of a centennial, no matter how effective their committee structure. Working with a volunteer staff, confronting problems without solutions, checking factional strife before it becomes explosive, trying to please all segments of the community—these are not easy matters. Too often trivia consumes the attention, patience, time, and money of the various staffs. Someone misplaces an important letter, another fails to answer a request for brochures, a clerk is rude to a prospective donor, the expensive publication which the president of a garden club requests eight hundred copies of for her next meeting runs short, newspapers garble an important news item, the best secretary resigns to have her baby, an important speaker is scheduled for two engagements on the same evening or is unavailable to an important group at a crucial time.

Grievances pile up. Within the office discrepancies and intemperance in the use of credit cards, travel sheets, insurance, and liquid refreshment may appear. Untrained personnel can mishandle office equipment. Criticisms appear through the mail, over the telephone, and in the news media. Harassment comes in strange packages—from the man in the street who feels uninvolved, from those who can do the job better, from those who feel the job should not be done at all, even from those who have no idea what the bloody centennial is all about anyway! And always there is the pest who uses friends in high places to pressure for an important job.

4. Fischer, *Concepts*, 1.

It is also difficult to keep good people on committees. Threatened with numerous time-consuming meetings, the industrious desert the committee for other interests. It is imperative that chairmen recognize this possibility and try to make the organization work as efficiently as possible, so as to keep the highest caliber of representation. Sometimes there is also the problem of how to get rid of a committee member. Though he may prove lazy, indifferent, callous, insensitive, or self-seeking, dismissal can create dissension within the ranks as well as political repercussions outside.

Planners will do well in these initial discussions to consult state and local historical societies for counsel. These organizations have trained personnel, facilities, resources, ideas, and pipelines to other services that local planners cannot afford to overlook. The daily life of the local historian is involved with commemorating the past, and he has already grappled with many of the problems facing the Bicentennial planners.

If final results are to be more than memories of parades, pageants, contests, and frivolity, then significant objectives must command planners' initial attention. Objectives differ from community to community, but they give focus and direction to committee actions. St. Augustine, Florida, stressed local interests in its four-hundredth anniversary with building plans that included a research library, an exhibition center, and a park. Only the exhibition center materialized. In 1946 Iowans sought with some success to establish a historical society in every county of the state. Kansas hoped to tell the Kansas story to more than a million people in 1961, and did. Talbot County, Maryland, spurned the prospects of an $85,000 pageant proposed by commercial representatives to give its citizens a chance to produce their own program in a "dignified yearlong observance." Waterloo, New York, accomplished its objectives—congressional recognition of Waterloo as the birthplace of Memorial Day and a proper celebration for such a centennial—

by keeping centennial observances on Memorial Day, 1966, simple, short, and to the point.

In its 1970 Centennial, Kansas City simply stressed civic unity and pride. British Columbia, in its initial meeting, set up two ambitious objectives: its Centennial was to be "based on a community level," not directed "totally from the top," and it was "not to be primarily . . . a tourist attraction." Minnesota stated the principal objective of her 1958 Centennial very simply: "Sell Minnesota to Minnesotans—and to the world."

States have used slogans and symbols to good effect in past centennial observances. Slogans and symbols have appeal, they can be publicized, they can represent something important in the community's past. They often establish an instant identity as image and metaphor. Alaska used its state motto, "North To The Future," as a Centennial slogan in 1964. Mankato, Minnesota, stuck with the more conventional "Century of Progress" for its Centennial in 1952. New Jersey selected its slogan from a statewide competition: "1664 to 1964—For Three Centuries —People, Purposes, Progress." South Carolina's recent Tricentennial was a "Festival of History."

Symbols have been just as important in arousing community interest. After all, a centennial is in itself a symbolic occasion. The six stacked "cannon balls" on New York's Bicentennial letterhead have already caught on as a symbol throughout that state. The Massachusetts Bicentennial Commission chose the Liberty Tree—symbol of freedom throughout the Colonies— to signify commemorative events. For her Centennial, Alaska adopted a seal of commemoration that sported a totem pole with the several stages of the state's historical development cut into it. South Carolina may have overdone symbolism by using three designs for its Tricentennial in 1970. One was a simple but attractive logogram—three slanted parallelograms clustered atop the dates 1670 and 1970. The official Tricentennial seal appeared in two other designs, the formal one showing "a triangular design of the official South Carolina seal resting atop the seal of the Lords Proprietor . . . and the royal British seal of the House of Hanover," while the popular seal pictured a palmetto tree in a circle with the lettering: "South Carolina Tricentennial 1670–1970."

Whatever the larger themes of nation or state, the local community should discover its own particular theme and identify and create its own symbols—keeping them in line with the sentiments of the larger issues when possible. Though the American Revolution Bicentennial Commission has issued an official symbol for the Bicentennial, states and communities are already at work devising their unique designs. Many have used contests as a popular and productive means of selecting symbols and seal designs. Contests may involve local schools, art departments, creative citizens, and interested outsiders. Talent and enthusiasm often blend to create a symbol of dignity and lasting quality.

Symbols, slogans, and objectives become tools which effective publicity committees and good public relations teams employ to communicate the developing program to the larger community. The chairman of the publicity committee should be an expert in his field, informed in the patterns of operations of all the available communications media,[5] and capable of using these media to build enthusiasm. He should be flexible, conscientious, energetic, and adept in self-expression. He should also be familiar with his total program, keeping abreast of the latest developments, conveying all pertinent facts to the public with speed and color. His committee should have a voice in policy-making and the support of all the other committees.[6]

Newspapers, radio, and television are first lines of presentation, but publicity committees should also enlist the support of community leaders, organize speakers' bureaus, issue bulle-

5. In some Southern states, for instance, there is better afternoon newspaper circulation than morning.

6. See Fischer, *Concepts*, 33–55, for an analysis of public relations proceedings.

tins and news releases, advertise in significant places, and sponsor special events and contests that will promote interest. Good publicity teams will capitalize on the historical events of their own communities as well as on all other local resources, as they spread the word of the Centennial events. They will feed material setting the tone and spirit of the occasion to the publications of schools, businesses, churches, local clubs and organizations, and ethnic groups. Public relations efforts will be geared to "a gradual, steady intensification of publicity, widening the area of interest, and informing more and more people as plans develop." [7]

Publicity must be a sustained effort, dignified but simple, and stimulating to all different elements of the community. Close ties with state and national agencies in a large commemoration will provide copy and ideas for publicity, but in the final analysis local publicity will capitalize on understanding of local community spirit. Not only will the local PR man write copy, he will inspire others to use their own means of publicity: window displays, newspaper ads and features, local lectures, forums, films, slides, posters, and other ways. Though every committee must be involved in publicity to some degree, the ultimate burden will rest on the publicity chairman and his staff.

A survey of the publicity committees of several past centennials has produced the following list of suggestions for those committees now going into action for the Bicentennial: (1) Begin your work by making a survey of all historic actions, personages, and places that relate directly to the local scene, stressing those with a direct tie-in with the commemoration; (2) Publicize local concerns in articles, pictures, and other news releases; (3) Use pictures of yesterday and today for colorful contrast; visit all local media—press, radio, television, etc., informing them of centennial activities, requesting their sup-

---

7. Manitoba Centennial Corporation Annual Report, 1965–1966, 37.

port, and offering your own co-operation; (4) Invite all media to centennial meetings, providing them with photographs and press releases of all announcements;[8] (5) Use special stationery, colorful brochures, and impressive signs to attract attention; (6) Use the centennial symbol, local or otherwise, in all forms of publicity—making it a familiar sight throughout the community.

Publicity efforts will be more successful if large numbers of people are involved. Public forums and discussion groups will increase local interest and broaden participation. Key people and organizations should be enlisted and youth involved in responsible ways to carry centennial messages to a larger constituency. Special events, observances, and visiting speakers should be played up, with subcommittees appointed to handle special projects and programs. All those who participate should be recognized with letters of commendation, badges, or special mention, with such actions publicized in the name of the Centennial.

Good publicity committees will find helpful the suggestions offered by a New Jersey Civil War Centennial guide as significant issues to stress in any centennial: the importance, fascination and drama of history; "the qualities of life . . . needed for a worthwhile and meaningful existence in the preservation of our society"; men and ideals that give larger meaning to commemoration; understanding of central issues that gives the Centennial contemporary meaning; "mission and destiny," or how men turned the tide in crucial times, how events of the past shaped the contours of the present. This is really a plea for reassessment and rededication to principles that give meaning to that which is being commemorated.

Good publicity can also help resolve one of the most pressing concerns faced by commemoration planners—finances. Finances

---

8. The National Trust for Historic Preservation suggests printing an invitation to newspapers to reply to "What Would You Like to See Saved in Your Community?," *Preservation for the Bicentennial,* 1.

come into focus quickly. Some central committees will begin with a nest egg, an allotment of funds from state or local sources to be used at their discretion. Others will obtain funds from donations of public-spirited citizens. Most, however, will not be so fortunate and will be forced to operate for long periods of time with limited funds or with what funds they can raise from their own endeavors. This is why white elephant and bake sales, telethons, tag days, flea markets, car washes, lotteries, door-to-door solicitation, subscription dinners, pageants, and other money-making enterprises appear so prominently in much of today's celebration. Other means of local fund raising include sales of publications, programs, and medals, setting up booths at fairs or on the streets to peddle items of every description, and selling tickets to programs and tours. Personal solicitation is popular and effective. If handled properly, these means of money raising can engender enthusiasm that carries over into more concrete programs. Commercialism of any sort, however, poses dangers. It may become an end in itself and siphon enthusiasm away from objectives. It may also desecrate an otherwise exemplary program.

What can be done about finances? Too often committees must tie themselves too closely to their sources of revenue to give their programs the full range of their expectations. Strictly local programs probably have little hope for outside assistance unless the event can be associated with something larger. Planners should expect some outside help in a national Bicentennial, however. The case studies of national and state centennials already described give clues as to how a few programs raised funds, but a study of many past centennials in this country indicates that there is just no pat way to keep money flowing steadily into commemoration coffers.

Some communities will turn to professional fund raisers for at least part of their finances, as did New Jersey in its Tercentenary and Indianapolis, Indiana, in its Sesquicentennial. While in some cases this can be a profitable venture, the dangers are the same as those involved in hiring a professional firm to plan a celebration—local initiative is lost, a sizable fee is charged, and the natural spontaneity and larger involvement of citizens is threatened. Again, however, each community must judge its own potential and then decide its own direction.

Much can be said for matching grants in financing centennials. Matching grants in Canada, Great Britain, and in American colleges, universities, and philanthropic groups have produced tangible results. In the Bicentennial of the American Revolution they would stimulate projects on every level of participation. Matching grants could inspire local communities to their most creative efforts. They would open the way for planners to approach local organizations, businesses, community leaders, and other citizens for co-operation and financial support. They would encourage more concerted effort within and between communities, more co-operation and studied planning in presentation, and a continuing appeal to community spirit. This would have the double-barreled advantage of encouragement and control—encouragement to proceed with a good program despite limited resources; control, not to restrict, but to develop exciting and worthwhile presentations in the proper spirit of celebration.

While the danger of "pork-barreling," misappropriation of funds, favoritism, and mediocre projects accompanies matching grants, a screening committee could offer controls. This committee would consider plans of all sorts—from the building of health centers, museums, libraries, and art galleries to attacking identifiable community problems or iniatiating experimental or remedial education programs. Even unusual projects, as the rebuilding of the town privy in British Columbia certainly was, may be appropriate.

Journalist Kevin P. Phillips has suggested a larger Bicentennial project which would relate well to matching grants—a major federal effort to recapture our physical and cultural pasts:

There are historic sites and buildings to be restored and
repaired; old villages, factories, farmsteads and ports to be
researched and then reconstructed as they once were; wild rivers,
national parks and scenic areas to be improved or cleaned up;
and historic books and guides to be written to catalog every
facet of Americana.[9]

Phillips' suggestion would also have the positive effect of providing jobs for young men and women interested in local
history and archeology, but who upon graduation from college
have found no jobs.

Local committees could work up their plans, present them
to a central committee for a review, then if properly encouraged
proceed to raise the necessary matching funds. In this way they
would arouse enthusiasm for the project itself. Parades, pageants, costume parties, beard growing, and medallion striking
would follow only as corollaries to the original goals. Strict
controls would nip in the bud the undesirable projects: the
elaborate pageant; the extravagant musicale; the costly parade;
programs with prejudicial racial and ethnic overtones; and even
the undue cluttering up of the countryside with historical
markers, an expensive practice that has already reached a saturation point in many places.

Matching grants are no cure-all, however, and funding a
Bicentennial program on any level will continue to present
problems. The ways and means subcommittee must be a strong
one, staffed by individuals who know the community and how
to raise money. They will have to promote their program to
industrial and business leaders; solicit funds from civic groups,
clubs, and other community organizations; and devise other
dignified ways to acquire capital for their community programs,
realizing all the while that all these sources of income are subject to repeated solicitations. John F. von Daacke, former head

---

9. *New Jersey Historical Commission Newsletter*, 2 (April 1972), 6. This
syndicated newspaper article was recently written into the *Congressional Record*.

of the local history section of the New York Office of State
History, has suggested, however, that if all the other "committees are well formed, the work of the finance committee will be
greatly simplified." [10] He stresses the importance of "starter
funds" in towns' annual budgets as well as special funds allotted
for unusual purposes. Raymond S. Sivesind in Wisconsin agrees
that the ways and means committee has a heavy responsibility
"for raising money as well as disbursing it." [11] He even suggests
the possibility of borrowing money in order to get the wheels
in motion. Borrowing, however, can be a dangerous practice,
and committees should initiate their drives for funds as soon as
possible to reduce the need for borrowing. Fund raisers should
be well prepared in advance to present an over-all plan. They
should always have a clear idea of their project, making personal
solicitation when possible. They must always be able and willing to justify the amount for which they ask, though they
should not hesitate to ask for more than they expect to receive.
Mailing requests for money is a poor substitute for the face-to-
face encounter. The follow-up is also important, if just to thank
the donor. [12]

Even in the midst of solicitation and fund raising, planners
should keep another point in mind: some of the best programs
will be those that require very little funding but capitalize on
creativity. John Cunningham of New Jersey once stressed that
communities can do a great deal without large sums of money,
with some of the best and most creative programs emerging
from communities that are forced to work with a bare minimum of financial contribution. Therefore, it is imperative that
enthusiastic and creative people become involved quickly in all

10. John F. von Daacke, *Presenting the Past* (Albany: Office of State History,
State Education Department, 1970), 14.

11. Raymond S. Sivesind, *How to Organize a Centennial Celebration*, Bulletin
of the State Historical Society of Wisconsin, No. 100 (1956), 5.

12. See "Programming for Fund-Raising," in Preservation for the Bicentennial Series, National Trust for Historic Preservation.

phases of planning—to promote the best interests of the community as well as the larger themes suggested by the exciting occasion itself.

The money problem relates directly to the main function of the steering committee, the creation of a program. Here again the planner faces many difficult questions. When is the most effective time to present a program? What type of presentation will be best for the occasion? What personnel and equipment resources are available? What long-range effects can be drawn from the accomplishments of the moment with the talent at hand? How can the community best utilize its time, money, and personnel?

In the preface I suggested that to produce more than "sound and fury," Bicentennial planners must recognize man's search for identity, his needs for festivity, and his innate urge to create. Planners must work toward these goals within the limits of available resources, personnel, and leadership. In addition, they must select practical projects to celebrate. The following suggestions offer some procedures for program-developing: (1) Choose the program or project and begin working at it early. It takes time to stimulate interest, organize committees, and do all the homework necessary for good programs and projects. Even two years is a short time for a community to organize a committee and produce a program. (2) Build programs on the needs and strengths of a community rather than upon its weaknesses. (3) Become familiar with the state and national commissions. Close association is almost always valuable to local planners. (4) Take cognizance of all disadvantaged groups in committee structure and programs and insure more than their token involvement. (5) Formulate programs that appeal to the largest possible community interest, encouraging maximum participation. (6) Keep in mind that this is the Bicentennial of the American Revolution, a significant event in our nation's history. It is a time to focus on the nation's revolutionary beginnings, its two centuries of growth, developing patterns of life that have become models for other nations, and its promising future in the midst of complex crises. Communities in states beyond the original thirteen need not, however, depend solely upon Revolutionary War battles, struggles in colonial legislatures, and eighteenth-century heroes. In the hands of enlightened leadership, local programs will join local and national themes and interests to increase knowledge and insure greater understanding.

Local centennial celebrations in the United States are not as complex or as demanding as national ones, but they are numerous and increasing every year. Some are well planned, emphasizing long-range goals and utilizing local talent and resources to best advantage. Others depend more on the outside agency or the imported leader to stimulate programs and events. Still others are just days of poorly directed frivolity, dreaded for months preceding the time of celebration, forgotten or regretted in the aftermath.

Though many communities and counties have celebrated their pasts in special ceremonies, the available research does not lead to absolute conclusions. A casual study of many of them, however, seems to show that when a community had a centennial that was more than just a holiday it had one or more of the following assets: (1) a historical agency, library, or museum that seized the initiative and pushed toward historical understanding; (2) a single citizen or a citizens' group that moved in fast, took over planning the celebration, and gave it firm directions; (3) economic and personnel resources that enabled political leaders to initiate a program; (4) the presence of a pride or love of community already demonstrated in community actions—its concern for civic beauty, for its disparate groups, and for its cultural growth; (5) a historical event of some importance in the community; and (6) energetic and co-operative communications media. Some of these resources will be noted in the following case studies of community centennials. Among the hundreds of case studies available, the following introduce centennial arrangements in several types of communities, including one university community. Most of them parallel earlier arrangements demonstrated in the larger case studies. In reality the small community faces the same problems as the largest unit, but in the end these communities usually concentrated on a shorter period of celebration and a single project for commemoration.

SAGINAW TREATY SESQUICENTENNIAL

The Saginaw Treaty Sesquicentennial commemorated an actual historical event—the signing of a treaty between area Indians and government representatives that transferred more than six million acres of land to the United States. This then is a celebration of beginnings, and historical persons and scenes commemorated relate to the fact. Saginaw wisely chose to celebrate, however, its entire 150 years, and its exhibitions, pageants, and other activities related to the longer period.

A local committee of interested citizens supported by "an endless number of committees" prepared the many events of this Sesquicentennial.[13] The committee worked for several months putting together a varied program for a community that seems to have shown very little initial interest. They publicized their proceedings extensively through the two local newspapers and radio stations. Speakers at local clubs and schools told of Sesquicentennial arrangements. A Saginaw Treaty Sesquicentennial symbol, an outline of the state of Michigan with treaty acres darkened, appeared on plates, glassware, ashtrays, clothing, and other items to publicize the Centennial in other areas.

Saginaw concentrated its Sesquicentennial celebrations into eight days in September 1969. Festivity dominated the proceedings. Festivity included many of the usual centennial activities

13. Mayor Warren C. Light to the people of Saginaw Valley, quoted in *The Saginaw Treaty Sesquicentennial Historical Program.*

—antique car parades, a snowmobile race, rock concerts, nightly fireworks, a pancake and sausage outing, and many water sports. Two queen contests eventually drew sixty contestants, and the usual beard growing, fashion shows, and bargain days were held. The main program was a pageant, *The Valley People,* directed by a visiting professional company. This pageant followed the standard theme—the presentation of the history of the community—and a common format—the participation of hundreds of local citizens in the production. This was not a "play," said one of the company directors; it was "a chronological progression." Players pantomimed seventeen episodic sequences, including stories of the trappers, lumbermen, farmers, Indians, Jesuit Fathers, Lewis and Clark, swaggering rivermen, soldiers, and even the French observer Alexis de Tocqueville. Performed on a 250-foot-wide stage, lighted by 4½ tons of equipment, the pageant was indeed spectacular. Live animals pulled wagons and coaches across the stage before 18-foot-high backdrops. Rear screen projectors showed historical scenes and created unusual visual effects. The costumes of the local players were elaborate beyond description.

Though newspaper editorials praised the Centennial committees for their actions and spoke enthusiastically of the days of celebration, the "tight smiles" and "crossed fingers" that promoters of the extravaganza had before the performance continued well beyond the conclusion of all the ceremonies. *The Valley People* was supposed to draw 20,000 paid admissions; it drew only 5,000, leaving a remarkable deficit. Twenty-five hundred Sesquicentennial books containing the program of the pageant remained unsold, also a great loss. Nearly a month after the pageant had ended, Sesquicentennial leaders were still appealing for the return of unsold consigned items in order to help balance the budget.

There were other complaints. One large institution claimed that it had been left out of the Sesquicentennial book. Involvement of ethnic groups seems to have left something to be desired. Some citizens wrote the newspaper that they were ashamed of Black women who dressed up as part of the "good old days." One of the Blacks countered by asking whether they were supposed to "wear slave chains, head rags, torn and dirty clothes." The greatest misfortune to some was the fact that more than a year after the Centennial ended, "a number of large bills incurred by the Sesquicentennial were still unpaid."

A larger historical perspective may yet give the Saginaw Treaty Sesquicentennial continuing meaning. It appears to have become the springboard "for a permanent memorial to the Woodlands Indians," the former occupants of that great region. Eventually they hope that this area will become "a forest preserve in which ecological and environmental research could be conducted by university specialists." [14] Another interesting and unusual aspect of the Sesquicentennial was the "sister-city" project. Saginaw's sister city in Japan, Tokushima, sent its mayor and his wife to the celebration, as well as a $300 donation toward the establishment of the Saginaw Japanese Gardens. The Japanese also added two large lanterns especially designed by Japanese sculptors for the gardens.

Depending almost exclusively upon the pageant to raise its funds, the Saginaw Sesquicentennial did not reach the expectations of its planners. Many people had fun, but until the larger memorial project is completed, little more was accomplished than calling attention to the historical dimension of the actual treaty signing and the well-defined effort to relate that heritage to the modern Saginaw Valley area.

EVANSTON (ILLINOIS) CENTENNIAL

Centennial format, objectives, and programs have become so standardized that it seems obvious that celebrations now more or less follow a pattern. Saginaw's celebration is typical. It is

---

14. Editorial, *Saginaw News*, September 17, 1969.

helpful, then, to find a centennial where planners tried the unusual, related it to the particulars of the community, and
depended upon the creativity of their own citizens for the
program. Evanston broke the patterns of pageant-oriented celebrations in its Centennial of 1963.

Evanston hates debt, and its planners were reluctant to spend
city funds for a celebration. The City Council took charge of
the Centennial proceedings, placing one of the aldermen in
charge of the standing committee selected to plan the ceremony.
The chairman was a capable but somewhat conservative leader,
and the program followed the patterns of his leadership. Objectives were commendable: helping shape the future of the
community, improving understanding, recognizing past Evanston accomplishments, and encouraging organizations to produce their own programs.

Evanston had many ingredients for a productive celebration.
It was near enough to Chicago to enjoy the facilities of that city.
It had an excellent museum and a historical society that gave
enlightened leadership. Its industries were willing to participate and its university supported the celebration. It had its
share of imaginative, intelligent, responsive, and energetic
citizens; and a friendly hometown newspaper covered the Centennial in detail.

A small executive committee directed most of the Centennial
activities, operating on a low budget and without the usual
hoopla of beard growing, phony arrests, and dressups. The
executive committee also developed a complex subcommittee
system with heavy representation from business.

Planners chose for Evanston's Centennial symbol a sketch of
the city fountain—in itself a symbol of temperance and so-
briety—which had been set up on a Fourth of July several
years back in the hometown of the national WCTU headquarters. Each citizen received a decal of this symbol with the
suggestion that he display it in a prominent location. The committee also mailed out a questionnaire soliciting program

suggestions. A series of newspaper cartoons showing late nine-teenth-century factionalism in city politics also helped publicize the coming celebration.

The four-day celebration began on July 4. The morning of the Fourth was devoted to sports events at the high schools and the playgrounds. "Let Freedom Ring," a preliminary to the noon ceremony at the municipal building, featured the ringing of bells and a reading of the Declaration of Independence. A parade, a twilight show, and a fireworks display at the stadium were followed by a pageant written and performed by local citizens.

The second day's main event was a visit to many of the beautiful homes of the city. The third day was a "Salute Evanston Industry Day," with open houses and descriptive lectures. The day ended on a festive note with dancing in the streets. Sunday morning, the last day, featured commemorative church services —but the afternoon was given over to boating, water-skiing, and skits on the waterfront. The climax of the day came when the committee gathered for a large ice cream social to commemorate the invention, in Evanston, of the sundae—created by an unknown fountain clerk who was circumventing a blue law stating that no soda water was to be used on the Sabbath.

During the four days the arts, especially music, were also prominent, with festivals of school children singing folk music and the classics. Local choirs and orchestras vied with visiting artists for the music stage, but the community took pride in its own music, using "two fully competent Evanston orchestras" to provide much of the music. The city named a new park Centennial Park for the occasion, and the city government sponsored an exhibition.

The amazing thing about Evanston's program is the low cost, though many people did donate time, services, and talents. The final income from all sources to the Centennial commission totaled $7,799.79, which included $6,271 in contributions. Few communities have gotten as much mileage from Centennial funds and preparations. Though no great breakthroughs in community development resulted, the community did build a Centennial Park and take a new look at their past.

Indiana University's elaborate Sesquicentennial program in 1970 called for a year of "dedication, commitment, and festivity." The general theme emphasized "The Pursuit of Light and Truth, Pathway to Enduring Greatness." Its special planning committees included representatives from the staff and faculty, students, alumni, and community leaders. Planners focused on four special days to commemorate four special events: the signing of the legislative act creating the university, Founder's Day, Commencement, and the beginning of the new academic year.

The university listed three major objectives: to honor the university and the people who had made up its complement for 150 years; to commemorate the achievements of the university, past and present; and to examine critically the new directions in which the university should move. The Board of Trustees divided the planners into two major groups, one to handle fund-raising, and the other, celebration ceremonies and activities.

The Sesquicentennial Birthday Fund Program was co-ordinated with the first major fund-raising campaign which Indiana had conducted since 1922. University officials announced eight major projects for this fund, six of them on the Bloomington campus. These projects focused on improving academic, artistic, cultural, historic, and sports pursuits. Major construction included a musical arts center; an assembly hall, one of the largest convention centers in the Midwest, with a theater for 8,000; a basketball arena seating 17,500; an auditorium for 20,000; a Hoosier Heritage Hall, dedicated to preservation of history artifacts and folklore; and a fine arts pavilion. This fund also supported endowed professorships, scholarships, and important library acquisitions. Planners predicted accurately that the momentum of the Sesquicentennial would add much to the enthusiasm for a birthday fund.

The second committee made and carried out elaborate plans for programs and events for the centennial year. The entire program was generally oriented toward the academic, but certain special programs were set aside for dances, rock bands, and light drama. Student- and faculty-wide colloquia probed major questions in chemistry and mathematics. Special Sesquicentennial lecturers elaborated on biological concepts, literature, "Man's concept of reason," biochemistry, dentistry, and the history of the university. The University School of Law held a symposium entitled "The Response of Society to Unusual and Extreme Pressures by Organized Groups." Exhibits in the Fine Arts Museum represented good balance: "The American Scene: 1820 to 1900," "Indiana University: Past-Present-Future," "Young Print Makers of 1970," "The American Scene: The Twentieth Century," "American Painting 1960-1970," "Islamic Art," "One Hundred Master Prints," and "Masterpieces of Sculpture." Of special interest was a Black Arts Festival in November with exhibits of the leading American Black artists appearing under the title "An Ebony Excursion." An opera, a convocation of a modern dance group, a Broadway musical, several special School of Music concerts of different instruments, and a faculty music series presented variety.

University participation in centennials, alas, is usually lukewarm, its constituency often cold to the festive nature of such affairs. Universities can find help in planning special Bicentennial services of programs, however. The film of Indiana University's Sesquicentennial activities, which is available from the university library, and the well-filled Sesquicentennial calendar produced for use during the year provide practical "how-to" knowledge and inspiration.

POTPOURRI

A look at certain aspects of several other local commemorations shows individual differences that appear even in similar experiences.

The Yorktown Sesquicentennial of 1931 featured three historical pageants, presented on successive days. They were "A Pageant of the Colonies," "A Pageant of the Yorktown Campaign," and "Yorktown Anniversary Day Pageant and Masque." Thomas Wood Stevens, a professional director of pageants, wrote and produced all three productions. Approximately 3800 people participated, with the leading actors drawn from as far as 75 miles away. Two regimental bands from a nearby army base provided music.

Yorktown's Sesquicentennial was actually a national affair, with a special congressional appropriation of $200,000. The state of Virginia added $12,000 and set up a commission of ten members to handle the intricacies of celebration. Visitors, who numbered over 300,000 in the four-day celebration, participated fully in the festivity—visiting homes and local gardens and getting a feel of the rich heritage of a colonial setting. Besides the pageants, tours, and special exhibitions, there were many dedications, and important speakers included dignitaries from the United States and abroad. Both Marshall Pétain and General Pershing sat on the speakers' platform on the third day of celebration. President Hoover gave an address on the last day.

San Diego's 200th anniversary celebration in 1969 extended its activities over "4,000 square miles of San Diego County, plus special programs in Tijuana, Mexico." It included a wide variety of festivities—"fairs, fiestas, music, drama, major sports, with an emphasis on water recreation, and spectacular parades." Its special programs included a salute to the Fifty States program, each state invited to select a week, during which time it would display exhibits, send dignitaries, have its flag honored, and present a military review and a "State Day" picnic. Another special program was a ham radio operator's program, with 7,000 operators daily sending anniversary information out of San Diego. There was an oceanside sport-fishing derby, a flower of the month program, and an industry open house. In the "Warm Lights of Welcome" program, San Diego businessmen trimmed their buildings with Christmas lights, with the lights changing colors on the first of the year and remaining lit throughout 1969.

Something seemed to be happening every day throughout the entire year of celebration in San Diego: swimming contests, ski-fests, opera performances, exhibitions, ice skating, local drama, elaborate musicals, all sorts of sporting events and contests, personal appearances of dignitaries, spotlight on other countries' programs, church services, flower shows, and an outstanding Shakespeare festival in Balboa Park's Old Globe Theater.

Planners attempted to include an important ethnic culture in the fiestas and special programs, emphasizing Mexican art and dancing. Though these programs attracted great tourist interest, they also produced cries of tokenism and discrimination from some elements of the Chicano population, who felt that they were not receiving proper recognition as part of the city's history. The critical felt that the Centennial expression was not exemplary of the other cultures, nor concerned with more immediate needs.

On paper this Bicentennial appears as an unusual community effort, with leadership creativity at a peak. Its *Official Souvenir and Program Guide*—with its interesting maps, its color photo graphs, its short historical narrative, its guides, and its stories of contemporary San Diego—is one of the finest. This bicentennial attracted much attention and represents a peak in festive celebration—sometimes at the expense of more enduring projects.

The Canadian Centennial Committee of Burnabee, British Columbia, informed a large number of people of a series of programs through a special newsletter. Their programs also represent sort of a collage of festivity—a miniature chuckwagon race, a period-dress garden party, and a giant birthday cake with a hundred girls dressed as candles dancing around it. Other programs included "Scotch on the Rocks," an ice-filled pool of performing polar bears in January; the *Best of Barkerville;* a women's pageant entitled *A Hundred Years of Progress,* a Scouts' Centennial action show, a clean-up program, a local drama players' festival, and a series of miscellaneous programs designed for nearly every taste.

Calgary, Alberta, also showed regional festive variety in its celebration of the same Centennial. Horses were popular in races, rodeos, and shows. Frontier influences prevailed in western barbecues, trail rides, trap-shooting tournaments, stampedes, square dance jamborees, horse shows, and a western ball. Cherbrook in the same province decided not to have a "big bash" and instead erected two illuminated fountains in the community square and added a reading room to the public library. What started out in Calgary to be a two-day celebration turned into a nine-day affair with over 30 major activities developing—"Centennial Fever," one person described it. Baltimore's "Star Spangled Banner Sesquicentennial" of 1964 focused on art films, classical and pop concerts, baseball games, tours, horse shows, battlefield tours, sailing regattas, and special musical and dramatic shows. The highlight of the program was a pyrotechnic re-enactment of the bombardment that inspired the writing of the National Anthem. The program guide of this sesquicentennial is well worth adding to any collection.

The Golden Spike Centennial at Promontory Summit, Utah, in 1967 featured the famous driving of the final spike, with music and a pageant supporting the occasion. Planners prepared the participants for days in advance with art and history exhibits, a railroad pictorial display, a symphony concert, a railway history symposium at the University of Utah, a convention of the Brotherhood of Locomotive Engineers, a steam train excursion, a gun-collectors' show, and a literary workshop.

Oakland County, Michigan, extended its Sesquicentennial of 1970 over six months. Crafts and art displays were among the exhibitions seen in museums and open houses. Photographic displays with themes on communications, education, government, culture, and recreation appeared in the Old City Hall and on the mall. A special Sesquicentennial "history day" focused on library materials, and a "heritage day" program probed deep into the history of the community. In the Meadowbrook Musical Festival some of the nation's best classical, popular, and jazz artists presented the *Heart of the Hills,* a well-received concert. Western Electric Company's colorful Centennial Exposition was an illustrated history of communications in the state. Other activities included boat races, a fifty-mile bicycle race on an Oakland parking lot, a Sesquicentennial soapbox derby, a metropolitan youth fitness tourney, a zoo day featuring "Back to School Animal Antics," and a musical salute to the State of Michigan with the performance of Meredith Willson's *The Music Man.*

The Bay St. Louis (Mississippi) Centennial; the Mankato (Minnesota) Centennial; Warsaw, New York's 125th Anniversary celebration; South Carolina's Calhoun County Golden Jubilee; and the McKenzie (Tennessee) Tri-county Centennial —to name only a few—all employed the Rogers Company; and their pageant titles have the familiar patriotic ring: the *Bay St. Louis Story, Century of Progress, Warsaw's Yesteryears, A Century Turns,* and *Our Golden Heritage.* Each focused on a week of activity, had beards and bonnets, a centennial queen and her entourage, special days, and wide local participation in the pageant.

Bay St. Louis personalized its celebration with a distinct Dixie flavor in its grand ball, beauty and "century of styles" contests, and parade. Mankato's Centennial was in the tradition of the West, with many of its exhibitions aimed at farm family viewing. Warsaw also appealed to agricultural interests with quilt shows, white elephant sales, cooking exhibitions, horse shows, greased-pig contests, milking and wood-cutting contests, and its dog and horse shows. McKenzie generated a festive program under an active local committee structure. The most progressive event of the program was government day, when young people took over the city government and many of the activities of celebration for the entire day. Only white youth participated. Calhoun County had a great deal of music presented by orchestras, pipe organs, and a band. One unusual event that attracted both black and white members of the community was a lecture on county history by a *white* speaker using the famous Gullah dialect.

Benson, Minnesota, in its Centennial of 1970, dispensed with the pageant and held a series of important special days. Flower displays, arts and crafts shows, teas, style shows, and special exhibitions of interest to the homemaker marked ladies' day. A special outdoor theater program, including music by one of the male groups, brought this day to its close. Agriculture day included a farm-city softball game, music appropriate for the farm community, sweet-corn-eating contest, and an Old Fiddlers' Contest. The highlight of the day was the gigantic sweet corn feed, and the program ended that evening with a square dance in the streets. Transportation day saw the dedication of a new airport, and finale day was a time to bury a time capsule and commemorate the season of celebration in the churches. A gigantic beef barbecue in the heart of downtown Benson ended the day and the Centennial celebration.

In the 75th anniversary jubilee in New Castle, Wyoming, in 1964, planners focused on a historical pageant of the city. An "outsider" directed the show, an action which one of the writers called "the wisest move made by the Pageant Committee." One of the most interesting events in New Castle's Centennial was the Jubilee Wagontrain, thirty-two wagons traveling across the state on an old pioneer trail with every driver responsible for his own wagon and team, food and shelter, and willing to abide by the laws of the wagontrain.[15]

These are only a few of hundreds of examples of local centennials that offer some of the similarities and differences that mark celebration on any level. There were no final answers or supreme authorities to whom the program committees turned. Aid and advice were available through many sources, but the committees made final decisions in line with their own resources, needs, and orientations—or with the special advice of an outsider. As we have shown, many of the better celebrations were accomplished without outside help, but if a community feels it must resort to a professional company, then checking of credentials becomes important—comparing past performances with promises. In nearly all the local celebrations, the outside source concentrated on a single event—usually the pageant. Pageantry does have its place, but its focus is one-dimensional—"the fleeting passage of an event without perspective of time, concept of space or reality of life."

A good program should be large and provide many possibilities for important residual effect—instructive and constructive. Programs should be neither cheap nor tawdry; they should enlighten as well as entertain. In the many centennials noted above, the artist, the musician, and the poet have commanded the stage on equal footing with the speaker, the actor, and the academician. Pictures, paintings, slides, movies, and television programs also reached deep into the community minds. Exhibits and tours offered real possibilities to other creative instincts. Panels, forums, and symposia brought issues and people together to search for new understanding.

San Diego's Bicentennial pointed up another dilemma of planners in the modern "celebration" of centennials in these days of urban deterioration, ethnic problems, and shifting populations. Is it enough merely to show off community assets,

---

15. Letter from Mrs. Mabel Brown to author, October 17, 1971.

even to build the significant memorial—park, library, museum, or community building? What is the planner's responsibility in the allotment of funds and the selection of projects in terms of the acute problems of the community? Is it enough for ethnic groups to dance in splendid costumes of their past, to have their literature and artifacts highlighted in exhibitions, to participate in all programs on an equal basis when they are still not equal partners in the daily routines of community living? Many ethnic leaders will feel that the Bicentennial must deal first with the harsh problems they face daily in community life. They will dance their cultural themes only when they dance hand-in-hand with the rest of the citizens!

Still there is no pat blueprint for a program of excellence. To lift celebration to a higher plane would require, in the words of Allan Nevins, "plans and sustained effort with brains behind the plans and time behind the sustained effort." [16] Many of the above centennials were too much the products of canned thinking—celebrations that ran down in a flow of tired rhetoric and boisterous merrymaking. Centennials that made their mark by building and rebuilding—that left memorials of achievement that bettered men's lives and expanded his hopes—did not come easy. Intelligence combined with hard work, sustained interest, and tangible goals generally produced such memorials. There must be talent and hard work—at the top and in the ranks.

Many excellent programs have come from centennial celebrations in past years. Certainly a first step for planners is to look at what others have done. The next chapter surveys many of the projects and programs of centennials that have taken place across the country in years past. Many of the projects are hardly worth recounting; others command respect and attention. In the number of ideas which emerge, however, I hope that centennial planners will find two important aids: activities

16. Letter in Allan Nevins papers, Civil War Centennial files, National Archives, Washington, D.C.

which may actually be used as Bicentennial projects on a modified basis, and projects that will inspire planners to new ideas not yet thought of by other planners. This list of projects is by no means exhaustive, nor does it pretend to do more than skim the surface. The creative mind can discover and devise programs and projects that will give new meaning and importance to our two centuries. Whatever his method of celebration, the planner must keep in mind the suggestions of Richmond D. Williams of the Eleutherian Mills Historical Library: find out just what is being celebrated, and through the use of projects, publicity, and events, make the community aware of what the celebration is all about.[17]

17. *History News,* 16 (November 1960), 10.

Projects, Programs, and
Events of Celebration

This chapter is primarily an outline of what planners have done to celebrate other centennials. In selecting these particular items, I have tried to keep in mind my original contentions that celebration must release festive spirit and individual creativity and search out personal identity. I have arbitrarily listed these items in five general categories: Heritage, Ethnic Affairs, Fine Arts, Service, and Pageantry. Naturally, there will be overlap. A few projects are called "Miscellaneous," because they seem important but defy categorization.

The listing of a project is not necessarily a recommendation for Bicentennial consideration. Some of the projects cited were products of planners deeply committed to the search for substantive centennial fare; some had value only as part of a larger mosaic. Others are listed merely to show what has been done in the name of a centennial; they may only suggest what not to attempt. I made the list because I felt that planners should know what has been done and react to it—basing final judgments on what the Bicentennial means in the history of the nation and their own community—and I was hopeful that they would raise their standards as a result of reading this book. My own bases are simple ones: I feel that a centennial celebration should help us understand the past and should leave something tangible that will always remind us of a special moment in history. Frivolity comes only in the wake of serious performance. I listed "Heritage" projects first because, in the final analysis, heritage is really what the Bicentennial is all about.

HERITAGE

A country's heritage is the real purpose of centennial celebration. The Declaration of Independence two hundred years ago announced certain fundamental principles of the American credo: equality, the "unalienable rights" of life, liberty, and happiness; government by consent of the governed; and the right to alter that government if it usurps unauthorized powers. "The history of the American Revolution," wrote Henry Steele Commager, "is very largely the history of the actualization, the legalization, the institutionalization, of these principles."[1] The purposes of a Bicentennial should parallel those suggested by historian Boyd Shafer as the primary purposes of American historians: "To tell a story in literary form, to win an audience, . . . to point out moral lessons from the past . . . to reconstruct the past as accurately and fully as research in primary sources would permit, and . . . to increase citizens' understanding of the present through affording them knowledge of the past."[2]

The Bicentennial is a time to honor the aspirations, actions, achievements, and human shortcomings of the revolutionary generation. The contradictory themes of their actions still serve as guidelines and inspiration to the nation they produced, and to others around the world who hope for such success. Heritage programs should recognize some of their themes: love of liberty, willingness to face the realities of change—even revolution— their sacrifice and devotion to gain legitimate ends, their cre-

---

1. Quoted in Leder, ed., *The Meaning of the American Revolution*, 182.

2. Boyd C. Shafer, Michel François, Wolfgang J. Mommsen, A. Taylor Milne, *Historical Study in the West* (New York: Appleton-Century-Crofts, 1968), 176.

ation of a tradition rooted firmly on moral principles, and their willingness to accept equality as an article of faith. The Bicentennial, wrote Robert Moses (of World's Fair fame), is "an excellent opportunity to present in its most graphic forms, not the American millennium but what we have been able to accomplish in two centuries toward realizing the aspirations of the founders."

Planners can deal with the heritage of this nation in many ways. Some call for extensive research, study, and publication; some require large sums of money; some are little more than the passing fancies of individuals or groups, seeking only group emolument or self-gratification. The following list of projects, programs, and events offers examples of what others have done, in hopes that what is done to celebrate 1976 will truly reflect twentieth-century people in the stream of the past in order to give deeper meaning to the future. Any program without a serious and objective concern for heritage misses much of what our Bicentennial is all about, and from my observations of other celebrations, heritage is best portrayed in programs that give us new insights into our past.

Exhibitions—Few projects are more popular or varied in scope for a heritage presentation than exhibitions.[3] Numerous exhibitions appear in the case studies. Some other examples include one thousand photographs arranged chronologically on six-by-twelve-foot easels to tell Ohio's history in Stark County; the series of exhibitions of original American documents displayed by the Educational Foundation of the Automatic Retailers of America, Inc., in museums, colleges, universities, and libraries; the Vermont Historical Society's use of local items to show "The History of Your Town," its organization, early life, everyday life, important people, industry, and fun; and the New York Historical Society's 1963 display of paintings, prints, and maps depicting the buildings, streets, and landmarks of

---

3. AASLH is planning a new publication on Bicentennial museum exhibits by Arminta Neal and Holman J. Swinney.

eighteenth-century Manhattan. Relating live demonstrations with craft activities, models in period costumes, or dramatic performance of the historical events depicted adds a special dimension for understanding.

Variations on exhibitions can be seen from the following programs and projects of past centennials.

(1) Historical Cartoons Display: One of the most interesting displays that appeared in Illinois was a historical cartoon program. Cartoons from 1776 to 1781 would make an educational display as would other cartoon sequences dealing with the importance of the cartoon in American history, both as a political venture and as part of the *Zeitgeist*.

(2) Historymobile: This popular exhibition facility, which is discussed in several of the centennial case studies above, is a popular form of traveling exhibition which combines a series of dioramas with other types of exhibits to bring a well-rounded presentation of a period of history to audiences who are often excluded from such presentations by distance or limited community resources.

(3) History Suitcases: A modification of the historymobile, the suitcase is used widely by historical societies to display historical artifacts and other materials difficult to transport. The suitcases, usually topical, hold the advantage of being inexpensive and easily portable.

(4) Distributing and Exhibiting Paintings: A centennial period is an excellent time to place paintings with Revolutionary period themes or historical themes peculiar to a state's or community's history in strategic places in community government offices and other public places.

(5) Industrial Exhibits: Industries can exhibit their past history—their development, achievements, methods of operation, and prospects for the future in their own facilities. Olmstead County, Minnesota, an agricultural area, placed new farm machinery alongside older models in an interesting exhibition of present and past.

(6) Achievements From the Past: One of the exhibits in the Jamestown Festival outlined the contributions that the Jamestown settlers made to the society they founded and to the later United States; this exhibit depicted men, events, and achievements that make up much of the main stream of contemporary American life.

(7) Our Parliamentary Heritage: Ottowa celebrated the 175th anniversary of Ontario's first Parliament with an exhibit in the main parliamentary building. This exhibit outlined, by means of documents, pictures, and other materials, the establishment and development of the parliamentary system of government in England and later in Canada. Copies and reproductions of the original acts of Parliament, personal letters, newspapers, woodcuts, engravings, old photographs, and colored transparencies illustrated the exhibition.

This project would be a good model for similar projects in the Bicentennial. Interrelationships between governmental practices of England and the United States and among the various states could well be illustrated in a similar series in courthouses, state capitals, and even in cities that are not directly associated with government.

(8) Continuing Exhibitions: The Butler Institute of American Art in Youngstown, Ohio, has begun a continuing series of displays of American art and history—displays presented each May indefinitely to commemorate the Bicentennial. Continuing displays offer the community a chance to develop its own exhibits and to include the history of its own community in the Bicentennial proceedings.

(9) Library and Museum Presentations: Larry Wolters, publicity chairman of the Illinois Sesquicentennial, suggested special evening programs featuring literature, history, poetry, fiction, music, or art to Illinois libraries as especially attractive to select audiences. By using posters, picture arrangements, foldouts, standup displays, and figures made of construction paper and papier maché, librarians could supplement the regu-

lar program with permanent or semi-permanent displays to illustrate some historical event of the Revolutionary War period or of the state or community's history. Book displays, children's library or reading projects, films and slide presentations by individuals who have traveled in other celebration areas would be appropriate. Boards bearing copies of documents of the historical period under consideration could be strategically placed through library rooms.

Libraries might also look to the Buffalo, New York, Historical Society, which set up a street scene of the early period of its history as an open exhibit on a main floor as part of its centennial planning in 1962.

One of Canada's library projects was a display in libraries across the country of a hundred essential titles for the educated citizen. Princeton University library has already set up a Bicentennial bookshelf, featuring books, reprints, and catalogs of the Revolutionary period. This could both be models to community libraries which could also include displays of local history as special Bicentennial projects.

In museum exhibitions, the written word should be minimized. Visitors enjoy walking through the displays, turning handles, feeling shapes, hearing sounds, experiencing with all of their senses. The museum, "a receptor of all kinds of Americana," will be a prominent feature in Bicentennial activities, and the best museums will resort to new methods, new techniques, and experimentation.[4] Short, exciting, and very expressive films, those two to three minutes in duration, can set a mood in a kaleidoscopic survey of a particular topic such as immigration, the human revolution, or ethnic achievement.

The Bicentennial is an excellent time for the museum to expand its program to relate to social purposes—"exhibition, education, programs, dance, song, music, children's activities,

4. Daniel R. Porter, "Giving Your Museums a New Look," *History News*, 15 (March 1960), 62; Minnie Harris Hanson, "Seattle Museum of History and Industry," *History News*, 23 (September 1968), 171.

publications on the popular level." [5] Museums have an excellent opportunity and even responsibility to tell, through the many different facets of their facilities, the true stories of minorities.[6] Recently the museum has been heavily criticized as little more "than an institution of the upper middle classes" [7] and must do something to shake this image. During the Bicentennial museums will have an excellent chance to open their doors to those put off by the barriers erected by our educational system and become more attractive especially for children.

(10) Museum "Project '70": British Columbia's four centennials presented a special long-range museum project that has possibilities for our own "76." This project set up a series of exhibitions that traced the history of the country from 1741 to 1971, beginning with the metropolis, 1921 to 1971; urbanization and industrialization; the gold rush era; fur trade and exploration. Visitors to the exhibit first noted the present, working back through time to earlier days. Planners hoped that visitors to these "galleries devoted to contact" would be struck by the sense of cause and effect while simultaneously making the mental jump between the white and native cultures.

Museum Confederations—Museum confederations like the one in Orange County, New York, a confederation of eleven local museums that have worked on problems of mutual interest for the past several years, may provide solutions for certain museum problems during Bicentennial years. Small museums will do well to work in consort with other museums to provide various programs and displays in the Bicentennial season. Company museums also may expand specific themes in their own Bicentennial museums. The exhibits of early American tureens, bowls, and labels of Campbell Soup Company, Camden, New Jersey, are setting a pattern that may become popular.

---

5. William A. Burns, "Museums and the Social Crises," *Western Museums Quarterly*, 7 (March 1971), 7.

6. See Ethnic Projects following.

7. *The German Tribune*, September 30, 1971.

Preservation—The National Historic Preservation Act of 1966 is a strong factor in helping states consider preservation as a Bicentennial project. Preservations of buildings, relics, documents, clothing, books and many other items have been centennial projects that carried the spirit of commemoration beyond the days of celebration.

Models of preservation appear all across our land, highlighted by Old Sturbridge Village, Shelburne, Colonial Williamsburg, and Old World Wisconsin—to name only a few. The National Trust for Historic Preservation specializes in this phase of history and offers counsel and illustrations to all interested persons. The American Association for State and Local History also has a special interest in preserving the past and has a publication program to keep people oriented to the latest developments.[8] There are many possibilities under the general heading of preservation, but these are a few that illustrate what others have done.

(1) Saving Landmarks: When the 230-year-old Bettin Oak, a landmark of the American Revolution, finally fell in 1971, the Department of Interior had it cut into souvenirs with sizable cross-sections of the historic tree given to the schools and museums to put on display.

More important projects are possible, however. Pierce, Idaho, kicked off a Territorial Centennial by making a museum out of the town's first jail. The preservation of barns, old courthouses, movie houses, and other historic landmarks often requires professional help, but this is a major area of concern as more and

---

8. Many of the current problems of preservation and restoration are discussed from two different viewpoints in an Old Sturbridge Village article "Preserving What Is Best from the Past—Two Points of View," *OSV Intelligencer* (February 1972), 1. See also AASLH Technical Leaflets: Nina Fletcher Little, *Historic Houses: An Approach to Furnishing* (17); Shirley P. Low, *Historic Site Interpretation: The Human Approach* (32) ; Paul L. Benedict, *Historic Site Interpretation: The Student Field Trip* (19) ; Penelope Hartshorne Batcheler, *Paint Color Research and Restoration* (15) ; Lee H. Nelson, *Nail Chronology as an Aid to Dating Old Buildings* (18) .

more landmarks fall victim to the "progress" of an industrial society.[9]

(2) Salvaging Historical Relics: Salvage, an important operation during the Civil War Centennial, was highlighted by the successful raising of the Union ironclad *Cairo* and the Confederate gunboat *Neuse*. These expensive projects require special funding, but they are popular actions where some historical relic is known to be under water.

(3) Painting and Photographing Landmarks: An interesting corollary to saving landmarks is painting or photographing those that are on the verge of being destroyed. Marion Cook, a young artist from Goodlettsville, Tennessee, already has a very fine collection of paintings of old barns that will someday make an excellent display of a past now rapidly disappearing. Paintings and photographs of old mills, covered bridges, and outdated farm equipment have also been projects of several New England artists and photographers.

(4) Local History Preservation Day: For several years Aberdeen, Mississippi, has celebrated a "local history preservation day," which has possibilities for small communities in the Bicentennial. Word-of-mouth publicity, radio, television and newspaper announcements, and community bulletin boards urge people who have documents to place them in the library collection. This culminates in a community open house where the citizens view their documents on public display. There is special emphasis on church records, war letters, old photographs, Bible records, and old currency.[10]

(5) Preserving and Displaying Flags: Ohio's Centennial was the occasion to preserve and display more than 400 bullet-riddled regimental flags carried by Ohio's 230 regiments during the Civil War.

---

9. Wolf von Eckardt described some of the possibilities for sparing old buildings in "Saving Our Landmarks," *Saturday Review* (September 5, 1970), 52.

10. Lucille Peacock, "A Little Town's Unique Celebration," *History News*, 9 (November 1953), 3.

(6) "Historic Revelation": Canada had a project by this name which related specifically to preservation. This project called for combining historical identification, preservation, and community beautification. Each community was to survey its buildings and select several for special centennial restoration, both to help the community establish its historical identity and to renovate a rundown area of the city. Facades, painting, planting of trees, flowers and shrubs, removal of extraneous detracting features, and complete renovation were suggestions eventually followed by many communities. In a special guidebook the Centennial Commission suggested the following steps for a community "revelation" project: Select the building carefully, keeping it in mind as part of a larger display; for promotional purposes, make a photographic record of the building —before and after; clean up and beautify the lot; clean or repaint the walls of the building; repaint the siding and clapboard; accentuate the good architectural features of the building as part of a larger display.[11]

Mobile, Alabama, has long had a similar program. Renovations of historic buildings and cleaning up of lots, disguising parking lots, and so forth, has encouraged "clean-up" of other facilities and buildings.[12]

(7) "Operation Clean Attic": This interesting Canadian program induced citizens to deposit old documents, letters and records of historical value, and other materials in the Provincial Archives. Brockville, Ontario, was especially successful in its "Attic Day." The project brought a great deal of valuable information into the Archives.

(8) Relic Hunting: Relic hunting is a variation on accumulating information from the past. Students near Kingston, North

11. *Historic Revelation,* Action Pamphlet No. 9, Community Improvement Program Bulletins (Canadian Centennial Commission, 1967).

12. Mrs. Nicholas H. Holmes, Jr.. "The Mobile Historic Development Commission, *History News,* 23 (April 1968), 73.

Carolina, looked for shells and Indian relics in nearby fields as a Tercentenary project.

(9) Preserving Tradition: Going beyond preservation of buildings, the Ranch Headquarters Museum of Lubbock, Texas, has plans for preserving the ranching traditions in the state by creating an educational facility for all age groups. Earmarking 20 buildings for restoration, the faculty will stress architecture, history, art, landscaping, and park and recreation administration. Conferences, seminars, and retreats will offer themes of discussion of ranching types as well as exploration into how ranching serves as a "twentieth-century expression of the American Revolution." [13]

This is a suggestion for communities far removed from the scenes we normally associate with the American Revolution. Capitalizing upon their own specialties and their own historical motifs, communities can deal with their own traditions as they relate to the larger traditions expressed by the founding fathers.

Restorations—Restoration goes hand and hand with preservation as a centennial project. A few projects will indicate possibilities: Hamilton, Ontario, restored and planned a sound-and-light production around Dundurn Castle, a 132-year-old mansion that had long been the property of the city. A Wisconsin community, encouraged by the state historical society, restored one of its main streets with all the stores that had formerly been there. Old Salem, Massachusetts, has had many interesting restorations and today can be seen to some degree as it was in colonial times. Restorations are already being talked about in Philadelphia, Boston, and Niagara, New York, as Bicentennial projects.

Publications—Few activities relate more to understanding heritage than do the many publication projects that centennials spawn. Publications appear in many forms. Some past projects include local history books in the New Jersey Historical Series;

---

13. *Bicentennial Era,* 1 (June 1970), 2.

thoroughly edited documents in the North Carolina Colonial History Series; the many state and county histories motivated by centennials; the many documents produced by the Library of Congress, the National Archives, and other important government agencies; pamphlet series like that of the New York State Department of Education in its 1959 Centennial; bibliographical studies like the bibliography of theses and dissertations pertaining to Kansas history that came out of the Kansas Centennial of 1961; an anthology of local works, stories, plays, as developed by the British Columbia Centennial Commission in its first centennial; histories of businesses, labor movements, and other community institutions; the many monthly Centennial releases; and the novels, poetry, and other writings that line the shelves immediately after the centennial is past.

The publication of city, town, county, and state histories is a popular centennial activity. Local histories became so numerous in the Canadian Centennial that they eventually inspired the publication of several "how to" publications.[14] The Glenbow Library of Calgary, Alberta, has an interesting collection of all the local histories written in that Canadian province. Unfortunately, too many local histories are marred by poor scholarship.

Other publications include the following:

(1) *"History From The Bottom Up":* A recent New York *Times Magazine* article suggested a special research project to uncover material that shows "the experiences and perceptions of the often inarticulate lower classes rather than on the elite who often dominate traditional narrative history."[15] Writings of several historians including George Rude, Jesse Lemisch,

---

14. One of the more interesting is by Hugh A. Dempsey, *How to Prepare a Local History* (Calgary, Alberta: Glenbow-Alberta Institute, 1969); see also Donald D. Parker, *Local History: How to Gather It, Write It and Publish It,* rev. and ed. by Bertha E. Josephson (New York: Social Science Research Council, 1944).

15. J. Anthony Lukas, "Historians' Conference: The Radical Need for Jobs," New York *Times Magazine,* March 12, 1972, 38.

and Stoughton Lynd have already explored some of the possibilities in this area.

(2) *"Bicentennial Tales"*: There are many precedents for the publication of a series called "Bicentennial Tales." Louis L. Tucker's "Vignettes of Local History" during his tenure as historian in Cincinnati, Ohio, generated interest in the past and presented interesting accounts of unusual information. John Fisher's reports in Canada are in many ways vignettes of centennial happenings in that country. The Independence County Historical Society of Batesville, Arkansas, published fifty-two similar articles in its *Chronicle,* a program well enough received to merit an award from the American Association for State and Local History. The Bay State Historical League *Bulletin* has been preparing "Yankee Sketches," tales about local people, places, incidents, and events for some time. The most popular of this type of writing is that of John T. Cunningham of New Jersey, whose *Tercentenary Tales* were described in the chapter on New Jersey.

(3) *Historical Maps:* The National Bank of Detroit recently published an interesting city map entitled "Historical Tour of Greater Detroit." It lists the major points of interest in two maps, a large one illustrated with pictures, and a small one which helps orient the visitor to the city projects. Short explanations of the history of each project appear on the back of these maps. This would be an excellent project for any town rich in history.

Updating local maps is a project often associated with centennial activity. The National Park Service can sometimes help in this matter. The Historic American Building Survey has been of service also, sometimes even supplying resources.[16]

(4) *Document Projects:* Several documents projects emerge from a study of other centennials: publication of selected documents concerning a particular community (constitutions, spe-

---

16. The Address: HABS, 1730 North Lynn Street, Arlington, Virginia 22209.

cial laws, official public documents, etc.) ; reprinting newspaper issues that relate specifically to some historical aspect of the community; donating of documents, either actual or Xeroxed, by citizens of the community to the library; accumulating documents from other places. An excellent example was noted in the New Jersey Tercentenary when the commission sent Professor Richard P. McCormick of Rutgers to Europe in search of documents that would shed light on New Jersey's early history.

(5) *"Liberty and Learning":* This Bicentennial project of the Library of Congress calls for extensive publications, exhibits, and other learned, educational, and cultural programs on the American Revolutionary period in American history. Several professional historians on the library staff are working with librarians, bibliographers, subject specialists, and editors in preparing "guides to original sources, bibliographies, facsimile reproduction of historical prints and documents, exhibits, and other special programs."

Tours—One of the simplest tours is the walking tour, adequately described in a pamphlet entitled "Historic Preservation Through Walking Tours," available from the National Trust for Historic Preservation. This pamphlet describes in detail how a walking tour can be set up and conducted. The use of bicycles provides a variation of the walking tour.

South Carolina focused on the development of several specific trails in its Tricentennial. The tourist who followed these trails could trace the state's history from a colonial to a modern state. The Pennsylvania Trail of History reveals the past in the same way. Package tours were part of the Illinois Sesquicentennial, and travel agents distributed them to visitors.

A canal boat tour in New York's Centennial illustrated both the means of transportation and what the countryside was like a hundred years earlier. New York also had bus tours in the rural areas and in the cities. In 1965 Maine looked toward the Bicentennial by setting up Revolutionary War tours, including Benedict Arnold's expedition to Canada. Interpretive display signs, placed at selected sites, lead the tourist to the important historical sites.[17] The following are also possibilities:

(1) Mystery Bus Trips: Washington Rock, New Jersey, is currently offering a "mystery bus ride." Students leave on a bus hike without knowing their exact location. Through hints they guess their destination, usually a specific historical location.

(2) Retracing Trails: A project in the California Bicentennial of 1970 retraced the Old Spanish Road from Rancho San Antonio to San Pedro, via the San Joaquin Valley, on horseback. It took a little more than a week to master the nearly five hundred miles of trail. Supplementary shorter rides over special trails were included for those who did not undertake the whole trip.

(3) Trail-chasing: Though not a specific centennial project, "trail-chasing" has possibilities as a Bicentennial project for a small community located in a rich historical area. Two professors at Wichita State University initiated a project to trace all the trails which crossed Kansas from the days of Coronado through the period of the settlement of the state. They have already uncovered more than 120 trails.

Special History Conferences—Special history conferences like one held at McGregor Memorial Conference Center at Wayne State University, April 14–15, 1972, entitled "Michigan in Perspective," make excellent Bicentennial orientation programs. Wayne State called on Canada's John Fisher to speak on "Lessons from Canada's Centennial Experience." Additional features of the two-day program included a series of films on American backgrounds, lectures, and photographs on what Michigan is planning for the Bicentennial, specialized subject matter in Michigan's background from the point of view of

---

17. Howard H. Peckham described how to set up a local historical tour in *History News*, 4 (May-September 1949), 168. Modifying Dr. Peckham's suggestions, students could draw up their own map of the main activities of some Revolutionary War general or campaign and follow the course of the action.

archaeology, sociology, history, and geology. This low-cost program was open to the public.

History Symposia—Bicentennial planners might note the three-day seminar held in Williamsburg, Virginia, in 1960. This symposium, entitled "Perspective on the American Revolutionary Era," examined and clarified historical interpretations of the impact of the American Revolution on England, Canada, and America in the late eighteenth and early nineteenth century. Historians from each country were on the program.

The Bergen County (New Jersey) Historical Society brought more than a thousand local citizens into a series of symposia on its local history.

History institutes and seminars are merely variations on the symposium and are often employed on a short-run basis in communities and by schools. All of these are popular forms of expression by academic communities.

History Workshops—Workshops, including sessions on bibliography, community resources for Civil War exhibits, Civil War folklore, arms, and accoutrements, were a popular feature of the Civil War Centennial. The workshops were held on a national basis and were also very popular local features.

Roundtables—Revolutionary Roundtables similar to the popular Civil War Centennial roundtables, are already appearing. Groups of interested citizens assemble at homes, schools, club buildings, or churches and discuss specific topics of the war period. While meetings are usually led by one of their own members, guest speakers, especially on important dates, are also popular. Roundtables often inspire other community activities.

Travel Symposium—In the North Carolina Tercentenary, the state commission sent brochures to its various committees suggesting a travel symposium or workshop on how better to relate Tercentenary affairs to the incoming tourists. A group of experts helped the community put its own resources into perspective for best appeal to its visitors.

Forming a Historical Society—The Bicentennial is an excellent time for communities, both large and small, to form historical societies.

Dedications—Three River Falls, Minnesota, dedicated a bridge; New Jersey and North Carolina dedicated large state archival and library buildings; and Canadians dedicated many national Centennial projects.

Possibilities for dedication are numerous. It is appropriate for a community to commemorate one of its own historical events as well as the national ones. North St. Louis, Minnesota, commemorated a great fire that destroyed much of the community at the turn of the century. Chicago has commemorated its fire on several occasions. Floods, tornadoes, and riots offer other possibilities, especially if the emphasis is placed on community co-operation in crisis.

Commemoration Services—For the Bicentennial year the New Jersey Historical Commission recommends that each community in the state have at least one major commemorative observance. Some suggestions include: reading the Declaration of Independence, ringing church bells, raising a liberty pole, dramatizing a historical event, with appropriate music and short addresses by the community leaders who use history and community achievements as basic themes.

Stamp Study—The study of commemorative stamps should inspire stamp programs for libraries, museums, and schools. Many modifications of stamp programs will be possible, depending upon the resources and personnel.

Excavations—A centennial is a good time to begin excavations. The United States Military Academy is already planning to conduct archeological excavations and the restoration of Revolutionary War sites at West Point. The Hampton (Virginia) Arts and Humanities Center has several interesting excavations underway. Communities with excavation possibilities will do well to consult such projects before planning their own.

Building Programs—Buildings have always been popular centennial projects. Hundreds of Canadian cities built museums, libraries, archives, and other buildings that related directly to their history. Examples of centennial building in the United States occurred in New Jersey and North Carolina, where important projects now stand for public and private use —more permanent reminders of the past than parades, pageants, and re-enactments.

Iowa plans to build a large Bicentennial building, combining history, agriculture, industry, and the arts and sciences. Some cities are discussing art centers and theater as well as the more traditional libraries and museums. Skating rinks, basketball courts, swimming pools, and community centers will fill needs in many communities.

Community Famous Persons Project—The Tercentenary film committee of Guilford, North Carolina, staged and filmed historical documentaries about its famous personages—past and present—which included interviews of famous citizens as well as examples of their works. They also secured file films of citizens from the past, including those of Edward R. Murrow's World War II broadcasts from London.

The committee supplemented its program with library displays, musical programs of local composers, and drama work of famous sons—including O. Henry.

"Names" Project—Bedford County, Illinois, published a series of articles on its own place and family names as a project.

Immortalizing Country Folk Music—Warren County, New Jersey, is planning a Bicentennial project to "immortalize country folk music." Special equipment will be used to record mountain folk-singing, which will preserve a very rich heritage of Americana.

Sunday Afternoon Historical Series—Nebraska's special Sunday afternoon programs for collectors and hobbyists which featured stamp collections, dolls, fireworks of the frontier, coins, archeology, and folk songs.

Slides—Canada's "School Brigade" was a pilot centennial

project of Manitoba in which photographers recorded the geography and history of that state for a slide presentation to a sixth-grade class. These youngsters were so enthusiastic that volunteers were encouraged to take the slides to the room of every elementary school in the province. The instructors rotated the slides periodically, depending upon the criticisms of the students and the grades to which they presented them, eventually developing such a popular program that it appeared on television.

The Kansas State Historical Society prepared a set of 35mm slides of historic sites and buildings and presented them to local groups, clubs, schools, and churches during its Centennial. In Orange County, New York, thirty-six slides and an accompanying script told the county's history to clubs and schools.

Two immediate possibilities seem to emerge from this study of slide programs. The original thirteen states might develop slide series of projects they are developing for 1976, or of scenes in their areas that tell the story of the American Revolution, and make them available to states beyond the bounds of the original colonies. Slides might be taken from collections in the National Archives, narrative tapes prepared to go with them and the packages made available to states where there is a dearth of source material. These slides could be pictures of art works, forts, geographic scenes, drawings, or other historical items available from the Archives. One group of 143 pictures in the National Archives called "The Select Picture List—The Revolutionary War" could easily be made into a traveling display for use in schools where such items are hardly ever found.

States and local communities with programs and projects that lend themselves to photography could so record them for central distribution to other communities not so fortunate in historical background. AASLH might serve as a clearing house for such an endeavor.

Oral History Project—Recording comments of older members of the community is a popular project and, if properly done, can be a valuable addition to local archives.[18]

Microfilming—Microfilming of documents, newspapers, sermons, deeds, diaries, speeches, and the like is an expensive project, but one that can add much to a local archives. Indiana was quite active in this program during its Centennial, as was Illinois.

History Film Festival—This has been a popular feature of several centennials, and with the unusual films available, it should also command attention in the Bicentennial. Selecting the proper titles is very important, for many films have fallen short in terms of both quality and accuracy. One plan would be to have series of films stressing certain aspects of the Revolutionary period with small discussion groups after each film.

Club Presentations—Planning commissions should urge local clubs to use films, history lectures, and other programs on local history or the American Revolution to highlight their own weekly sessions.

Local Television Programs—Many of the programs listed above could be worked into television series. WOSU in Columbus has done much to bring educational television programs into central Ohio, producing an interesting series on the state in its Centennial year entitled *Ohio: The Seventeenth State.* The series included programs on Ohio presidents, archeology, birds and fish, and on the state's various historical sites. The Western Reserve Historical Society of Cleveland has developed an interesting TV history series called "Antiques Corner," a program that appears each Wednesday from 11 o'clock until noon. This program is set up so that the public can write and telephone questions about antiques and collecting and get unusual information from the station.

Information Booths—Information booths have been tried on several different levels in centennial projects. They generally

---

18. Willa K. Baum, *Oral History for the Local Historical Society* (Nashville: AASLH, 1971).

are set up in the heart of town and often manned by high school students who have been thoroughly instructed in the history and background of the community. Booth personnel are responsible for brochures and map-distribution, program sheets, book sales, pamphlet sales, mimeographed descriptions of the local museums and other historical sites, printed materials on the local libraries, colleges, and other special features. In some centennials these information booths have been on the malls and in others on college campuses. They are also good places for community businesses to publicize their activities.

Data Bank—In Canada one local commission set up a data bank, a compilation of information about the location of artifacts, manuscripts, books, and newspapers relating to a particular period of history. This could be a good project for states accumulating material relating to the Revolutionary War period or to other historical themes of particular interest.

Information Package—A good project for any community may resemble an Illinois Sesquicentennial project—developing packages of materials that can be available to communities throughout the state. This can be done on almost any level and can include a vast variety of materials, topics for discussion, projects, tapes, slide series, and films—all of which can be exchanged among the various communities of that state. "Information '68," an Illinois Sesquicentennial project, allowed anyone to call a set number and receive answers to any historical questions about his state.

Church Projects—In the large context of heritage, religion seeks some of the same answers that history does, raises many of the same questions, and is inclined toward similar expressions in a centennial. Churches looking for programs for centennials might use many recorded in this chapter. Some special programs as they related to other centennials include:

(1) Interfaith Programs: Interfaith programs are very appropriate for centennials because they encourage a wide community spirit. Pulpit exchanges, interfaith mid-week programs,

large Thanksgiving Day services, early morning interfaith services, and youth rallies are examples of interfaith activities from other centennials. The Canadian Interfaith Conference provided pamphlets and booklets to encourage the development of interfaith book shelves for research purposes. They made a placemat which included a short centennial blessing in English for all denominations on one side and in several different languages on the other. One project resulted in a laminated paperback *Anthology of Prayer* which contained English and French prayers for the different churches. One of Canada's leading poets, Robert Choquette, wrote a Centennial anthem.

(2) Memorials: Several Canadian churches were successful in placing memorial plaques in strategic places.

(3) Honoring the founders: This was a popular project in some Canadian areas, with churches honoring their own founders and those of the larger church. Some churches, like a Lutheran church in St. Louis, celebrated by preparing exhibitions, including collages, sculptures, photographs, art, and drawings.

History Themes—Sugar Bowl officials have agreed to use the Bicentennial theme for all their activities in 1976. This is a pattern that many organizations, clubs, and events will employ. It can be employed to good effect to publicize the Bicentennial in the totality of the American experience. Planners must be careful not to prostitute the significance of the term in overuse or in frivolous exhibition.

Youth Programs—Youth involved in a centennial provide excitement, creativity, and variety. Acting as individuals, members of a club or organization, or within a school, their projects are often models for other planners. Student debates on centennial topics took place in Canada and suggest similar Bicentennial debates on meaning and importance of the American Revolution. The Indiana Junior Historical Society Sesquicentennial Committee produced a Directory of Historical Markers of the surrounding area. Illinois youth not only followed traditional patterns of service in local government on Sesquicentennial Youth Government Day, but they acted out, in costume, the roles of local government of an era of Illinois history long past. Armed with 35mm cameras, both color and black and white, Allen County, New Jersey, students produced a centennial film on the vanishing one-room schools.

In 1957 the Chicago Historical Society announced a special slide program to supplement the social science curriculum of the nearby schools. Children also received free pictorial scrapbook material to provide their own historical record to supplement the slides, with prizes for the best scrapbooks. In 1964 students surveyed and listed the political actions, organizations, military units, flag presentations, military engagements, and other facts that took place in the community at the time of the Civil War. Then, working with the various clubs and associations of the community, they set up programs around the material they had found.

The Clinton (New Jersey) Museum Heritage Workshop offered three two-week sessions in an old seventeenth-century mill to educate young people in certain techniques of handicrafts. Businesses provide many of the tuition scholarships to help the young people participate. Candle making, bookbinding, tinsmithing, theorums (paintings on velvet), wood and linoleum block-printing, spindle spinning, knotting, broommaking, pewter molding, toleware, marbelizing paper, gravestone rubbing, and caning are among the many topics offered.

Washington Rock, New Jersey, offered, as a series of Girl Scout programs, workshops designed to develop special skills in several areas, including research methods, audio-visual equipment, the graphic arts, restoration, mapping, and museum techniques.

A group of students in Newton, Massachusetts, learned history by performing some of the tasks of their forefathers: they made soup in an iron kettle, dipped candles, worked a spinning sheel, and played games of an earlier decade.

The youthul members of the Shackamoxon Society combined

cookouts, hikes, athletic contests, and other fun activities with preservation, re-enactments, workshops, and other history projects.[19]

School pioneer days have been popular in some centennials, especially in communities that have close ties with their past. Activities include old-fashioned ball games under early rules, period costumes, square dances, home cooking, homemade candy, souvenirs made especially for the occasion, and husking or quilting bees, in programs that seek to capture a feeling of the past.

Timmons High School in Ontario in the Canadian Centennial had as its Centennial project the construction of a miniature scale model of the city showing its development from a Hudson Bay post and an Indian trading center to its present format. Manitoba thought highly enough of "History Fairs" to issue a special brochure describing how to produce one. The fairs emphasized history and student creativity in a series of displays researched and built by students. The unusual interest in history in a centennial year seemed to permeate the minds of younger people in New Jersey, Minnesota, and North Carolina, where organizations of junior historians made remarkable advances. New Jersey's Bicentennial group came out of the New Jersey Tercentenary and is now planning an extensive program. For help in organizing youth historians, the state historical association and AASLH are indispensable in providing counsel and programs.

Youth publications also played a prominent role in past centennials and hold many possibilities for the Bicentennial. In its Centennial Manitoba encouraged high school students to "collect, collate and write the history of their local areas" as a Centennial project, aiding them in maintaining quality and uniformity with a brochure entitled *Local Histories,* which included basic steps to follow, sources of information, how stu-

---

19. For a detailed account, see *History News,* 27 (February 1972), 38.

dents could work together in putting together a manuscript, and some topics for consideration.

Professor Jordan Fiore of Bridgewater State College in Massachusetts modified this program in his American Revolution course by engaging students to research particular communities in the Revolutionary War period and write papers on their findings. Professor Fiore filed the best papers in the school library and offered copies to the local historical societies and libraries of the community studied.

Foxfire, a quarterly publication from Rayburn Gap, Georgia, selected by ARBC for special support, is a model deserving the consideration of any local group planning a Bicentennial publication. Local history at its best, *Foxfire* stresses life in the mountains of North Georgia. Its staff, unusual because it is made up entirely of high school students, spends many hours combing the hills for local folklore, and they record their findings in verse, essays, feature articles, pictures, and drawings. The result is a publication that now commands national attention, providing the model for a similar publication now being published at a Sioux Indian reservation in Pine Ridge, South Dakota.[20]

In 1971, New York State American Revolution Bicentennial Commission published *The American Revolution for Young Readers,* a bibliography of books for students in the fourth, fifth, and sixth grades. This is an eleven-page publication listing 140 to 150 titles. The focus is on getting young people to read fiction, romance, adventure, history.

The chief librarian of Ottawa's National Library is enthusiastic about a youth project of the Canadian Centennial, in which young people made diagrams of various Ottawa architectural structures. These diagrams were then filed in the National Archives. As a result of unusual enthusiasm to creativity,

---

20. "Students Preserve Appalachian Folk Ways As They Uncover History From the Hills," *History News,* 27 (March 1972), 48.

some excellent diagrams of buildings that would be difficult to photograph are now available.

Youth Education—Education should possibly be given a special category of its own, but it is concerned with the understanding and interpreting of man's heritage. Education means encounter, a confrontation of people and ideas. If the encounter is significant and meaningful, it heightens awareness and enables us to understand each other and ourselves better. A centennial is a good time to bring education into focus and to challenge its devotees to greater efforts. A few special projects of the past indicate how education related to young people in centennial years.

(1) Special youth projects: Illinois's planners offered many projects for young people in its Centennial. Programs for junior high schools included suggestions of surveying buildings for historical importance and permanent recording; developing original research in terms of electrical equipment; collecting pictures that show the evolution in automobiles, trains, farm equipment, machinery, wagons, and buggies; arranging for communications with students in other communities; focusing study units on missionary work of Father Marquette and others whose achievements helped mold Illinois history; studying Illinois immigration patterns; and reading novels of Illinois authors.

Wisconsin's series of programs to stimulate young people's interests included: bulletin board displays; poster-making; producing film strips, motion pictures and recordings; collecting newspapers, magazines, brochures, and pictures; establishing correspondence committees with other schools; cataloguing records of work on Wisconsin history; organizing speakers' bureaus for group meetings; surveying county records; and listing materials in local public libraries that can be utilized in history projects.

North Carolina's youth committee organized a Bicentennial project in each high school in order to get similar tasks done.

These committees also set up contests in cooking, sewing, furniture-making, oratory, and other events.

(2) Seminars on restorations: The King of Prussia (Pennsylvania) Historical Society set up a seminar for junior high school students to study outdoor restorations including Cooperstown, Colonial Williamsburg, and Old Sturbridge Village. Local community Bicentennial seminars may want to extend this idea to local historic sites.

(3) Sharing materials from home: In Delaware, students brought materials from their homes to their classes to use as display materials in school exhibitions.

(4) Summer camp programs on peace and international understanding: Ottawa, Canada, held a summer camp for eleven-year-olds from ten nations to study peace and understanding. Few topics are more noteworthy for Bicentennial consideration.

(5) "1967" reading project: Canadians, in a program on improving and encouraging reading among students, purchased $50,000 worth of reading materials to be distributed among the various schools. The program, entitled "1967 Reading Project," solicited individual contributions of $19.67.

(6) Student House of Burgesses: Williamsburg, Virginia, students held a House of Burgesses meeting at Colonial Williamsburg as part of their commemoration. Secondary students from thirty-four foreign countries and forty-nine states attended. New York had a similar Bill of Rights meeting where students assembled and discussed freedom as a historical concept, dealing with John Peter Zenger, Quaker writings, Harriet Tubman, the early women's rights movement, and civil rights legislation.

(7) Education innovation in state history courses: Many states have used centennial periods to shore up state history courses with both methods and material including New York and Ohio.

(8) Student commemoration project: British Columbia had a province-wide Centennial commemoration project in which all school children could participate. This project provided rec-

reational and other facilities at certain children's homes. The students responded commendably, raising money enough to provide new materials.

(9) Education evaluation: A Canadian Centennial suggestion was an evaluation of educational programs by companies, organizations, and individuals, with stress on inequalities. This type of program could be very useful in certain areas in our own Bicentennial.

(10) Education week: Wonderful Wisconsin Week, a week of educational events and activities, might well serve as a model for local communities in our Bicentennial. Some of the projects outlined for this week included the following: community service projects; recognition days for adults who have served youth; project co-operation with all other youth groups, including the Boy Scouts; identifying community problems; participating in the open houses, exhibitions, demonstrations, and concerts of the week; paying special heed to the science fairs; participating in the various contests; serving colonial foods in the school cafeterias; recognizing the extra-curricular activities of young people in the newspapers; encouraging every facet of young talent to participate in some program that week; using the media to publicize student activity; holding library open houses; exhibiting school equipment and facilities—foreign language labs, science rooms, libraries, and gyms—setting up student-teacher panels on education-oriented subjects; visiting in senior citizens' homes; participating in local government, business, and church programs; and encouraging exchange groups and individuals with nearby communities.

(11) History for the seventh grade: In New York's Centennial of 1959, the State Department of Education urged a more intensive study of New York history in the seventh grade. They suggested a series of special student projects to stimulate interest in local history, furnishing several booklets to implement this program.

ETHNIC AFFAIRS

A section on ethnic projects, programs, and events points up one of the major dilemmas facing Bicentennial planners in a nation torn by racial and ethnic dissension. On every level, planners are facing the hard facts—some racial groups in America see little meaning in this particular birthday and will be uninterested in joining traditional means of celebration. Too long, leaders of these groups contend, some Americans have not shared in the bounty of the nation. It behooves planners, therefore, on every level, to look toward total involvement of *all* Americans as a Bicentennial goal.

Centennial programs will not solve inflammatory problems, but they do raise questions of priorities. Instead of creating inflammatory situations in the programs planners can anticipate potential explosive problems and effect courses of action that will at least smooth the troubled waters for the larger occasion. Of course the largest Bicentennial concern for all Americans is the greatest integration of all people into the total fabric of our way of life. On national, state, and local levels it is therefore imperative to include ethnic representation on planning committees and in some cases to encourage ethnic committees. Of course, ethnic groups must also respond and engage. Dialogue may be the only hope in many cases, but even this may be a step forward.

Where to begin in ameliorating ethnic problems in celebration is a concern of all planners. Leo F. Twiggs, an art professor at South Carolina State University, recommends the use of art forms as an initial approach. Unless citizens "think of their human interactions as sources for aesthetic experience," he suggested recently, "the possibilities of a rich common existence, nurtured by the richness of our diversity, is lost and we shall all suffer." [21] Supporting this view is a statement by art philosopher

---

21. Leo F. Twiggs, "The Museum and the Black Community," *Museum News,* 50 (May 1972), 8.

Edmund B. Feldman who wrote: "Increasing the role of art in our society is becoming one of promoting discourse—that of the exchange of feeling among citizens of a free society." [22]

Art forms may well help break down the barriers between races while preserving the integrity of each. "If you can show me how I can become a part of your world without losing that which is uniquely my own," concedes Black writer Ralph Ellison, "then I will not only sing praises, but I will help the desert bear fruit." [23] This attitude not only offers a new mandate to Bicentennial planners, but it also suggests a continuing concern which hopefully will be initiated in Bicentennial enthusiasm.

Canada's handling of ethnic groups, especially the Indians, has merit, in spite of some discrepancies and mistakes. In many cases there were ethnic representatives on Canadian planning councils and committees, and many communities drew heavily on ethnic resources for their programs. Many of the projects listed below are Canadian in origin and represent that nation's attempt at finding understanding and co-operation. Some difficulties have already appeared in Bicentennial planning, and others will appear. Selfish interests can confuse and garble ethnic problems. In the Bicentennial it must be possible for each community to commemorate what is important and interesting to its own culture. The Bicentennial should also be a time when different cultures can look at each other and say hopefully that because of, not in spite of, diversity of heritage and emphasis we will reach our national Tricentennial.

In the projects listed below a specific ethnic group may be referred to as in an actual case study. Planners for the Bicentennial will have to relate their own ethnic situations to the example or broaden the base to a program more related to their specific cases.

Ethnic Arts—There are few better places to approach ethnic expression than in the arts. Indian poetry contests in Canada

22. *Ibid.*
23. *Ibid.*

were popular. Blacks have made a musical contribution to several centennials. The Chicago Jazz Show in the Illinois Sesquicentennial was an interesting example. Black art and literature also have appeared in centennials, and both are live issues for any program stressing our Revolutionary Era. Handicrafts also offer many opportunities, and the Canadians did an unusually good job in stressing this art form for its Indian communities. Indian handicrafts and arts played strong roles in exhibitions, symposia, and in school programs all across the nation.

Drama and artistic dancing have also served to highlight ethnic particulars. Canadian Indians specialized in tribal dances, including a unique rain dance, in several of the western provinces.

Few places have given such publicity to ethnic culture as did San Diego in her Bicentennial in 1969. Fiestas of modern Mexican dance, combined with the ancient rituals of Aztec and Mayan cultures, entertained large numbers in an outdoor arena on the grounds of Fiesta Two Hundred at San Diego's Centennial. Colorfully costumed dancers acted out the saga of ancient peoples, symbolizing their different attitudes about life and death, illustrating patterns and rituals unusual in the modern day. Folk ballet was also popular in these exhibitions, as were marionettes of Mexico, a charming puppet performance, and the Magic of Mexico, a professional demonstration of sleight-of-hand and other magic tricks. Ethnic leaders in the area criticized these events, however, as poor substitutes for more positive and creative actions.

Indian art, colorful and expressive of the particular Indians it represents, speaks volumes for a culture seldom recorded in written documents. The many Indian collections in centennial exhibitions in Victoria, British Columbia, were appreciated by many viewers.

Relating the Museum to the Black Community—Leo F. Twiggs sees the museum as having a very great potential for the future, but immediately he sees that it still lacks rapport with the Black community. In a recent article Professor Twiggs enumerated several suggestions that will relate not only to museums but to other aspects of Bicentennial planning.[24]

(1) Develop exhibits that will inspire the Black community to visit the museum. "Thirty Contemporary Black Artists" was a successful venture along this line. "Harlem on My Mind" was a Metropolitan Museum of Art production of high caliber.

(2) Develop the one-man show, using a Black artist as featured guest in a program which will give the public "greater insights into an artist's creative endeavors."

(3) Determine what resources are available in the community that the museum appeals to. This includes both resources and personnel.

(4) Bring in people from the neighborhood as apprentices, as on-the-job trainees, or as qualified curators.

Ethnic Exhibitions—One of the finest exhibitions now on display is Peter McCloud's "The Legacy," a contemporary British Columbian art exhibit at Victoria's National Museum. Important in the display are weaving, silver carving, special chests, totem poles of all descriptions, facial masks, silver dishes, bracelets, the famous beak headdress of an important British Columbia Indian ritual, and many red cedar products. Displays cover nearly an entire floor and include not only actual and simulated material but descriptions in print and on tape of how these Indians accumulated their materials and how they made the finished products. Periodically, Indian lecturers and demonstrators take part in ceremonies and programs to highlight the particular exhibition. Watching people walk through this exhibition is a thrill in itself, especially observing the children as they identify with the various items.

Many of our own states, including Kansas and Nebraska and most of our Western states, already have interesting centennial Indian exhibits. A new Indian museum opened in Minnesota

---

24. *Ibid.*

in 1960, organized around the story of the native Chippewa through four seasons of the year, might provide a pattern for other museums to study not only Indians but other ethnic groups.[25]

Canada's interesting Ukrainian museum in Manitoba is also a product of Centennial action. This museum, originally an old Ukrainian home, now gives a vivid panorama of a prominent ethnic group long associated with Canadian life.

Ethnic Days—Ethnic days have been very popular in centennials. During the many Indian days in Canada, communities recounted the glories of Indians as they related to that particular region. Indians generally participated in these activities. New Jersey invited Indians in to its Tercentenary for a special occasion.

Many provinces, especially those in the west, celebrated Canada's National Ukraine Festival. Traditional dances, foods, and folkways were highlights of such occasions.

Edgartown, Minnesota, dedicated its ninth annual Dutch Festival to the state Centennial and prepared a special program which attracted one of the largest crowds of the year. They highlighted the accomplishments of the Dutch, with pageantry and frivolity in the best sense accompanying these activities. New Jersey also celebrated several Dutch Days, as well as special days for other national groups.

Ethnic Pageants—The Six Nations Pageant in British Columbia was an outstanding success. The Indians brought their culture into focus with dancing, singing, and plays that spelled out certain group patterns of living, culminating in a community ox-roast at the end. Canada also sponsored a large Indian Princess contest, choosing twelve princesses from as many different tribes. Selections were based on leadership ability, poise and personality, and a knowledge of their own

---

25. See Doris Platt, "The Youthful Outlook," *History News*, 23 (September 1968), 158.

people. This is a counterpart to the beauty or queen pageant which too often discriminates against minority groups.

Indian war games, races, archery, and original Indian lacrosse were featured in a special Canadian Centennial program offered to all the provinces. This was quite a popular program. Combining such a series of activities with an ethnic dinner, a slide series, or a film broadens the possibilities for educating the public. Powwows were very popular all across western Canada and into Ontario in the Canadian Centennial. Indians came into central locations selected by their chiefs, had discussions, shared cultural activities, and enjoyed dancing, singing, and other forms of festivity.

Miscellaneous Projects—In the Illinois Sesquicentennial a book of biographical sketches of famous Blacks of Illinois made its appearance. Canadian planners in 1967 sponsored special instruction in courses on Indian history, social, legal, and economic forces in Indian communities, and other important subjects. Canadian educators also examined the degree to which they were patronizing and degrading their Indian groups. Mariapolis, Manitoba, set up programs for grades three, four, and five, which showed Indian and Eskimo clothing, tools, and household items. Written and oral histories interpreted ethnicity in Canada; researchers and interviewers often visited Indian communities for material.

Genealogy also makes an important contribution to understanding special cultures. One Black group in Virginia is searching to see whether it can find members of its race who are eligible for entrance into various patriotic organizations. Illinois made a Sesquicentennial project of its general "open house" program, which brings neighbors together in an integrated situation and points up the prospects for extending such activities to larger communities.

Several days honored Canadian ethnic leaders, and a booth at *Expo* recognized achievements of national groups across the country. Ottawa's summer village brought children from different ethnic backgrounds together to promote friendship and understanding. Across the nation exchange groups took part in pow-wows, talent shows, and other programs. School groups and local clubs found this activity especially effective.

ARTS

[We go to see *Macbeth*] to learn what a man feels like after
he has gained a kingdom and lost his soul—Northrop Frye [26]

Driving along America's highways, crossing her muddy streams, hiking through her denuded forests, or watching the flashing panoply of a city's lights shouting out their incoherent themes at night—all stamp upon the individual a vivid realization of what ugliness is all about. What great need we have for a new consideration of beauty for our everyday lives, and what better time is there than a Bicentennial to put a new emphasis on the arts to provide us with hopes for new beauty. Centennials are times of opportunity, and planners in many of the case studies above effectively highlighted arts features into their programs—both to entertain and for new emphases. Already much effort is being expended to bring the arts into 1976 celebration on every level, with the exciting new roles being played by the National Endowments for the Arts and for the Humanities offering encouragement to all.

What do the arts offer a planner as he looks toward his Bicentennial program? One critic recently gave a partial answer to this question, saying "The most valuable function of artist and his art is to tell us who we are and help us to see ourselves for what we are." [27] He might also have added, to help us know where we are going. Art then is involvement with, and not escape from, reality. The arts criticize: they zero in on the weak-

---

26. Northrop Frye, *The Educated Imagination* (Bloomington: Indiana University Press, 1964), 63.

27. John R. Watts, "Why the Arts," *Boston Art* [Massachusetts Council on the Arts and Humanities] (April 1970), 19.

est links of our society and bring them to the attention of those who can correct them. Arts reflect the temper of our times as do very few other aspects of our culture. "They have a . . . forceful and direct delivery," says Watts. They get directly to the heart and to the mind. Art is "an international language," wrote the late Yale president A. Whitney Griswold. It serves "as a passport through time and space." [28] Art then is an effective means of communication.

Art is also good therapy. It is an excellent means of education, since good art reaches large audiences. Art is disciplined, yet it offers imponderable variety. It crosses ethnic lines, or it recalls ethnic particulars in support of a people's heritage. It knows no age bounds. It provides entertainment in the finest sense of the word. It gives unusual release to the creative spirit of man and offers special appeals to the disaffected youth of our present world. "Arts . . . have been a unifying force in the affairs of man," recently said Robert Shaw, conductor of the Atlanta Symphony Orchestra. [They] "have promoted understanding and affection rather than half truths and no trust." [29] Finally, an arts emphasis in a centennial gives opportunities and encouragement to the artists themselves to perform and create at their best.

It will indeed be the wise planner who looks to the arts to express some of the complex themes that will reveal and express the various spirits of celebration in the Bicentennial. Art programs, projects, and events are as varied as the people who design them. Quality is heavily dependent upon resources available. But even with minimum resources good arts programs are possible. Some of the following programs may be helpful as models, they may stimulate new activity, or they may just show what others have done in times of celebration.

---

28. A. Whitney Griswold, *Liberal Education and the Democratic Ideal* (New Haven: Yale University Press, 1962), 84.

29. Quoted in Nancy Hanks, "Government and the Arts," *Saturday Review* (February 28, 1972), 32.

Exhibitions—Earlier we saw exhibitions related to heritage, but they deserve special consideration under Arts. Exhibitions of the arts, especially the plastic arts, can focus on three-dimensional materials, a collection of photographs, or a combination of the two. They can be static—objects arranged in stationary patterns—or they can be live, combining features that will appeal to the other senses—smell, taste, touch, and hearing. Collections may be permanent, kept in the same location for long periods of time, or they can be mobile. Some displays will show only actual historical materials, some will use reproduced items or symbols, still others will combine reality and reproduction. Exhibitions can take the form of collages, historical scenes, window displays, maps, arrangements of documents and papers, and many other possibilities that experts will devise. They may have Bicentennial themes of courage, democracy, freedom, liberty, individualism, and beginnings, or they may deal with more specific topics that include uniforms and clothing, maps, guns, and transportation, among many others. Exhibits may present something of the period through focus on the life of a single figure, or they can feature a community or even a larger political unit. Comparison also offers many opportunities for creative efforts.

In addition to special arts shows of individual artists, other possibilities for exhibit include stamp exhibits; pictures and models of architecture; unusual sculpture; handicrafts; paintings of people, scenes, buildings, and battles; mosaics with certain parts highlighted by unusual techniques; and exhibitions that focus on various disciplines, including science, technology, medicine, psychology, and education. Railroads, canals, and farms make good exhibition topics because they reveal the past so vividly. Other possibilities for exhibitions are almost limitless; the range of possibilities will increase as planners conceive new ideas. Some of the unusual exhibitions of other centennials are listed below as examples of what other people have done.

(1) Mother and child exhibits: In the Canadian Centennial, Winnipeg planners developed a special Mother's Day project

entitled "Mother and Child Exhibits." This exhibition presented the art works of the great masters which dramatized the role of motherhood, mother-child relationships, and the many facets of the role of mother as seen by the artist.

(2) Dioramas: The diorama is a special three-dimensional miniature scene that is very popular in places where exhibition area is limited. Among the many dioramas that have been used in centennials two in New Jersey illustrate possibilities. The Wood Ridge diorama recreated that community as it was at the turn of the century. The students of the high school art department at Roxbury Township presented a diorama of an Indian squaw, Magepeta, which attracted enough attention to warrant display at the New Jersey Pavilion at the World's Fair. The Mariner's Museum at Newport News, Virginia, acquired its impressive diorama of the *Merrimack-Monitor* fight as a feature of the Civil War Centennial. This exhibit took more than a year to prepare and cost over $12,000.

(3) Son et lumiere (sound and light): The first *son et lumiere* came out of France about 1952 and holds great possibilities as a form of artistic expression for Bicentennial days. Paul Robert-Houdin blended interpretative lighting and sound with stable and moving objects for an entertaining and pleasing historical dramatization. Robert-Houdin may have been inspired by watching a historic European castle under the bombardment of an impressive thunderstorm. First reception of this new mode of presentation was good, and the idea spread to other parts of the world. Canadian planners, impressed by the reception of *son et lumiere,* decided upon an elaborate production for their own Centennial year.

During a *son et lumiere* presentation, no live performers appear, nor are there sets or films. The focus is on a building caught up in a barrage of sounds and flashing lights. A Canadian writer's description gives some indication of the impact of *son et lumiere* on an audience:

With the use of dynamic light alone . . . the building can begin to live—a light goes out in one room and appears in another, and we imagine the movement of an historic character from one place to another. Light floods out from a large room. It is interpreted frequently by something crossing the source and we imagine the room to be full of people. A light projector throws simulated fire on a high tower and we watch it burn. Tall flames leap into the sky. A wall crumbles as the lights on its separate bricks go out. An unseen carriage travels across the grounds, its flickering coach lamps lighting the lawns and trees it passes.[30]

Add sound to this and you get a vivid re-creation of an historical event.

Canadians focused on their impressive Parliamentary buildings in Ottawa for a *son et lumiere* in their Centennial of 1967. Action around these buildings produced one of the largest and most spectacular of such presentations. The flashing lights and recorded voices from the past told the story of a nation, its birth and its growth. The forty-five minutes of action filled eyes and ears with highlights of a nation's history and left the audience with an uncanny feeling that they had actually been there.

Dan Klugherz of New York City produced an interesting sound-and-light program for Independence Hall in Philadelphia entitled *A Nation Is Born.* Audiences were attentive to its "broad unfolding story of the nation's birth," and to the interspersed human sequences: "the secret removal of the bell from the tower . . . ; the sufferings of American prisoners in Independence Hall when it was a British jail" and others.[31] Klugherz is a pioneer in sound-and-light production and has several other productions for the Bicentennial in mind. *A Nation Is Born* is longer than most productions, but it relates well to the Bicentennial season.

---

30. *A Study and Recommendations for a Sound and Light Presentation on the Parliament Buildings Ottawa Prepared for the Centennial Commission* (Ottawa, Ontario, Canada: Legendrama Productions Limited, 1965) , 5.

31. Letter from Dan Klugherz to author, February 26, 1972.

An earlier sound-and-light presentation, *The American Bell,* with a script written by Archibald MacLeish, was held in Philadelphia in 1962. Frederic March was the narrator, and the voices of Broadway actors were recorded in the roles of Washington, Jefferson, and others.

Movie producer Charles Guggenheim is adding a new dimension to sound and light. He recently produced an innovative indoor sound-and-light representation of events at the end of the Civil War and the Lincoln era of reconstruction, which focused on Ford's Theatre in Washington.

Sound and light will make a significant contribution to the Bicentennial. Already the French government has expressed interest in co-operating to make some such ventures possible. Charles C. Wall, the director of Mt. Vernon, speaks enthusiastically of the possibilities involved in a *son et lumiere* for General Washington's historic home as a centennial project and plans are underway for such a project. *Son et lumiere* is generally an expensive proposition and requires talent and artistry, but the effect is magnificent if properly done. Audiences are highly receptive to well-done shows which strongly stir their imaginations. Poorly done, the show can be the most dismal of failures.

(4) Antique shows: An impressive show in Marlboro County, South Carolina, in 1970 focused on items loaned from individual homes. Documents, dolls, linen, china, silver, and other mobile items were included. Other centennial antique shows have included items from homes, shops, and other displays. Items must be carefully marked and properly insured.

(5) Wild flower show: A wild flower show featured in the San Diego Bicentennial was an innovation on the popular flower show. Flowers gathered from the desert and from the mountains made an impressive and colorful display at a local museum.

(6) Nature pictures: Though not a Centennial project per

se, Minnesota in 1964 released two portfolios of nature pictures, each print suitable for framing.

(7) Electric map: An unusual fourteen-foot electric relief map of Jackson's Valley Campaign, with 346 lights flashing the story of one of the war's most important campaigns, was a feature of the Civil War Centennial. Other communities have had modifications of this, but few were as spectacular as the "Valley."

(8) "Sketches From The Field": Indiana's impressive display may suggest something to local planners. This was a collection of drawings and water-colors by a captain in the 32nd Indiana Volunteers. This was a German regiment, and the one hundred sketches by the captain presented dramatic insight into an unusual military unit.

(9) Traveling replica: Traveling replicas have been popular in centennials because they offer excellent reproductions to areas that normally would not be touched by the larger traveling companies. Minnesota's famous Red River Ox Cart traveled more than 420 miles in that state's Centennial to illustrate an earlier means of transportation in many of the rural areas.

(10) Military medicine exhibition: The Armed Forces Institute of Pathology had a Centennial Room during the Civil War commemoration that told the story of wounds, suffering, and death in the Civil War. In this exhibition medical art, early photographs, actual materials including bone specimens, medical books, medical instruments, and historical writings tied together a stirring story of the development of military medicine.

(11) Period water colors and drawings: The National Gallery of Art's display of water colors and drawings from the soldiers in the field in the Civil War gave a panorama of an important era of American history when photography was still in its infancy.

(12) The Library of Congress Civil War Exhibition: This exhibition deserves special treatment. It consisted of drawings,

prints, photographs, maps, letters, historical documents, and books of the Civil War period.

(13) Public opinion profile exhibition: In the New Jersey Tercentenary, a specially trained staff, using information from the Opinion Research Corporation of Princeton, computed individuals' behavior profiles as compared with the national average for such activities as television viewing, political viewpoints, books read, theaters attended, and so forth.

(14) "Live" exhibitions: A New Jersey exhibition that offered a variation on other types of live exhibitions featured a young man dressed in Revolutionary War uniform standing in the midst of a period exhibition. Periodically he fired an authentic flintlock musket and an old French cannon, to the great delight of large crowds.

(15) Demonstrations: Demonstrations popular in centennial celebrations have included painting, ceramics, and wood carving. Glass blowing in the New Jersey Pavilion at the World's Fair and also at Jamestown show the educational value of this type of exhibition. Demonstrations also include equipment displays by manufacturers.

(16) Handicrafts: Handicrafts are popular for doing and for viewing. In "doing," people work together learning a new art form: candlemaking, broommaking, blacksmithing, toymaking, carving, papier-maché, bisque and other forms of pottery, and furniture making or refinishing are a few. In "viewing," participants exhibit their finished products.

(17) "Sounds" exhibition: One Civil War enthusiast recorded the actual sound of Minie balls and Civil War cannon, trying to capture the true sounds of combat a hundred years earlier. Reproduced, these became a three-dimensional "exhibition" when matched with weapons and pictures of battle scenes.

(18) Centennial dolls exhibition: In Canada an exhibition of four sets of period dolls was made available to women's organizations, schools, libraries, and other groups across the nation. These dolls were ten inches high and each had its own

hand-painted background. Primarily educational, the collection was also used for fund raising and for general viewing.

(19) Artmobile: Artmobiles carry not only paintings and other plastic arts displays, but they also explain the art with recorded tapes and helpful packets that educate people. They have been difficult to keep on the road because of the high expense. Two operated during Virginia's Jamestown Festival, but one of them had been in operation before the 1957 celebration. The second artmobile, which appeared during the Centennial, is still in use. New Jersey's endeavor to raise money for such a Tercentenary project failed.

(20) Graphic art exhibition: An interesting variation in exhibits appeared in the Frankfort (Germany) Graphic Arts Display in the summer of 1971. The emphasis was on content: reality and spontaneity blended to stress the fact that "drawing now as ever has an important function in many aspects of everyday life as a direct form of communication, notation and planning." [32] This is an excellent idea for communities which desire to broaden the base of participation in the arts, for at this level "there is consequently no difference with regard to effect between an artist and a non-artist."

(21) Bicentennial designing: The industrial education students of Glassboro (Pennsylvania) State College have attracted national attention recently in a showing of Bicentennial models. These exhibits, conceived and designed by students of the school, include designs of pavilions that these young artists believe will fit into the context of a Bicentennial fair. This program presents students with the opportunity to stretch their creativity into Bicentennial planning, placing an emphasis upon modern architecture and design. [33]

Students from 16 New Jersey counties recently participated

32. Ernest Gunter Engelhard, "Round The Galleries," *The German Tribune,* September 1971, 7.

33. *Bicentennial Era,* 2 (May–June 1971) , 3.

in a similar exhibition—designing potential models for a New Jersey pavilion in the 1976 Bicentennial Exposition.[34]

(22) Continuing exhibitions: The Butler Institute of American Art in Youngstown, Ohio, has begun a continuing series of displays of American art and history—displays to be presented each May indefinitely to commemorate the Bicentennial.[35] Continuing displays offer the community a chance to develop its own exhibits and to include the history of its own community in the Bicentennial proceedings.

Theater—With current interest in drama so high, community theater, which has already achieved prominence in local centennials, now can be used to celebrate the national Bicentennial. Many of these theaters are sponsored by local merchants and other community leaders and find most of their talent locally. Their patterns have already been set by local theaters, including Barn Theaters and community summer theater.

(1) Folk opera: The University of Mississippi prepared and presented two folk operas during the Civil War Centennial commemoration, one the story of the history of a military unit, the other, a study of life in Mississippi during the war period.

(2) Drama workshop: In Canada these workshops were generally a responsibility of the provincial or federal government; though in local centennials, schools, clubs, and individuals usually assumed responsibility.

(3) Experimental theater: Experimental theater is a variation of the community theater except that the emphasis is on new plays and new techniques in drama production.

(4) Drama reproductions—plays and operas: A popular project for a centennial is the reproduction of a period play or opera. South Carolina Tricentennial planners arranged for the reproduction of *Porgy and Bess,* an original musical about Charles Towne, and the opera *Flora.* A high school group in the

---

34. *New Jersey Historical Commission Newsletter,* 2 (March, 1972), 1.

35. *Bicentennial Era,* 2 (May–June 1971), 7.

state also did William Gilmore Simms' nineteenth-century play *The Yemessee.*

(5) Folk theater: Canada and North Carolina captured something of the heritage of the past in these presentations.

(6) Folk festival: Calgary's folk festival in the Canadian Centennial, *I Am An Albertan,* had twenty acts that represented the many ethnic cultures of Alberta. These acts ranged from Indian children's choirs singing "This Land Is Your Land," to bawdy, knee-slapping Bavarian folk dances.

Few American centennials have done as much with folk talent as North Carolina did in her Tercentenary. In *The Sojourners and Molly Sinclair,* a folk musical drama, local history came alive in singing, dancing, band music, and fiddlers.

(7) Children's theater: Programs of special appeal to the younger folk.

(8) Shakespearian theater: These productions appear in some form in many centennials, are appropriate for nearly all of them.

(9) Drama contests: The District of Columbia Recreation Department sponsored a series of one-act play tournaments in 1961.

(10) Festival of the arts (County Level) : A Festival of the Arts in Guilford County, North Carolina, appealed to the artistic sense of its citizens. Artists, craftsmen, dancers, sculptors, and musicians prepared and performed with highlights centering on the local scene.

Music, Art, and Literature—Music, art, and literature have engaged Centennial planners in a variety of creative projects. Some representative programs follow.

(1) Pro-musica: Professional musicians, including vocalists and instrumentalists, performed music of the seventeenth century for a select audience during the South Carolina Tricentennial.

(2) Choral festival: In 1970 Manitoba brought together choir groups from all over the province in a centralized choral

festival. They competed against each other and then also performed in hospitals, nursing homes, music centers, Y's, shopping centers, and schools. Bands, ensembles, and other special musical groups have followed similar practices—travel and service for the performers, entertainment and culture for the audience.

(3) Colonial music workshop and services: During the North Carolina Tercentenary, the religious activities committee of Guilford County, North Carolina, sponsored a workshop for choirs to learn and prepare colonial music presentations—with special emphasis upon the Christmas season.

(4) Mom-Pop festival: Here the usual pattern is to feature music of special interest to citizens over forty for part of the evening, and tying in with teas, tours, films, and fashion shows during the rest of the time.

(5) Local music: Brockville, Ontario, used local musicians in special centennial programs and performances.

(6) Centennial artists-in-residence: As did the Canadians and several states in their centennial activities, colleges in particular will do well in the Bicentennial year to sponsor some artist-in-residence. Teachers-in-residence is a variation that brings in new talent and ideas.

(7) Poetry festival: Canada, New Jersey, and Minnesota stressed composition and reading.

(8) Essay-writing: This is usually a popular and worthwhile form of centennial endeavor—though it can be used to promote narrow interests. Planners must check topics, supervisors, and the administrative problems in setting up such programs.

(9) Parents-children reading project: Several Canadian provincial libraries organized programs where parents and their children read and discussed books together.

(10) Paint-ins: The Manitoba *Centurion* of July 15, 1966, described a paint-in that must have been exciting. Art students, art directors, postmen, housewives, garage mechanics, and many others registered to fill 168 latex-covered panels attached to the

fence around the large Centennial Center then under construction. Despite prizes given, most artists admitted that these were not the primary objectives. In another Canadian community, a similar experience was called a "Paint-Out."

(11) Mosaic wall: Fifteen hundred square feet of wall space at the new cafeteria of a British Columbia secondary school served as a large easel for the students.

(12) Architectural survey: Several centennial projects have taken account of community architecture to record their community history, to survey possible historic sites, and to seek a better understanding of the arts in their own community.

(13) Japanese garden: This particular garden came as a result of Canadian friendship to Japanese immigrants into Canada. Located in Lethbridge, Alberta, it now commands attention throughout the province.

(14) Special carving projects: Centennial Canadian artists used soapstone and wood carvings in special projects and displays. British Columbia Indians excelled in this type of presentation with reproductions of the early relics of their culture, especially the totem pole.

(15) List of local artists: Every community should also list all local artists of every description—writers, painters, architects, and so forth, and record this permanently for the library. Newspapers perform a valuable service by publishing such a list during the Centennial year with some notations about each artist.

(16) Arts consulting service: The state commission of the Minnesota Centennial provided "a pageantry and drama consulting service" to assist all committees, schools, and other organizations to plan and present proper artistic programs which incorporated the Centennial theme. Communities would be wise today to work with a special consultant, perhaps someone from within their own area who would offer his services on a reasonable basis. Unfortunately, many communities do not have such an expert; thus community representatives should request such services of the state central committee.

The University of Minnesota drama advisory service eventually published a pamphlet entitled *History Through Drama,* a practical guide to planners considering programs relating to fine arts and pageantry. A second pamphlet offered the same guidance for musical programs.

(17) Inventory of American paintings: The National Collection of the Arts of the Smithsonian Institution is currently involved with an unusual Bicentennial inventory of American paintings. This is an attempt to get all paintings by Americans into a central file.

(18) Summer fine arts seminars: The New York Folk Culture Seminars included materials on customs, folktales, songs, dances, humor, art, religion, and handicrafts. Such seminars provide local historians and centennial planners with techniques of recording and portraying local history, organizing societies, planning outdoor historical dramas, and caring for maps, prints, pictures, and manuscripts already available. Many modifications could be made for summer seminars, to include music, drama, painting, writing, and all other forms of art expressions.

(19) Centennial workshops for strings and composers: Winnipeg held a four-day Centennial Workshop in 1967 as an opportunity for young musicians to work with a symphony orchestra under the immediate tutelage of eminent instructors. The Winnipeg Symphony Orchestra, in co-operation with Festival Canada, assumed travel and living expenses for those selected.

(20) "Lost arts" workshop: This workshop, sponsored jointly by the Washington Rock (New Jersey) Girl Scouts, the Union County Historical Commission, and the New Jersey Arts Council has recently revived interest and instruction in the lost arts, colonial art and handicraft long lost to the creative talents of man. These arts include: candle craft; decorative painting and stenciling, including theorum painting (stencil painting on velvet) ; papercraft, including filigree, pressed, tole, and poti-

chromania (similar to decoupage) ; dried and pressed flowers; woodcarving and treen; historical needlecraft; permanent flowers; tinsel painting; pierced and punched peddler tin; toymaking; marbelized bookbinding, and hairpin lace. Such programs draw a close tie between the present and the past to all age groups.

(21) Museum folk art project: Studio Watts Workshop is a recent endeavor which seems to offer possibilities for a similar Bicentennial project. Two museums in this highly volatile Los Angeles community have set up programs which use locally collected material in conjunction with their regular collections. The object is "to preserve the ephemeral art found in shop windows, back yards, rambling bungalows, and, increasingly, on walls and fences; to document its creations; and to develop new ways to integrate it into the sophisticated presentations of traditional museums." Beyond this they want to determine exactly what folk art is, who the artists are, and how they can bring the community into better relationship with these elements of society that have been so long unattractive to them.[36]

(22) Rip Van Winkle display: New York State seized upon the famous fictional character Rip Van Winkle as the focus for a Centennial art exhibition. Through Rip they presented the times, the place, and something of the history of the region. Options of other characters are open to Bicentennial planners.

(23) Special collections: Acquiring new paintings, musical instruments, and other museum materials provided valuable additions to collections in the Museum of Canada during its Centennial. This could be a way to centralize Revolutionary War items in our own museums.

Miscellaneous Art Projects—Other projects focus on similar

---

36. John M. Woods, John W. Blane, Will McWhinney, "Studio Watts Workshop," *Museum News*, 50 (May 1972), 17. See also Emily Dennis Harvey and Bernard L. Friedberg, eds., *A Museum for the People* (New York: Arno Press, 1971) ; "Anacostia," *History News*, 27 (May 1972), 102–103.

themes and ideas as those listed above and provide variety to the creative planner.

(1) Photography projects: Photography projects will appear in the Bicentennial in several different ways, if past centennial programs are any indicator, including photography contests— before its demise, *Life* magazine initiated a lively photography contest for the American Bicentennial—historical exhibitions, and photographs with social messages, such as the Canadian exhibition showing the role of the woman in Canadian business for more than a hundred years.

(2) Films: Films have been a vital part of every centennial in the past twenty-five years. Canada especially made great strides, using films as materials for entertainment, education, and public relations. The National Film Board of Canada offered assistance in the production of an extensive film program, including several designed especially for the Centennial.[37]

The Hundredth Summer, the story of Prince Edward Island's celebration of the Centennial, depicted well the fun of local festivities. *Celebration* told the story of a Canadian family celebrating the Centennial year. *Centennial Travelers* depicted a youth exchange program between a Quebec family and a British Columbia family. *Centennial Fever,* a lively film and an excellent model for local filming, was a perceptive twelve-minute inside view of Centennial activities in St. Paul, Alberta. *Helicopter Canada,* an ambitious effort received with only lukewarm appreciation by the people, was a fifty-minute "big beautiful, brash, and bright" portrait of Canada taken from a helicopter. There were also special films on the history of the Confederation, on explorers and discoverers of Canada, on some of Canada's leading citizens, and on unusual or special themes.

Filming is an expensive endeavor, and success does not come easy. Amateurs often fail to achieve desired goals. Communities

---

37. One of Canada's most innovative film experts has many ideas to offer Bicentennial film-makers. See Lawrence Elliott, "Norman McLaren: Gentle Genius of the Screen," reprint from *Reader's Digest* (August 1971).

planning projects would be well advised to employ skillful direction and use exciting themes. This area contains as many possibilities as there are artists interested in this medium.

(3) Central clearing house: In its official study of the arts, Canadian planners recommended a national clearing house for all artistic endeavors. This has great possibilities for local use. A clearing house makes certain that programs do not overlap, are shared with other communities in the same general locale, and that programming is arranged to meet a particular situation or cultural fete.

(4) Christmas open house: Connecticut's Danbury Scott-Fanton Museum and Historical Society sponsored an interesting colonial Christmas party that has possibilities for centennial expression. Young people made their own candles for the event and arranged music and refreshments. The party was strictly a colonial affair with only colonial activities involved.

(5) Manual training projects: Manual training programs have been used as centennial projects for many young people.

SERVICE

Canadians would probably have labeled this section "Action," or "Community Action," for most of these activities were attempts to involve community elements in dealing with some of the most obvious social problems of the day. Taking a cue from North Carolina's proposal of making the Bicentennial a time to renovate the spirit of nation-building of 1776, I have listed centennial projects that have achieved this end with some degree of success.

National Beautification—The Canadian Commission faced up to a shamefully neglected physical environment of noise and visual disorder, with an emphasis upon "a new stewardship of the land." Their program focused on two fundamental factors: Relationship—fitting the parts of the environment together;

and identity—enhancing the distinctive qualities of each community.

The Canadian Commission implemented its ecological concerns with a national beautification program in the name of the Centennial. They made available to all interested planners a series of ten *What-to-Do and How-to-Do It* manuals, a *Community Improvement Idea Information Bulletin,* a series of color slides, a 16mm motion picture film, and poster displays. They also compiled an extensive slide library on community improvement, including projects as they appeared. Revising and republishing the ten manuals, which were available in large supply during the Centennial, would be a good project for the ARBC or some other group. Some projects suggested by these manuals include:

(1) Cleaning up the "C" strip: The "C" strip is the line of commercial establishments that line both sides of highways approaching a community. Too often they demonstrate a total disregard for any kind of visual order. The Canadian Commission suggested preparation of a master plan and community cooperation in a "rehabilitation program." This program would eliminate "madvertising," the patchwork of signs and billboards that present "a cacophony of chaos" to anyone approaching the town and include service station beautification, planting trees and flowers along the main streets, eliminating overhead wiring, beautifying the highways, and eliminating or disguising auto graveyards and salvage lots.

(2) Community facelift: This project suggested improvement and beautification of the town center, including rearranging street furniture (benches, litter containers, telephone booths, signs, and lighting standards) ; adding floral display tubs, pedestrian walks, and crosswalk oases and landscaping medians; and beautifying parking lots. Trees and flowers to accentuate natural features and elimination of harsh street signs would restore beauty to the downtown area, as would beautifi-

cation of the "corner store," and homes and buildings along the streets.

These actions require extensive community co-operation. To initiate such projects the Canadian Commission suggested the formation of a Citizen Amenity Commission, to include people who had the visual as well as the economic interest of the community in mind. This commission handled the promotion of improvement and beautification projects within the framework of the community plan. It recommended a series of individual projects for change, outlined areas of discrepancy, and presented specific suggestions for total community improvement.

(3) Centennial clean-up: Part of a larger beautification program, Centennial clean-up directed planners' attention to certain basic aims: instilling an appreciation for community appearance; fostering permanent interest in community improvement; promoting good "outdoor" manners; developing personal consideration for keeping playgrounds and streets clean; and encouraging permanent litter-prevention programs.

To support these aims, all publicity stressed the need for clean-up by showing photographs and maps of discrepancies within the community. Committees from all clubs, schools, and organizations were mobilized, and business, labor, local government, and young people became vital forces in supporting local actions.

Canadian authorities eventually established workshops all across the country to work on the general theme of community beautification. In the final analysis, however, the local community had to make its own move.

Local Beautification—Several other beautification projects that appeared in centennials also might offer further suggestions to planners.

The Canadian village of Pointe Claire set a month aside to plant chrysanthemums at churches and schools. A Sesquicentennial "Let's Beautify Illinois" project included tree-planting on Arbor Day, beautifying the state's surviving covered bridges, and accumulating materials, publications, maps, and films, in the schools and public libraries to encourage further beautification programs. Wisconsin's *Community Achievement Day Handbook* suggested clean-up paint-up, and fix-up campaigns, with prizes going to the communities with the best performances.

Illinois's "Lonesdale Project" was a neighborhood beautification project, supported by several grants, which installed swimming pools, recreation areas, craft and fashion shops, and thus created a whole new atmosphere for living. Sculpture, art, and a free bookstore added other dimensions to this exciting new mode of living.

Brockville, Canada, made a clean-up project unique by concentrating on the town library. Many specialists donated their services, and others provided the labor for a total renovation of the reading rooms. Volunteer workers also installed electric baseboard heating and put in a drop ceiling, modern light fixtures, and carpeted floors.

Several cities may want to study the project of Edmonton, Alberta, as a prospect for their own Centennial. A scale model of Edmonton's plans for the future was constructed and placed in public view by the City Commission. Indians from surrounding areas, many of whom had no idea what the future city might be like, were especially interested in this project.

Ecology Programs—Suomi College, of Hancock, Michigan, in co-operation with several other schools and authorities, celebrated its seventy-fifth anniversary with a symposium on science and ecology.

The Canadian Wildlife Federation set up a Centennial project to inform children about the various aspects of nature. This included nature hikes, instruction, and examples of things they could do to improve the country's ecology. This program was so popular that it was repeated several different years after the Centennial.

In 1972 the United States celebrated the sesquicentennial of the birth of Frederick Law Olmsted, Sr., whom some historians designate the founder of the current ecology movement, dating back to the 1880s. To commemorate this birthday, the Olmsted Sesquicentennial Committee planned four major projects: collecting his unpublished papers; preserving his home and office in Brookline, Massachusetts; conducting a major public symposium entitled "The Great Parks of American Cities"; and preparing exhibits of his work.

In honoring this ecology pioneer, the sesquicentennial will also bring attention to bear upon a major social problem in the United States today—the preservation of our natural resources. Bicentennial planners may attract attention to other relevant issues by honoring other important men.

Peace Garden—In a day when peace is much on our minds, it seems that a Bicentennial should highlight peace concerns. The ingenuity of students and others interested in peace programs inspired several Canadian peace gardens. Numerous related activities included booths on streets and in parks to distribute literature and materials, decorated shop windows, a specially planted flower garden, and street pageantry on anti-war themes.

Bicentennial Garden Spot—Bedford County, Pennsylvania, has begun a project that could well start a trend in vacation-minded America. The county possesses a "charming rural area" in the Pennsylvania mountains and has long been known as a tourist and resort center. To celebrate their own Bicentennial, which is possibly just a preliminary to celebrating the nation's Bicentennial, they designated March through November of 1971 as a time of a special Bicentennial celebration. They opened up sports events to larger participation, touched them up with a colonial flavor when possible, set up trails and tours, brought in antique cars, had rifle shoots and bow-and-arrow contests, re-enacted an old Appalachian wagontrain trek across the mountains, presented a three-hour spectacular pageant, set up exhibitions, had costume parties and dances, and dubbed themselves the "Garden Spot of Pennsylvania."

Cultural Exchange Programs—Twinning of municipalities, begun in 1951 in France, included the promotion of cultural twinning or pairing of cities in different lands. Eventually the World Federation of Twinned Cities was formed, with its primary task to obtain universal co-operation centered on individual action at the municipal government level. Canada seized on twinning as a project for its Centennial in 1967, stipulating that twinning must go beyond open dialogue to produce continuous exchanges of people, services, and information. Everyone and every organization in the concerned municipality was involved. Canada also sponsored a school-twinning program in which schools were paired off and student exchanges arranged by school authorities.

Thirty people from British Columbia made a visit to Quebec, where they attended a series of six orientation sessions on social, cultural, and historical aspects of life in that province. The Canadian Institute of Mining and Metallurgy attempted unsuccessfully to establish a summer job exchange as a Centennial project. In spite of Canada's failure, this is an idea that businesses might adapt to Bicentennial proceedings.

Teen-age friendship programs brought young people together on common subject matter and are good projects for Junior Red Cross, municipal clubs, and school organizations. The Canadian Junior Red Cross initiated a productive series of annual seminars on various contemporary subjects, which stimulated dialogue and new friendships.

Some communities may consider a Canadian project that helped to pay the expenses of high school students visiting the exposition at Montreal. Each student was given a week in Montreal and allowed a certain financial limit. Organizations and clubs might consider a similar project for some of the less fortunate in their community.

Noble County, Minnesota, planners divided the county into

three parts for a good-neighbor program, with the towns in each division designated as hosts for a week's celebration. A large variety of programs appeared, and people crossed community lines to involve themselves with other celebrants.

A good project for automobile clubs, gasoline companies, and others interested in tourists' activities is to arrange a travel schedule, sending appropriate maps to travelers planning to visit a certain area. A counseling service could also be a part of this over-all program.

An interesting community open house in the Fulton County (New York) 1959 Centennial of that state included several tours, exhibitions, and other activities. The glove industry's factory tour was topped off by a pageant describing how the industry works. This program had strong appeal to Centennial visitors.

Rochester, Minnesota, invited all foreign-born residents to "get-acquainted teas," and teen-agers in a Canadian community opened the "Red Baron," a popular coffee shop that received high commendation for its activities. As one of its major Centennial projects, Brockville, Canada, set up a Centennial Youth Arena built with funds raised within the community. This arena consisted of areas for play, drama, and meetings.

Installations and Park Programs—As Centennial projects, Winnipeg placed in its parks a jet plane, an artificial ice rink, and several other youth-oriented projects. In its park, Sudbury, Ontario, put a thirty-foot model of a 1951 Canadian commemorative nickel and several other coins, including a 1964 U.S. Kennedy half-dollar. Other communities built up their parks with playground equipment, picnic and camping facilities, wading pools, tables and outdoor kitchens. One Manitoba community put in a nine-hole golf course, and another built a park museum.

Communities with planetariums or an observatory could put on certain programs to relate the building to the Centennial. Calgary, Alberta, did a fine job with programs like "This Land

Is Your Land," "Spaceship Earth," and "The Wanderers." The first was an introduction to the sky around Calgary, the second dealt with the geological and geographic aspects of the countryside, and the third traced the history of the stars and their names back to the Greeks.

Prince George Province built a Centennial fountain which, they contended, testified to the fact that the community *could* improve its culture and instill a new spirit. Ottawa, Ontario, built a Centennial fountain where people tossed coins for retarded children.

Architectural Surveys and Building Programs—The study of architecture in Illinois helped to reveal the state's history. Architectural surveys recounted the historical developments of Illinois as shown by the old buildings still standing and earmarked certain buildings for preservation and restoration.

The United States National Trust has already suggested how to conduct and organize an architectural survey in its publication, *Preservation for the Bicentennial*. Communities should make this survey as soon as possible, not just to save old buildings but to get a better understanding of the background of the community through its architectural history. Then some of the key buildings can be saved without so much debate and conflict.

Community building projects are good Centennial endeavors, but planners should be aware that they require concerted action of the community and large expenditure of funds. Colby, Kansas, built a large unmortgaged library, which was presented to the city as a Centennial project. The county historical society was pivotal in raising more than a hundred thousand dollars toward the construction of that library. Federal money will also be available in some instances.

Manitoba called one of her projects Operation Total Involvement. It involved people from every walk of life in a varied series of programs. A twenty-minute slide presentation on the many projects being planned through Canada was followed by reports on others. During the discussion period new ideas were pooled for other projects.

Programs to Help Ourselves and Others—Princess Margaret, Manitoba, gave instruction on what it means to be a citizen and how to become one in night citizenship classes.

Victoria, British Columbia, made a special study of European and other nursery schools during their Centennial in order to improve their own techniques and nursery school centers. In Illinois the Head Start and Upward Bound programs adapted their subject matter and direction toward Sesquicentennial themes.

Winkler, Manitoba, set up an industrial workshop for retarded adults as a Centennial project. This non-profit organization offered employment to some of the less fortunate members of the community. Several additional activities for the retarded included a special sports program which brought Centennial athletic awards to youngsters across Canada who took part in numerous sporting events. A program of this type would be a good one for Boy Scouts or other youth-oriented groups to supervise or even instigate.

The Salvation Army was quite involved in Canadian Centennial projects. They renovated a lodge for out-of-town girls, helped to extend the rehabilitation of alcoholics into a special center named Hope Acres, helped boy law-violators by placing them in certain homes under the supervision of older boys, and presented a film entitled *A Canadian Mosaic,* which told the history of the Salvation Army.

Communities will do well to follow Canada's example of engaging students and other youth in special centennial work projects. Work projects, building programs, decorating, clean-up, and so forth would be excellent vehicles of action for fraternities, local clubs, and youth organizations. A special centennial work project might provide free counseling service to young people, drug clinics, and tutoring services. Other subjects for consideration include law services, remedial reading and writing programs, and a job information center.

"Miles for Millions" called for young people to march or hike long distances, to be compensated by so much per mile donated by individuals of communities to a fund for underdeveloped countries of the world. International affairs institutes, folk-sing rallies, coffee house activities, and other projects produced additional monies. Young people were heavily involved in all these activities. Of thirty-five hundred walkers in Ottawa, more than eighty percent were high school students. Winnipeg accepted the challenge of Ontario's achievement, setting its own goals, matching "the capital blister for blister."

Rochester, Minnesota, and the Mayo Clinic sponsored a World Health Organization Day, acting as hosts to the international members of that organization who traveled to Rochester to participate.

Special seminars and other programs for senior citizens appear as regular features in many past centennials. Varied programs provide courses in instruction in real estate, law, taxes, music appreciation, art appreciation, photography, medicine and its use, community history, biographies of state and local dignitaries. Boston has an interesting publication project called *The Senior News,* published by the Commission on Affairs of the Elderly at City Hall. This publication contains articles that are primarily of interest to the elderly and that cover some of the same subjects suggested for seminars. It also serves as a calendar and guide for community events as well as a forum for some of the views of the older citizens.

"Dial a Dietician" was an interesting Canadian project which allowed one to dial a specific phone number and get a dietician who would answer a food problem or give information on better nutrition. This project of the Ottawa Home Economics Association was endorsed by the Academy of Medicine.

In Detroit, Michigan, an urban transportation center is being set up for the Bicentennial.[38]

Thanksgiving Day in 1970 marked the culmination of "Share Centennial Week" in Manitoba. Clubs shared meetings, churches shared religious services, and educational institutions exchanged teachers and students. Topics of the nine-day program included sharing of hearts, time, knowledge, clothing, food, heritage, future, faith, and homes.

Centennial Designations and Awards—The Illinois Sesquicentennial symbol appeared on the diplomas of graduating seniors in that state, and a Sesquicentennial program gave ham operators a special card for making a certain number of contacts. The National Council of Jewish Women of Canada selected eleven outstanding Canadian women for a special centennial award, and several Canadian communities made listings of scientific achievements in their areas. Businesses and organizations can designate their annual programs as centennial celebrations. Oregon planned and made available to local communities filmed documentaries on its twenty colleges as a Centennial project.

Projects in Business and Industry—Special centennial visitor programs were the concern of businesses in most communities. Canadians unified such activities as store decorating, displays of local goods, and community co-operation by displaying the Canadian symbol as a cohesive element.

In some centennials communities tried a low-key approach toward preserving their oldest buildings by converting them into business office complexes. This would appear to be an excellent Bicentennial project, now that money is available for preservation. A railroad depot, an old mansion, a church, a historic school building, and other important community buildings can be modernized inside and cleaned up outside to play a dual role: a good office building and a historic landmark.

---

38. See *Bicentennial Era Newsletter*, II (1971).

One can imagine old courthouses being used this way in the smaller cities, thus maintaining the distinctive mark they make on so many landscapes as period reminders of a significant past.

Canadian industry made several interesting contributions in the name of the Centennial. A Montreal chemical company stocked Canadian waters with young salmon. Some small companies set up Centennial fountain and flower-bed projects. A large bank gave scholarships. Large industries promoted scientific research. Businessmen and industrialists served on local committees, and several industrial organizations developed special in-plant tours for visitors. Probably the most popular feature of most industries was their display of goods and services. Some used actual equipment; others presented displays of pictures that told the story of their operations.

Labor unions in Canada staged seminars and conferences which outlined the labor movement's contribution toward strengthening democratic institutions. They published a history of trade unionism, made tape recordings of reminiscences of early pioneers, put up a series of commemorative plaques and markers and created a long-range program of scholarship and financial aid for students. Unions also sponsored student exchanges, provided social amenities for institutions that dealt with disabled workers, and built several special community centers, such as labor temples and union halls. In Brockville, Ontario, they donated two hundred dollars worth of books about trade unionism to the high schools.

The State Historical Society of Wisconsin held a "Wisconsin Week," recommending several projects that relate well to Bicentennial commemoration. The first was "America at Work" week, which included:

Honoring all those engaged in the process of business, with some special recognition to labor, citing men and women by name when possible; graphic presentation of the statistics of numbers employed, hours worked, pay received, and a profile of the workers themselves; parades and exhibits of products, including old and new models, recent technical developments, and performance demonstrations; open houses and tours, both of the factories and of the community in which the factories play a prominent role; speeches from area development leaders during the week; school presentations, exhibitions, and tours; concerts and other cultural programs, sponsored by business organizations; honoring the oldest enterprise and some of the oldest members of the business community at special cere- monies; outlining plans for future developments in various charts, diagrams, and in programs especially arranged to com- municate messages of the future.

Special Days and Weeks—Government weeks are ideal for centennial times because they deal with the problems of forma- tion of government and the way the community operates in political circles. Government days in Wisconsin were similar to "America at Work" days, and suggestions include the follow- ing: An exchange of mayors or other government officials; open houses and guided tours through the state buildings and offices with lectures on the historic and contemporary importance of each; encouraging citizens to visit government in session during that week; speeches from government officials at clubs, organiza- tions, and schools in programs that emphasize the importance of government and its role in the community; public forum with local politicians discussing some key issue; strategic place- ment of charts of costs, expenditures, and exhibits of govern- ment throughout the community; paying tribute to pioneer officials; programs which deal with future concerns, current problems, ecological problems, and what is being planned to improve the situation; government studies by retired officials and others with an eye to improvement; preserving government materials, documents, and so forth; clean-up and beautification programs; involving students in as many ways as possible, in- cluding exchanges with government officials, visits and tours into government officials' activities, youth panels, forums, and special study courses; encouraging the various elements of the community, including the sheriff, the fire department, the police department, the health department, and others, to stage special programs to indicate what they do in the political scene; involvement of women individually and by groups in special programs. Organizations like the League of Women Voters can provide leadership.

A transportation day can also provide excellent possibilities for centennial celebration. Transportation relates especially well to the Revolutionary period because transportation was just coming into its own at that time. Transportation days provide occasions for creative exhibitions in airports, railway stations, and automobile show windows. Contrasting modern equipment with the past is a popular approach.

Wisconsin suggests organizing transportation choruses to sing at various locations, putting up displays and exhibits in shopping centers and store windows, setting up a "great river-road art show display" in the bank lobby, touring facilities that relate to transportation, including the places where transportation is built, arranging for speeches and other presentations on behalf of transportation facilities, tying in beautification with transportation, arranging educational programs in schools and plants, having newspapers prepare special supplements with pictures and stories from the past, reprinting articles dealing with transportation from other publications, studying new ways to utilize public transportation, making graphs and charts to show how transportation affects the community, promoting programs on safety, and encouraging school students to arrange programs in schools on transportation subjects.

New Jersey, Wisconsin, and Minnesota had agriculture days. Variations on the suggestions for government and transportation days can be utilized for agricultural days.

Individual Projects—The Central Commission of the Canadian Centennial encouraged individual projects. Thousands of Canadians responded, and a list of some of their activities indicates what people might be able to do in a Bicentennial without even relating to a central planning commission.

The local Halifax Council of Women sponsored a room in a hotel where girls picked up by the police could stay instead of going to jail.

One man donated a small piece of land for a Centennial park.

An Albertan collected old photographs on communication, transportation, industry, agriculture, health, religion, and culture, cataloguing the photographs and making them available to other communities for display.

Shell Canada Limited had a Centennial rally of 100 cars and produced a bilingual brochure of Canada for school children across the country.

A Calgary native sponsored an exchange visit between his ten-year-old and a ten-year-old from Ontario. Several individuals followed suit.

One individual made a record as a centennial project. When the record was not published, he hawked copies on the street until the police picked him up.

The Glass Blowers' Union of Regina offered free labor for installation of all glass required for a new animal shelter in the Winnipeg area as a Centennial project.

A Manitoba University professor proposed a student-faculty alliance to help United States draft-dodgers locate in Winnipeg. While this was never a rousing success, with opposition strong and vehement, several young Americans did receive services.

A woman from Kleefeld, Manitoba, made a special quilt, which contrasted life in Canada a century ago with Canada at the time of the Centennial.

One Canadian spent about 130 hours on his Centennial project, a working model of a historic boat. Another individual's rolling railroad presented a historical record of the way life in western Canada focused on its railroad industry.

A teen-age club in British Columbia built a youth recreation center as its project.

A boy in Winnipeg collected pennies with which he built a tower twelve feet tall, seven inches in diameter and with eight windows. A Toronto weirdo tossed a hammer through the window of the U.S. Consulate, describing it as his Centennial project.

A retired school teacher wrote letters to her former students, exchanging pictures.

One Canadian woman made an individual Centennial project of teaching her special courses in every Canadian province and territory during the Centennial year. Her specialty was to teach typing to the beginner in seven hours, practical Spanish in seven hours, and shorthand in thirty.

A man in Alberta made a 250-mile dogsled trip into the snow country as his project.

A Quebec family, as their Centennial project, moved a gristmill ten miles to the site of the original mill. They sent out a family Christmas card with a picture of the mill and the family grouped around it and a poem describing the new experience written by one of the members of the family.

Doll projects were popular. Two women in Montreal dressed a large number of dolls in period costumes.

A Quebec couple made a "unity tent," which boosted the idea of Canadian unity. Two couples shared the tent, one French, the other English.

A Quebec woman wove a twenty-foot stairway rug, highlighting the figures "1867 to 1967" in bright red.

A Quebec couple made up a puppet show, a thirty-minute play which ended with a "Bobby Gimby" puppet's rendition of the popular song "Canada."

A girls' group from eastern Canada made a fourteen-hundred-mile bicycle ride from the Atlantic provinces to *Expo*.

An Ottawa woman collected 1151 salt and pepper shakers and arranged them into the figures 1967.

One of the members of the Centennial Commission decorated his house at Christmastime with the Canadian symbol and other decorations that reminded one of the Centennial.

Another member of the Commission took his family on a canoe exploration trip as his Centennial project. A coach took his family on a tour of Canada, something he had wanted to do for a long time before the Centennial roused the necessary enthusiasm.

A museum director took his family to visit fifty museums on a kind of "busman's holiday," because he felt it was important to understand his country and his profession better.

A Winnipeg woman whose house was on Centennial Street joined five other women to encourage planting petunias. They made a door-to-door plea for other people to plant petunias also, providing them with plants for a small fee.

PAGEANTRY

Centennial pageantry is usually viewed primarily as an expression of man's festive nature. Perhaps this is why pageants have dominated so much of the proceedings in past centennials and why it will be a vital part of planning for 1976. Pageants can be creative and historical, and it is the responsibility of planners to create this larger dimension.

Too often planners seize upon pageantry because it seems the thing to do and because others have had colorful experiences with it. As part of a larger celebration it can rouse interest, engender enthusiasm, and extend participation. But if these are its only functions, or its goal is merely to entertain, then its importance fades with the passing days, and the scenes it created become only dull memories without any lasting reference as to why the celebration was held in the first place.

Pageantry will be popular in the Bicentennial because so many themes from the Revolutionary generation will lend themselves readily to expression in this fashion. Though there are many varied forms of pageantry, the three most prolific expressions are pageants, parades, and fairs. Few groups will not consider one or more of these as a possibility for 1976.

Pageants—A pageant is a simple play, generally centering upon a single theme and making strong emotional appeal. As employed in many centennials, it has much rhetoric, broad local participation, music, dancing, and elaborate costumes. Variations, however, are common, providing many loopholes for local innovations and creativity. Commercial organizations specializing in centennial planning usually recommend a pageant as a focal point for the celebration, and for a fee or a percentage of the gate they will provide skilled leadership to organize and present a pageant geared especially to local needs.

The first book published on celebrating the Bicentennial is virtually a textbook on how to conduct a pageant, and its author supports the use of the pageant as one of the best forms of celebrating historical events.[39] Her purpose, however, is to show how to present a pageant, and planners interested in pageants should consult it as a guide. But they should also be aware that the major weakness of the book is its emphasis upon the pageant as a community's only endeavor.

In deciding whether or not to produce a pageant, planners should consider positive and negative features before beginning the extensive work necessary to make this a vital part of the program. Pageants do transmit historical themes effectively; they generally draw heavily upon local talent in many areas— writing, acting, singing, dancing, stagecraft, directing, even sales and publicity—they make excellent vehicles for crossing ethnic lines; they generate enthusiasm and encourage participation; they can be inexpensive if financial commitments remain modest; and they do present exciting do-it-yourself possibilities for community self-expression.

Too often, however, pageants evince mediocre or controver-

---

39. Adele Gutman Nathan, *How to Plan and Conduct a Bicentennial Celebration* (Harrisburg, Pennsylvania: Stackpole Books, 1971).

sial leadership, poor writing, faulty planning, and bad acting. Though they can be inexpensive, they can also create false hopes of profits that never appear. Too often pageants "grind axes," focus on prejudiced viewpoints, and overextend or oversimplify patriotic themes. Success in pageants is often tied to the availability of a large auditorium or an outdoor arena. Probably more important, planners tend to use them as oneshot affairs, devoting energy and resources to guaranteeing their success and thus neglecting opportunities for projects that would have a more lasting community effect.

Canadians took their pageants seriously in the Centennial of 1967. To guarantee a high caliber of production the Commission employed a team of distinguished writers to prepare scripts in French and English for both indoor and outdoor productions. They also provided money for Indians and other ethnic groups to write their own pageants. Though this centralized action sometimes hindered individual expression and do-it-yourself possibilities, it did provide themes that related directly to the Confederation and to the objectives of the Centennial.

In 1961 Kansas Centennial planners employed a commercial company to help them organize and present a pageant which many considered successful. Saginaw, Michigan, planners are less enthusiastic about their commercial pageant, since they are still paying the bill. In both cases the pageant stimulated enthusiasm and much participation. One was just too elaborate for the resources available.

Down Memory Lane, a New Jersey Tercentenary pageant, told the history of a town's fire and police departments, its parks, its schools, and its public officials by dramatizing them in speeches, slides, and exhibits. Another New Jersey Tercentenary pageant resulted in the participation of more than a thousand students who dramatized the community's history in a pageant written, directed, and produced by local citizens. The Parent-Teacher Association supplied the costumes and scenery, the YMCA furnished the stagehands, the Junior Chamber of Commerce served as directors, and the Boy Scouts and other youth groups acted in whatever capacity they were needed.

Several pageants that were already in existence, operating seasonally, joined their themes with Centennial celebrations to good effect. Among the most exciting were *The Lost Colony* of Roanoke Island, *Unto These Hills* in North Carolina, and *The Common Glory* at Williamsburg, Virginia.

Already New Jersey and several of the original thirteen colonies are planning pageants for 1976. New Jersey plans an outdoor musical drama dealing with the ten days Washington spent in New Jersey in the first winter of the war. To provide a valuable residual effect, this pageant will tie in with the establishment of the state park in the same area. The pageant will stress the beautiful setting, the use of an orchestra, and "startling" choreography.

Pageants need not be related directly to the Revolutionary period. Communities outside the thirteen colonies have many opportunities to use events from their own past to express the same themes as those offered by the Revolutionary generation.

Parades—Though the parade is not unique to America, it has become a distinctive part of our heritage. Many people cannot think of a celebration without recalling a long parade winding in and out of crowded streets: decorated cars filled with community dignitaries or laughing children; bands from high schools and military organizations interspersed among the floats, each playing its own particular tune in a bedlam of noise magnified by sounds of proud parents or little brothers and sisters along the sidelines spotting familiar faces among the marchers.

But the crowds are usually there whether the parade is an elaborate event marking Mardi Gras, Thanksgiving Day, or a local parade to celebrate the Fourth of July or a returned veteran. A parade can speak to almost everybody in the community. Its basic objective is essentially to erect a vivid and exciting show on the familiar streets of the community, and in its best form it becomes a backdrop for history and draws on the creativity of many different people.

Parades require co-operation, much money, sacrifice of time and energy, and good weather. As a popular expression they tend to siphon enthusiasm and creativity from other projects, though they can be organized to produce a completely opposite effect. If a parade emerges out of a larger project, if it brings together ethnic groups who have heretofore been unreceptive one toward the other, if it lifts the community above the commonplace of everyday life, then that parade can have meaning. If it is only fife and drums, the sounds of bands, competition between expensive floats, or flashing crepe paper that will glut the sewers before evening, then the community will do well to mark the Bicentennial another way. Under any circumstances planners should think of planning more than parades and consult one of the many guides suggesting techniques. Some of these guides are included in the bibliography.

Fairs—Fairs take many different forms, from the complex international exposition to high school, club, or even community fairs. Like parades and pageants, they have deep historical roots, and their multifaceted programs give many opportunities for expression. A fair on any level usually generates excitement, enthusiasm, and fun. Because of midways, side shows, clowns, and races it is easy to associate fairs primarily with festivity. Their exhibitions, however, can give full range to man's creative instincts and offer opportunities for historical expression. A fair is a common carrier of local pride and individual accomplishments, and though one may often think only of surging crowds, hawkers, flapping banners, and garish colors everywhere, fairs do bring people together regardless of race, creed, or color, and provide avenues for creative expression. Fairs also provide an excellent locale for displaying centennial symbols, features, and wares, for exposing centennial costumes, and for presenting historical themes through artifacts, pictures, fine art, and even pageantry.

Pageants, parades, and fairs are so commonplace as to be treated more generally than many of the other items listed below. Many of the reservations connected with them, especially as they promote entertainment at the expense of other aspects of celebration, also apply to many of the other programs that appear under the broad designation of pageantry. My general feeling is that pageantry too often dominates celebration proceedings, and to start thinking Bicentennial in terms of pageants, parades, and fairs is to miss the larger issues and possibilities of such an occasion.

(1) Modified pageants: Modifications of pageants often have a distinct modern or regional ring to them. One such example was a street pageant held in a Manitoba city. Several blocks of the street were roped off, and in each block a specific series of activities took place. In one block were eating places where one could order food from several different countries. Another block contained several crude stages upon which various groups performed from time to time, to the appreciation of large audiences. In still a third block bands of all types competed for the attention of the passer-by. In a fourth block vendors sold flea-market goods from hastily devised but period-oriented counters. In my opinion, this type of pageant offers possibilities for both individual creativity and joy of participation.

The fascinating and controversial stage musical *Hair* has also had an important influence on pageantry. Its unusual music, settings, and performances relate more than most to abstract and primitive ways of expressing important themes. Using freely all new media, especially amplified sounds, psychedelic lighting, and natural acting, these productions stimulate the emotions and the senses to add new and exciting feelings to old themes.

Ontario's *Oktoberfest,* an annual affair that offers possibilities for any centennial, has an air of the pageant about it. This suds, sausage, and oompah binge lasts for several fun-packed days in the month of October. German bands provide background music for patrons who sit at long wooden tables, their arms interlocked, their bodies swaying back and forth as they sing German drinking songs. German sausages and beer are generously distributed by German waiters in lederhosen. These programs vary from place to place, but generally they combine parades, celebrity appearances, and display of locally grown meats and baked goods with dancing and singing for a gala affair. One additional attraction is the annual *Bogenschuetzenfest* archers' shoot, in which archers attempt to shoot down a styrofoam eagle with a seventeen-foot wingspread.

(2) Special holiday pageants: Planners interested in local pageantry associated with special holidays might modify the Canadian Centennial activities of Sorel, Quebec. In its project of 1967 Sorel chose Christmas as the special holiday upon which to focus the Centennial interest. Townspeople placed a large and attractive tree in the center of the community square, lighted it with 2,000 lights supplied by an electric company, and put up a stage nearby. Under the lights of the giant tree, local citizens presented a special community pageant which outlined the history of the community's past. Music and drama blended to remind the citizens of Christmas seasons that had gone long before, but which left their impress upon the citizens of another day.

(3) Vaudeville: A New Jersey town presented a vaudeville performance, another variation on the pageant. The New Jersey commission invited all local talent to participate and held auditions all during the winter months to decide upon the participants. Eighteen vaudeville acts resulted, and under skilled leadership some were so good they were featured later at the New Jersey Pavilion at the World's Fair.

(4) Marionette and puppet shows: Though not a specific centennial project, marionette shows in Boise, Idaho, several years ago communicated important history lessons. Like the pageant, these marionette shows mixed fancy with fact for grade school children who presented a short play describing the role

of the donkey in the early gold mining days. The show was written by local people and performed by marionettes carved and costumed in local surroundings. An interesting marionette show in the South Carolina Tricentennial of 1970 depicted the Revolutionary battle of Fort Motte. Many other centennials also employed marionettes to develop interesting and worthwhile historical themes.

Puppets are simpler to construct and operate than marionettes and offer a wider range of participation, especially on the grade school level. Most public libraries have ample material on puppets for general use.

(5) Talent shows: Talent shows offer unusual opportunity for identifying local artists as well as for providing popular entertainment. Several centennials successfully modified the talent show by setting aside a place for various musical groups to perform and letting them attract their own audiences. Some of these were rock groups, others were country or pop, and some were undesignated.

(6) Tattoos and other military pageantry: The Canada Centennial highlighted several popular tattoos—military formations that displayed the color and fine drilling of men and horses to musical accompaniment. Small military units have performed with less spectacular results in local centennials in this country.

(7) Zoo programs: Canadian zoos offered special Centennial programs, including parades, animal shows, name-the-animal contests, folk singing, and other fun activities, many designed especially for children.

(8) Fun days: Flin Flon, Manitoba, headlined "fun day." Planners called on all clubs and organizations to contribute some idea or project to a special day of fun and entertainment. There were dances, interfaith choir-sings, a modified version of *South Pacific* performed by the local glee club, a music festival, a trout-fishing contest, a Flappers' Flip in which costumed ladies revived the life of the '20s, ceremonies to several Centennial projects, a student exchange program, a flower show, a talent

show, and numerous teas, banquets, and fashion shows. Small communities intent upon celebrating for only a short period of time might enjoy a "fun day," but it should be tied to something a bit more lasting.

(9) Balloon race: A balloon race during the Canadian Centennial engendered a great deal of enthusiasm among its viewers. Not only were they interested in who the winner might be, they were also interested in the specially stamped postcards which would serve as mementoes of the occasion. Eight balloons carrying the world's greatest balloonists were covered by television and radio as they took off from Calgary and flew eastward across the prairie. The program excited one of the members of the Centennial Commission, although he did comment that it was very fortunate that no one got killed.

(10) Youth rallies: Youth rallies are very similar to "fun days," except that they are handled by the young people, usually through the schools. Dances, photograph showings, art displays, school fairs, choir concerts, and various contests are examples of the multiple activities associated with these rallies. The emphasis is on getting all the youth in the community involved in a creative and festive way.

(11) Fireworks: Fireworks displays are popular but expensive. They have been part of centennial programs the world over. Fireworks usually mark some special occasion, often an opening ceremony.

(12) Centennial balls: Centennial balls are generally formal affairs in which costumed citizens dance to the music of earlier times. Modifications of the centennial ball include centennial street dances, rock sessions, and popular dances. Dances bring members of the communities together to eat, drink, converse, and mingle in a festive atmosphere. They also are excellent media for raising funds. South. Carolina had a great ball in its Tricentennial, and there were many popular Civil War Centennial balls—especially in the more prominent Confederate cities.

(13) Re-enactments: Re-enactments are difficult to classify by topic, but they often result in colorful pageantry. They are popular because they involve large numbers of people, allow for costume pageantry, and recall days of noble deeds. Battle re-enactments, already discussed, are very popular, but re-enactments of many other activities of the past show the great variety of possibilities.

In the Illinois Sesquicentennial a community had a timberjack contest which included wood chopping, crosscut sawing, rail splitting, and chain sawing. A flatboat race on the Sangamon River topped off the day.

British Columbia held a 540-mile stagecoach run from Bakersville to Victoria to re-create the early days of settlement in that province. A long wagon-train trek from Independence, Missouri, to Independence, Oregon, celebrated a centennial. Planners added realism, if not historical fact, to a Canadian stagecoach re-enactment by including a hold-up.

South Carolina's several re-enactments in its Tricentennial in 1970 included the landing of the first settlers, the firing on Fort Sumter, a restaging of America's first opera, an eighteenth-century ballet, and the re-enactment of a balloon ascent of 1773.

New Jersey co-ordinated the Tercentenary re-enactment of Washington's retreat across New Jersey with the historic evacuation of Fort Lee. One New Jersey community re-enacted the first public meeting held in the colonial period in that community. Actors wore authentic costumes and used the language of the period.

Dress-ups are really a form of re-enactment. One of the most interesting ones, in Shelby County, Illinois, in 1969, entitled "Hoops to Hippies," told Illinois history through seventy different costumes. Manitoba had an interesting women's dress-up in 1967 which featured gowns complete with bustles, and a special display of early period pantaloons. This could be a way to attract larger crowds.

A hundred-day voyageur canoe pageant marked the Canadian

Centennial in 1967. Experienced canoeists re-created the early settlement and exploration of western and central Canada by following the original routes of explorers and fur traders from Edmonton to Montreal, a distance of about 3500 miles. All ten provinces entered canoes, named after the original voyageurs, with the winner receiving large money prizes. Highlights of the pageant for viewers occurred at the seventy portages where the canoers stopped to rest and re-equip. These became occasions for local Centennial celebrations, with many Centennial projects making the short period a dramatic one.

MISCELLANEOUS PROJECTS AND PROGRAMS

Many activities of centennial planners defy categorizing, but some of these programs have attracted attention. There have been "Baby Days" for the newborn of the Centennial year; postage stamp souvenir booklets that reviewed history through stamp collections; time capsules; the Canadian program "Wild Bells," in which bells all over the nation pealed out simultaneously at the beginning moment of celebration; antique car shows and parades; barbershop singing exhibitions and contests; centennial dinners, breakfasts, and picnics; a "bean soup" memorial commemorating Civil War hardships; a "jumping frog" contest in San Diego; bazaars; reunions; camporees; special commemorative license plates. Other projects that need elaboration include:

(1) Window decorating: This may not be a planner's idea of pageantry, but some communities make this a gala affair. Decorating in gay colors with historic materials and themes of past days gives a festive air to a community. An especially attractive display occurs when all the stores in a block join in presenting exhibits of the same period. A modification of this in one Centennial was a clock display, in which several store windows used various clocks to represent the continuity and change in the history of the community.

(2) Models: Models are reproductions of items of former times. Liquor companies take pride in special commemorative bottles and decanters. One bottle which sold filled for $9.95 during Illinois's Sesquicentennial was recently priced by collectors for at least $65.00—empty.

Eighth-grade students at Gibbsboro, Manitoba, constructed a four-by-eight-foot model of their city, including the streams, the mills, and the farm lands. As a Centennial project, three eleventh-grade students of the MacGregor Collegiate Institute made a very accurate model of Manitoba's legislative building out of sugar cubes. They used seventy-five pounds of sugar cubes—eight thousand small pieces glued together—with styrofoam for domes and portico peaks.

Dolls dressed in period costumes have also been popular, and Canada again had an interesting example. In the Canadian Centennial, Alberta nurses put together a display, dressing their dolls in uniforms that illustrated each era of their profession back through the history of nursing.

(3) Commercial tourism: Already many states are beginning to use the Bicentennial as a spur to greater travel and touring possibilities. Pennsylvania says "put your kids right in the middle of a revolution," as it informs parents of many historic events in the state in festival Pennsylvania, sporting Pennsylvania, honeymoon Pennsylvania, historic Pennsylvania, and outdoor Pennsylvania. Each of these specific historic areas is outlined and brochures are available on all.

(4) Quilting parties: Quilting parties combine many festive features. Old-fashioned quilting parties were very popular in the South Carolina Tricentennial, in Illinois, and in several Canadian provinces. The major purpose of the quilting bee is often primarily to bring people together in a festive spirit—the quilt may be only incidental.

(5) Gathering recipes: This is similar in many ways to the focus of quilting parties. This brings people together to try different recipes from the past and it usually results in the pub-

lication of a new recipe book. Centennial cookbooks have been good moneymakers on several occasions.

(6) Contests: Contests are also as varied as communities and very popular in centennials. New Jersey was especially prolific in its offerings of contests. Tercentenary queens from all surrounding towns appeared in Bergen County in a Queens' finals. There was an old-fashioned recipe contest at Park Ridge. Several communities had barbershop quartet contests. Volunteer firemen used handpumps of 1852 vintage for their own special contest in Tenafly. There was a state Green Thumb contest, a slogan contest, and a contest to see who could write the best "Welcome" sign. Many contests in this and other centennials dealt with essay-writing, music, and poetry. Canada and several states also had contests in plowing, milking, bee-raising, and baking.

(7) Pioneer days: Pioneer Days usually honor senior citizens. Canada also extended this distinction to those who had been in the country a long time. Family reunions are often stressed as a part of this type of celebration. Several New Jersey communities had "Old Timers' Day," at which time senior citizens enjoyed special programs geared to their own interests. This is a good way to give recognition to people who otherwise are often omitted from consideration in centennial affairs.

(8) Goodwill ambassadors: A centennial is a good time both to send and receive ambassadors of good will. This is an especially good project for youth planners to consider.

(9) Gifts given, not received: This special Canadian idea, in which a person gives gifts on his birthday rather than receiving them, appeared in several western Canadian provinces. Gifts were directed toward the underprivileged both at home and abroad.

(10) Special day programs: One way for communities to highlight festivities in centennials is to choose special days for special programs. This can be done in two ways. The program can be related to the actual birthday of a particular event, or it

can be centered on one of the regular holidays like Hallowe'en, Fourth of July, Labor Day, Christmas, or Thanksgiving.

Re-creating the past in the drama of an oldtime Fourth of July celebration is an especially popular activity. An interesting program at the Chicago Historical Society building marked the Chicago Tercentenary. Naturally, oratory was a high point of the day. Illinois also had a Constitution Day on August 25, the hundredth birthday of the Illinois Constitutional Convention.

Veterans' Day, Thanksgiving Day, and Christmas also have had special meaning, and many centennial programs relate to these important occasions. In San Diego's Bicentennial year in 1969 much of December was devoted to Christmas pageantry, which included setting up a "Christmas Center" around a great tree, a "parade of home decorations," a special Christmas lighting service, several ethnic Christmas programs, a toyland parade, a Christmas flowers exhibition, several pageants, and a Christmas Day swim. Canada also showed unusual interest in Christmas displays and pageantry. Veterans' days spawn parades and special commemorations. Thanksgiving provides many historical themes as well as ideas for pageantry.

A more festive air usually appears at Hallowe'en programs. Again San Diego offers an interesting study. Students decorated store windows in several shopping districts with Hallowe'en symbols, with prizes to the best display. A lively pancake breakfast followed.

(11) Centennial novelties: Since this is an attempt at a comprehensive coverage of at least most types of centennial events, mention of commercialism in a centennial must not be omitted. Commercialism is part of every centennial, reaching unusual proportions in certain phases of the Civil War Centennial and others. Our Bicentennial offers many opportunities for exploitation. Already commercialism has appeared, and the following examples will illustrate its many faces.

Davison, Newman and Company, tea merchants of London, are preparing packets of tea for the United States which they hope will have a better reception than those in the Revolutionary period. Another London firm has cast twenty-four hundred copies of the Liberty Bell in one-fifth size. Other British firms are offering varied novelties, modeled after products traded with the colonies just before the Revolutionary War. One interesting and novel idea is a British firm's sale of decks of cards which have the faces of American or British Revolutionary War heroes superimposed on the kings, queens, and jacks. Donald Crawford, the English lawyer who devised the novelties, commented on this endeavor: "We are attempting to give a commercial bias to the bicentenary by using historically authentic and high quality items," he said. Let the buyer beware!

(12) Sports events: So much has already been said about centennial sports that extensive coverage of most centennial sports events seems unnecessary. One has only to read the Manitoba vignette or look through Canada's official *Programme of Events* to appreciate the extensive role that sports played in recent centennial observances. Still sports play a significant role in commemorating men and events, and a few examples stand out.

Celebrating regions often like to affiliate championship matches of all kinds with their centennial program. Halftime activities also appeal to sports enthusiasts, and the Bicentennial has already been the theme of at least several major football halftime festivals. At a recent professional football game in Texas, two hundred members of a high school band and the "Pepperettes" recounted the two-hundred-year "history" of the United States in various formations that included Paul Revere's ride, the Liberty Bell, and a large birthday cake with two hundred candles—all inside a huge outline map of this country. Other halftime festivities have also presented patriotic and Revolutionary War themes, including a musical re-enactment of the Battle of Bunker Hill. This is only the beginning of extravaganza and hoopla to challenge the stamina of even the staunchest fan in the coming years. Sugar Bowl officials have agreed to use the Bicentennial theme for all their activities in 1976. Bicentennial symbols will also appear on athletic equipment, in sports advertising, and in hundreds of minor events that will take place as the result of the actions of committees set up especially to press a popular image on the sports scene. Other special sporting events will appear, including programs for young people, with competitive sports for the retarded, for elementary and high school youngsters, and for university students. Special centennial events will occur on every level in just about every sport.

The following samples illustrate some of the additional activities happening in past centennials: a Centennial soap box derby, a Red Cross swimming safety show, swimming contests, yacht cruises, regattas, horse shows, driving clubs, a fish derby, mountain climbs, figure skating, and too many others to list. More unusual events iclude: the Huck Finn paddle boat project of Illinois, in which fourteen young people and two adults paddled a forty-foot boat of their own construction 1462 miles down the Mississippi River; a kids bike parade, held by Wichita, Kansas, in its Centennial; the physical fitness program that was so popular in the Canadian Centennial; the Alpine Centennial expedition, in which men climbed the newly designated "Centennial range" on the Alaska-Yukon border in 1967; and the Canadian voyageurs canoe pageant, described earlier.

Though hardly recommended for the average centennial program, the New Year's Splash was an unusual event. The San Diego Rowing Club swam in the cold waters of San Diego Bay to celebrate the city's Bicentennial in 1969. The splash, long an annual event, took on a new emphasis and stimulated new interest in its centennial affiliation.

The most valuable programs seem to be the ones which open up sports to the largest number of individuals, and de-emphasize professional and organized sports activities. The building of new sports arenas, especially the more modest ones designated for community service, which include cinder tracks, curling rinks, skating rinks, and swimming pools, can be fine additions to the community to the extent that they offer opportunities to the underprivileged, to ethnic groups, and to the general public.

On With Celebration

To celebrate,
We remember—
Remember That which gives fullest meaning
To Life!

God?
Perhaps.

A sense of being?
Someone who opened the right door
When I stood waiting—
Scared?
Heroes of the Now:
  Neighbor, Friend, Postman,
  A servant for my personal cause?
Heroes of the Past:
  Some martyred soul who knew
  That Life and Liberty and Joy
  Not only opened doors for him—
  Or Her—
But could open doors
For EVERYONE!

Today we celebrate our being—
Our being here!
We celebrate our love—
Loving those who yet do not celebrate
With us—
Hopeful that this celebration
Commemorates that which we are—
That which we hope to be—
That which we can be!

We celebrate new knowledge
About old Truths,
New relationships with old friends,
New dreams
That only add texture and meaning
To old dreams we had before.

We celebrate with a drop of morning dew,
Burning deep in the liquor of the vine.
A pinch of bread—
Our Souls—
Trembling hands touching trembling hands!
Faces smiling once more,
With eyes lit up, softening lines
Cut deep into our brows;
Sharing a golden moment of Peace
Together!

The Elements only say:
"This is Now!"
But we may touch hands again,
And also say—
Together—
"This is Tomorrow!"

THE Bicentennial Era moves on—slowly, but with an unrelenting pace—and more and more eyes turn toward '76.
Will this celebration enrich lives, strengthen unity, and leave
lasting memorials that future generations will view with pride?

Will our nation embrace the dignified historical perspective noted in the Jamestown Festival, the North Carolina Tercentenary, and the British Columbia centennials? Will it capture the rustic midwestern local historical patterns of the centennials of Minnesota, Illinois, and Manitoba? Will it focus on the arts as Oregon did in its Centennial and New Jersey in its Tercentenary? Will we discover the same elusive spirit that the Canadians found? Will Americans recover from the unproductive first phase of national planning and move to a creative and innovative second phase? Will we retain our Bicentennial enthusiasm over the long period suggested for celebration? Answers to these questions relate to the state of mind of the nation at the time of the Bicentennial, the spirit deep inside the heart of a nation, as it plots solutions for its numerous problems. Much depends upon the President, the Congress, and those agents they have appointed to set the wheels in motion for celebration. Much depends upon the American people themselves.

Gaining the support of many Americans for the Bicentennial will be an uphill fight. Still, no one should take lightly the opportunity to participate in a Bicentennial celebration. Two hundred years of change, triumph and tragedy, hopes fulfilled and frustrated, giving and receiving, pondering the future, and recording and recovering the past—this is the heritage we celebrate.

The American Revolution stands out in our history, not only as our age of beginning, but as a monument to the vitality and inventiveness of a particular age, a seminal event in the history of men. It is an event worthy of celebration. We will celebrate, and planners must devote themselves to encouraging a positive national celebration. "It must be the kind of celebration," said Senator Charles Mathias, "that enables and encourages the American people—of every region, every race, every religion, every age, every ethnic group . . . every income level—to discover and develop a greater sense of common purpose, of sharing common aims and ideas, of belonging to the same country." [1]

What we need, then, is a new strange and mysterious "Spirit of '76" to underline our own actions for that year and the years following. This spirit has been tossed by wind and tide and battered by the storms of politics and economics—but it still lives. It is this spirit that can command poets, novelists, and artists to produce the Bicentennial sonnet, epic, or painting. It can control and humanize the forces of change even as they threaten to tear our society apart. It may bring men of different persuasions toward great understanding and a common brotherhood of human beings.

Our celebration, therefore, must somehow reflect the idea of what it means to be an American. Our hearts are touched in *Fiddler on the Roof* when the two persecuted Jews who have known so much travail in their lives decide to seek refuge in the United States. Somehow, when these two old men find comfort in their belief that America really is the right place, we share that belief with them—America *is* the right place! This intangible spirit—seen so simply in their expression of faith—is what we celebrate in the Bicentennial.

But celebration alone is not enough. We must use the Bicentennial to work toward an America where these men and others can find lives and explore worlds about which they have only dreamed. The Bicentennial is indeed the time to praise famous men, but let us, in our time of celebration, also include "our fathers who begat us," and the great mass of humanity both within and outside our national bounds who have never known their dreams.

Abraham Lincoln once wrote that Jefferson "had the capacity to introduce into a merely revolutionary document an abstract

---

1. U.S., Congress, Senate, *Congressional Record,* 117, No. 186 (Dec. 2, 1971), pt. 2:S 20265.

truth applicable to all men and all times." [2] What a time and opportunity the Bicentennial Era offers for Americans to amplify the meaning of such sentiments! Even patriotism, which too often loses ground to overenthusiastic nationalism, may gain new meaning and importance. Real patriotism is knowing and appreciating what it is to be an American, while disdaining all false rhetoric and gross exaggeration. True patriotism has a seedbed in the American Revolution. In the local community it has its most ardent spokesmen. Americans may still find their Bicentennial a congenial moment to *celebrate,* in the largest sense of the word, a continuing nationhood—created in the Revolution, meeting its responsibilities to all mankind in another revolutionary age.

To realize the hope of more than passing success, the Bicentennial of the American Revolution must attempt to create something more than programs, simple themes, new buildings, and dancing feet. It must have at its heart the celebration of an idea—"an idea so simple, so consonant with justice and morality, so powerful in the strength it released, that all manner of people, great and small, high and low, rich and poor, has understood it and responded to it: the idea that everything rested upon and within the individual human being; that each individual possessed within himself something sacred and inviolable; that no government, group, or authority in any form or in any sphere of society could encroach upon that sacred core of right, save by consent of the individual." [3] If Bicentennial planners can keep the spirit of this idea at the heart of their actions, we may look at our nation in 1976 and say, with Hernando Cortes' captain, "I stood looking at it and thought that never in the world would there be discovered other lands such as these."

---

2. Quoted in Lawrence H. Leder, (ed)., *The Meaning of the American Revolution* (Chicago: Quadrangle Books, 1969), 67.

3. Quoted in William II. Nelson, "The Revolutionary Character of the American Revolution," *American Historical Review*, LXX (July 1965), 1013.

Bibliographical Essay

Research for this book led me to national, state, and local archives, offices of former centennial officials, libraries, museums, conferences, and celebrations in progress. A complete bibliography of the works consulted would be of little value to the average planner, but some of the gleanings from the sources listed should offer new areas of consideration for his own Bicentennial participation. Therefore in this bibliography I stress those items which readers might consult to add new dimensions to their own programs. The other items I used are reserved for the footnotes and for the permanent files which can substantiate the material of this book otherwise not footnoted. Though personal interviews of many of the officials and many "people-in-the-street" gave me many insights and helped me understand how and why celebrations take place, it was books and written records that determined much of my presentation. Two books provided historical background on how Americans celebrated in 1876: Dee Brown, *The Year of the Century: 1876* (New York: Charles Scribner's Sons, 1966) ; and William P. Randel, *Centennial: American Life in 1876* (Philadelphia: Chilton Book Co., 1969). Two other works describe aspects of that same Centennial: H. Craig Miner, "The United States Government Building at the Centennial Exhibition, 1874–77," *Prologue,* 4 (Winter 1972) , 202–219; and

David B. Little, *America's First Centennial Celebration* (Boston: The Club of Odd Volumes, 1961). For information on the fiftieth anniversary celebration of the Declaration of Independence, see Daniel Boorstin, *The Americans: The National Experience* (New York: Random House, 1965); and Page Smith, *John Adams* (New York: Harcourt and Brace, 1962).

To learn more about the meaning and historical background of the American Revolution, I recommend the following from a long list (most of these have appeared in paperback editions): John R. Alden, *A History of the American Revolution* (New York: Alfred A. Knopf, 1969); Hanna Arendt, *On Revolution* (New York: Viking Press, 1965) and *On Violence* (New York: Harcourt, Brace and World, 1970); Bernard Bailyn, *The Ideological Origins of the American Revolution* (Cambridge: Harvard University Press, 1967); Max Beloff, ed., *The Debate on the American Revolution, 1761–1783* (New York: Harper and Row, 1960); Cecil B. Currey, *Road to Revolution* (Garden City, New York: Doubleday and Company, 1968); Jack P. Greene, ed., *The Ambiguity of the American Revolution* (New York: Harper and Row, 1968); Merrill Jensen, *The Founding of a Nation* (New York: Oxford University Press, 1968); Martin Kallich and Andrew MacLeish, eds., *The American Revolution Through British Eyes* (New York: Harper and Row, 1962); Milton M. Klein, "The American Revolution in the Twentieth Century," *The Historian,* 34 (February 1972), 213–230; Dan Lacy, *The Meaning of the American Revolution* (New York: The New American Library, 1964); Walter La Feber, "American Historians and Revolutions," *Colloquium,* 8 (Spring 1970), 1–6; Heinz Lubasz, ed., *Revolutions in Modern European History* (New York: Macmillan, 1966); Edmund S. Morgan, ed., *The American Revolution* (Englewood, New Jersey: Prentice-Hall, 1965); Richard B. Morris, *The American Revolution Reconsidered* (New York: Harper and Row, 1967), and ed., *The American Revolution 1763–1783, A Bicentennial Collection* (New York: Harper and Row, 1970); William H. Nelson, "The Revolutionary Character of the American Revolution," *American Historical Review,* 70 (July 1965), 998–1015; J. R. Pole, ed., *The Revolution in America* (Stanford, California: Stanford University Press, 1970); Norman K. Risjord, *Forging the American Republic 1760–1815* (Reading, Mass.:

Addison-Wesley Publishing Co., 1973) ; Clinton Rossiter, *The First American Revolution* (New York: Harcourt, Brace and Company, 1956) ; Arthur M. Schlesinger, *Prelude to Independence* (New York: Random House, 1957) ; Eric Sevareid, "The American Dream," *Look*, 32 (July 9, 1968), 17–28; James Morton Smith, "The Transformation of Republican Thought, 1763–1787," in *Indiana Historical Society Lectures 1969–1970* (Indianapolis: Indiana Historical Society, 1970), 22–60; and "Wisconsin and the American Revolution Bicentennial," *Historical Messenger of the Milwaukee County Historical Society*, 28 (Autumn 1972), 82–95; Paul H. Smith, comp., *English Defenders of American Freedom, 1774–1778: Six Pamphlets Attacking British Policy* (Washington: United States Government Printing Office, 1972) ; Arnold J. Toynbee, *The Continuing Effect of the American Revolution* (Williamsburg: Virginia Institute of Early American History and Culture, 1961) ; Alden T. Vaughan, ed., *Chronicles of the American Revolution* (New York: Grosset and Dunlap, 1965) ; and Gordon S. Wood, *The Creation of the Republic, 1776–1787* (Chapel Hill: University of North Carolina Press, 1969). An excellent series of articles on this important period of American history and its impact on the present is Laurence H. Leder, ed., *The Meaning of the American Revolution* (Chicago: Quadrangle Books, 1969). The Library of Congress has a helpful publication entitled *The American Revolution: A Selected Reading List* (1971), and the New York State American Revolutionary Bicentennial Commission has issued *The American Revolution for Young Readers, a Bibliography* (1970). Two other articles make interesting background reading: "The Spirit of '70: Six Historians Reflect on What Ails the American Spirit," *Newsweek* (July 6, 1970), 19–34, and Clifford Geertz, "Is America by Nature a Violent Society?" New York *Times Magazine* (April 28, 1968), 25.

The following offer ideas on the spirit of celebration: Bruce Catton, *The Meaning of the Civil War* (Chicago: Chicago Historical Society, 1961) ; Merle Curti, "America at the Worlds Fairs, 1851–1893," *American Historical Review*, 55 (July 1950), 833–56; Johan Huizinga, *The Waning of the Middle Ages* (New York: Doubleday and Company, 1924) ; Richard D. Mandell, *Paris 1900: The Great World's Fair* (Toronto: University of Toronto Press,

1967) ; and Eileen Power, *Medieval People* (Garden City, N.Y.: Doubleday and Co., 1924) . Pierre Goubert, "Local History," *Daedalus,* 100 (Winter 1971) , 113–28, deals with the importance of local history.

Publications from other centennials offered much valuable material, with special kudos to Bernard Bush, *The New Jersey Tercentenary 1664–1964* (Trenton: New Jersey Archives and History, 1966) . Other similar works include: *Canada One Hundred 1867– 1967* (Ottawa: Canada Year Book and Library Division, Dominion Bureau of Statistics, 1967) ; *Final Fiscal Officer's Report to the State of Oregon Centennial Commission* (Portland: Oregon Centennial Commission, 1960) ; *Final Report* (Minneapolis: Minnesota Statehood Centennial Commission, 1959) ; *Manitoba '70* (Winnipeg: Manitoba Centennial Commission, 1970) ; *Report of the British Columbia Centennial Committee* (Victoria: Office of the Commission, 1959) ; *Report of the Carolina Charter Tercentenary Commission* (Raleigh: State Department of Archives and History, 1964) ; *Report of the Virginia 350th Anniversary Commission,* House Document 32 (Richmond: Commonwealth of Virginia, Division of Purchase and Printing, 1958) ; *Saskatchewan Golden Jubilee Committee Final Report* (Regina: Printer to the Queen's Most Excellent Majesty, 1956) ; *The Civil War Centennial, A Report to Congress* (Washington: U.S. Civil War Commission, 1968) ; *The Manitoba Centennial Corporation Sixth Report* (Winnipeg: Centennial Concert Hall, 1971) ; and *The Yorktown Book: The Official Chronicle and Tribute Book Issued by the Yorktown Sesquicentennial Association* (Richmond: Whittet and Shepperson, 1932) . *Centennial Facts,* a publication of the Canadian Centennial Commission, gave detailed outlines of projects and programs of that celebration, as did *100 Years After,* a comprehensive newsletter on the Civil War Centennial. *Illinois: The Challenge of the Sesquicentennial* (Chicago: Illinois Sesquicentennial Commission, 1968) , outlined the organization, programs and projects, and presentations of that celebration. Three other important inspirational accounts of other centennials include: Willard E. Ireland, "British Columbia Centennial: A Provincial Birthday Celebration," *History News,* 15 (December 1959) , 22–26 (this is one of the best articles planners can read) ; Allan Nevins, "A Conflict that was Big with Fate,"

History News reprint, 11 (July 1956), 65; and Anne Hanna, *The Canadian Centenary Council* (Ottawa: Centennial Commission, 1968) (excellent on organization). These reports and the personal interviews I conducted with many of the officials of the same celebrations form the framework of my case studies.

Guidebooks and articles from other centennials on how to organize and present various aspects of a celebration include, among many discovered in files of the archives: *Centennial Guide for Local Committees* (Raleigh: North Carolina Tercentenary Commission, 1961); *Centennial of Confederation Information Manual for Isolated Communities* (Ottawa: Centennial Commission, 1967); *Festival Canada* (Ottawa: Centennial Commission, 1966); *Greatest Hour, A Manual for Local Observances of the Centennial of the War Between the States* (Jackson: Mississippi Department of Archives and History, 1961); *Seminar '65: Canadian Conference of the Arts Report* (Toronto: Canadian Conference of the Arts, 1965); Raymond S. Sivesind, *How to Organize a Centennial Celebration,* Bulletin 100 (Madison: State Historical Society of Wisconsin, 1956); and John von Daacke, *Presenting the Past* (Albany: State Education Department, Office of State History, 1970).

Many publications on the various phases of celebrations are discussed in this book. Some illustrative examples are: *A Study and Recommendations for a Sound and Light Presentation on the Parliament Buildings, Ottawa* (Ottawa: Legendrama Productions Limited, 1965); Dan Klugherz Productions, 155 West 68 Street, New York, 10023, also furnishes a brochure on sound-and-light activities; Joseph O. Fischer, *Concepts for the Development of Local Arts Councils and other Art Groups,* 2d ed. (St. Louis: The Missouri State Council on the Arts, 1972); Nancy Hanks, "Government and the Arts," *Saturday Review* (February 28, 1970), 32; George McCalmon and Christian Moe, *Creating Historical Drama: A Guide for the Community and the Interested Individual* (Carbondale: Southern Illinois University Press, 1965); Wolf von Eckardt, "Saving Our Landmarks," *Saturday Review* (September 5, 1970), 52–53 (raises questions as to what to save); and Roger Stephens, "America's Stake in the Arts," *Saturday Review* (February 28, 1970), 18. AASLH, 1315 8th Avenue, South, Nashville, Tennessee,

37203, will send on request a list of technical leaflets and books which offer similar presentations.

The following periodicals contain many articles and views of what kind of projects and programs go well with celebration: *Humanities,* the quarterly of the National Endowment for the Humanities, keeps readers up to date on Bicentennial activities; *Museum News,* the journal of the American Association of Museums; *Prologue,* the journal of the National Archives; *Preservation News,* the publication of the National Trust for Historic Preservation; *The Capitol Dome,* the newsletter of the United States Capitol Historical Society; and the Library of Congress *Press Releases* and *Library of Congress Information Bulletin.* Representing other interests are *The Arts Reporting Scene,* the publication of the Arts Reporting Service, Silver Springs, Maryland, and *The Medallion* of the Texas State Historical Survey Committee, Austin.

Several publications are already beginning to focus on the Bicentennial, with newsletters being the most prominent. One of the first in the field was the *Committee of Correspondence,* of the Massachusetts Revolutionary Bicentennial Commission of Boston, which began in 1966. New York's *The Correspondent,* the newsletter of the New York American Revolution Bicentennial Commission, also appeared early in the field and deserves special consideration for its organization and varied presentations. Though not concerned exclusively with the Bicentennial, the *New Jersey Historical Commission Newsletter,* also of high quality, focuses much of its material toward 1976 activities. *The View from Washington Rock,* a New Jersey Girl Scout release, is a local publication that concentrates on programs and projects that relate to the Bicentennial, and the Massachusetts Revolutionary War Bicentennial Commission published in 1971 *Massachusetts in Ferment,* a chronological survey of the events leading to the Revolution.

All Bicentennial planners must make two periodicals from the American Revolutionary Bicentennial Commission part of their continuing fare. They are *Bicentennial Newsletter,* begun in 1970 as *Bicentennial Era*—rich in programs and projects that are being set up all over the country for the celebration—and *Bicentennial Bulletin,* their weekly newsletter of briefs. These publications are available at ARBC headquarters, 736 Jackson Place, Washington,

D.C. 20276. ARBC also has a fourteen-minute 16mm film for national distribution, entitled *A Call to Action.* Most of the original
thirteen states and several states beyond their perimeter also have
begun Bicentennial newsletters. Two commercial publications of
contrasting styles are the *American Bicentennial Newsletter,* a
Kiplinger-type letter published monthly by the Bicentennial Service
Corporation, and the more popular *Bicentennial Chronicle,* published eight times a year by the Colonial Historical Publishing
Company of Philadelphia.

Three publications detail specific aspects of the Bicentennial as
seen from the view of certain groups: "America's 200th Anniversary,
the Report of ARBC," is a government publication setting up the
objectives and plans of the American Revolutionary Bicentennial
Commission. *American Revolution II* (Raleigh: North Carolina
Bicentennial Commission, 1971) details highlights in the nation's
and in North Carolina's coming plans for celebration. *Focus 1976* is
the guide for the Daughters of the American Revolution and has a
strong patriotic flavor.

One last item deserves a special listing. Critics of Bicentennial
planning have already appeared, and their attacks and concerns
have been duly recorded. Besides the *Congressional Record,* which
has recorded much official concern, some of the criticisms include:
William T. Alderson, Jr., Editorial, *History News* (April 1972), 74;
Arts Reporting Scene, 2 (August 7, 1972), 2; Julius Duscha, "An
American Tragicomedy," *Saturday Review,* (July 1, 1972), 28–33;
Editorial, Nashville *Tennessean* (January 7, 1973); Paul J. C.
Friedlander, "Lack of Celebration Site Puts Damper on '76 Spirits,"
Nashville *Tennessean* (June 11, 1972); "General News," *Arts Re-
porting Scene,* 3 (September 4, 1972), 3; Eric F. Goldman, *The
Tragedy of Lyndon Johnson* (New York: Dell Publishing Co.,
1968), and "Topics: The Real Revolution—Or Doodle Dandy?"
in New York *Times* (September 27, 1969); Robert Hartje, "American Bicentennial," *History News,* 25 (August 1970), 194; Walter J.
Hickel, "Report of the Secretary of Interior to the American Revolution Bicentennial Commission," 1970 (less a criticism than a
report that offers constructive programs that have not seen much
action); Marianne Means, "Nixon Aims Slogan at Bicentennial
Year," Philadelphia *Inquirer* (February 19, 1971); Eugene L.

Meyer, "Bicentennial Commission" (three successive articles), Washington *Post* (August 14, 15, 16, 1972) ; Eugene L. Meyer, "Bicentennial Ignoring Minorities," Washington *Post* (December 5, 1972) ; Robert Moses, "Bicentennial Time," New York *Times* (October 31, 1971) ; Anthony E. Neville, "Bicentennial Blues," *Harper's*, 245 (July 1972), 32–39; Kevil P. Phillips, "Bicentennial Planning Kitschy," Cape Cod *Standard Times* (July 1, 1972) ; Jeremy Rifkin, "The Red, White, and Blue Left," *The Progressive* (November 1971), and, with Erwin Knoll, "The Greatest Show on Earth," *ibid.*, 36 (September 1972), 14–24; "Come Home, America," *The Progressive*, 36 (September 1972), 3–4; "Towards a New Spirit of '76," *Avant Garde* (March 1969) ; "Visual Arts and Museum News," *Arts Reporting Service*, 2 (April 17, 1972), 2; "When in the Course of Human Events It Seems Necessary to Celebrate a Bicentennial," Washington *Post* (September 19, 1971) ; and "Who Stole the American Revolution," *Fact* [Publication of the Democratic National Committee], 2 (August 13, 1971), 7–11.